The War on Privacy

The War on Privacy

Jacqueline Klosek

Westport, Connecticut
London

Library of Congress Cataloging-in-Publication Data

Klosek, Jacqueline, 1972-
The war on privacy / Jacqueline Klosek.
  p. cm.
 Includes bibliographical references and index.
 ISBN 0-275-98891-0 (alk. paper)
  1. Privacy, Right of. 2. War on Terrorism, 2001—Law and legislation. 3. Privacy, Right of—United States. 4. War on Terrorism, 2001—Law and legislation—United States. I. Title.
 K3263.K56 2007
 342.08'58—dc22   2006028565

British Library Cataloguing in Publication Data is available.

Library of Congress Catalog Card Number: 2006028565
ISBN 10: 0-275-98891-0
ISBN 13: 978-0-275-98891-3

First published in 2007

Praeger Publishers, 88 Post Road West, Westport, CT 06881
An imprint of Greenwood Publishing Group, Inc.
www.praeger.com

Printed in the United States of America

The paper used in this book complies with the Permanent Paper Standard issued by the National Information Standards Organization (Z39.48-1984).

10 9 8 7 6 5 4 3 2 1

To Grace Young, a true friend and inspiration.
Your support, friendship and laughter has meant everything.

Any society that would give up a little liberty to gain a little security
will deserve neither and lose both.

—*Benjamin Franklin*

Contents

Sadly, terrorism is far from a new phenomenon. While the attacks of 9/11 caused many in America who had previously given very little thought to the subject of terrorism to become increasingly focused upon the issue, the reality is that terrorism has been a feature of society for centuries. In fact, the word "terrorism" is believed to have originated back sometime between 1793 and 1794 during the French Revolution's "Reign of Terror" when Robespierre's Jacobins was reported to have executed more than 12,000 people who were deemed to be enemies of the Revolution. Robespierre was unapologetic about the use of terrorism as a means of achieving political goals and is reported to have said about his actions: "Terror is nothing but justice, prompt, severe and inflexible."[1]

Since its origins, various societies have had to deal with the plague of terrorism. Although specific types and phases of terrorism have arisen for a multitude of reasons, the essential challenge for societies confronting such threats has remained the same: that is finding a means to an end to the scourge of terrorism, while preserving the essential liberties and freedoms upon which modern democratic societies have been based.

Terrorism is not a recent creation; however, it is also undeniable that the current terrorist threat presents new and special challenges to our society. Indeed, the recent wave of terrorist activity has been particularly damaging and profound. The effects of the terrorism of the past few years have transformed and will long continue to influence the way we live for decades, if not centuries, to come. While many of these changes have occurred as a direct result of the acts of terrorists themselves, others have followed and will continue to grow out of our collective response to the acts of the terrorists.

History demonstrates adequately that caution must be exercised before undertaking a reactionary response to a new threat. Still, evidence suggests that all around the world governments have been responding in a very rapid and extremely over-broad manner to the current perceived risk. Consider, for instance, the singular but incredibly significant example of the Patriot Act, fully titled, the Uniting and Strengthening America by Providing Appropriate Tools Required to Intercept and Obstruct Terrorism Act of 2001 (USA PATRIOT Act). This very lengthy and extraordinarily detailed legislation was passed on October 26, 2001, only six short weeks after the terrorist attacks that devastated the country. The text of the USA PATRIOT Act exceeds 100 pages, making it the longest piece of emergency legislation passed in the shortest period, in all U.S. history. Such a rapid and utterly transformative response is sufficient cause to sound the alarm bells.

After the terrorist attacks, there was much speculation that many of the measures undertaken would be temporary in nature. However, all indications are that governmental powers continue to increase and expand in ways many of us never imagined would be possible just a few short years ago, while personal privacy rights and individual liberties continue to diminish. Now, more than five years after the attacks that devastated the country, it is time to take a step back and analyze whether the measures that have been taken in an effort to protect the country have truly been in the nation's best interest. If proper care is not taken and due consideration is not given now, it is more likely than not that the changes caused by our collective response to the terrorist acts will be largely negative.

In light of the foregoing, this book shall explore how the ongoing global war on terror has led to a global war on privacy. *Introduction* will introduce preliminary evidence supporting the notion that the war on terror has resulted in a war on privacy. It will examine the ways in which, led by the United States, various governments around the world have been responding to the threat of terrorism and will show how these responses have been eroding well-established privacy rights and individual liberties.

Chapter 1 will present a general overview of privacy rights in the United States before and immediately following September 11. Specifically, the chapter will present an in-depth examination of the trends in privacy regulation as they existed before September 11, 2001. The chapter will demonstrate how various factors, including the advent of new technologies, were leading to the enactment and enforcement of more stringent legislation concerning individual privacy rights. This chapter will explore some of the most prominent privacy rights laws that were passed in the United States during the 1990s and early 2000s. It will then show the general trends in privacy rights that had begun to develop just after September 11, 2001.

Having introduced the privacy regime, as it existed in the United States before September 11, Chapter 2 will move on to examining how the events of September 11 (and the legislation passed as a result thereof) have resulted in a startling and significant erosion of privacy rights in the United States. Significant focus will be placed on the USA PATRIOT Act and similar legislation. This chapter will also highlight the government's data mining efforts and, in doing so, will show how corporations, educational institutions, and other private entities have been drafted into becoming foot soldiers in the government's war on privacy. Such draft has, of course, put many such entities in the impossible position of having to choose between responding to governmental demands for information on the one hand and honoring privacy commitments made to individuals and complying with privacy laws on the other.

Then, in Chapter 3 the discussion will shift to an analysis of privacy rights in the Middle East and Africa and will examine how such nascent rights have also been impacted by the global war on terror. While neither privacy rights nor Internet usage was very well developed before the attacks on America, generally in most countries in the region the slow march toward enhanced privacy protections was stalled considerably by the attacks against America and the governmental response that followed.

Chapter 4 will examine the impact that the war on terrorism had on privacy rights in Europe, with a particular focus on countries that are members of the European Union (EU). Privacy rights have long been respected in the Europe. In fact, in many European countries, privacy is considered as a fundamental human right. Member states of the EU have to implement in their local laws the requirements of the Data Protection Directive, a very comprehensive legislation that provides individuals with comprehensive privacy rights and places restrictions on the export of personal data outside the EU. At the same time, however, European countries have been battling terrorism for many years, and in the wake of the September 11 terrorist attacks against the United States and those that followed in United Kingdom, many European jurisdictions demonstrated a willingness to adopt tough new anti-terror measures, many of which had a palpable negative impact on privacy rights. The horrendous transit bombings that followed in Madrid and London only strengthened the resolve of many European countries to take all actions deemed necessary to reduce the likelihood of future terrorist attacks.

Chapter 5 will focus on our northern and southern neighbors: Canada and Mexico. As an important trading partner and close neighbor of the United States, Canada has been particularly impacted by US efforts to combat terrorism. Like the EU, Canada has comprehensive privacy legislation, enacted in advance of the 2001 attacks. Therefore, Canada has been trying to balance the need to collect, disclose, and use personal data with the need to protect the privacy rights of its citizenry. Mexico, as well, has been impacted in a dramatic way by the U.S.-led war on terror. Mexico has become a higher priority for law enforcement because of a growing concern about the porous southern border and the potential for terrorists and/or dangerous materials to be smuggled into the United States.

Chapter 6 will focus upon Latin and South America. Privacy rights were somewhat slow in coming to the region of South America. Even today, there are many countries in South America that have not enacted any privacy laws and do not provide any constitutional protections to privacy rights. Nonetheless, in the late 1990s, a handful of South American countries did begin to consider and enact privacy and data protection laws. It is likely that such efforts were encouraged at least, in part, by the enactment of the European Data Protection Directive, which prohibits the export of personal data from the EU to third countries that do not provide adequate protection to personal data. For the most part, efforts to enact new privacy laws and strengthen existing legislation were diminished by the war on terrorism. At the same time, local governments found that they had a very clear basis for strengthening a wide range of anti-terror measures.

In Chapter 7, attention will shift to examining the privacy rights in the South Pacific and Asia. This chapter will demonstrate how the war on terrorism has been having a very negative impact on the privacy rights in many countries of the region. Like in many other regions examined in this book, privacy rights were largely under development at the time of the terrorist attacks in the United States. The growth and development of these privacy laws took an about-face in the wake of the terrorist attacks and in response to increasing demands for information from the U.S. and other governments. At the same time, many countries in the region engaged in increased surveillance and enacted various anti-terror measures, all of which had a negative impact on privacy rights.

The final chapter will argue that the erosion of privacy rights on a worldwide basis is fundamentally detrimental to a democratic society. While it is clear that efforts to prevent terrorism are essential, it is the position of this publication that such efforts can be carried out with greater respect for individual privacy rights. This chapter will also demonstrate why aggressively pursuing efforts to prevent terrorism and apprehend terrorists with little regard for privacy rights and civil liberties will lead to far-reaching negative consequences on a worldwide basis.

ACKNOWLEDGMENTS

I gratefully appreciate the research assistance of Dale Fulton, Haseeb A. Chowdry, and Elizabeth Weill-Greenberg, the secretarial support and laughter of Edwina Battle, and the encouragement of my supportive and highly talented colleagues at Goodwin Procter, LLP, including, most notably, Steven G. Charkoudian.

Introduction

OVERVIEW

Privacy is a relatively new concept. While it is true that today most jurisdictions around the world recognize privacy in some respect, the right to privacy, particularly as an enforceable legal right, is a relatively new creation. Moreover, there continue to be tremendous differences in how privacy is viewed, let alone how and even if, individuals may enforce their privacy rights. In certain jurisdictions, including most European countries, privacy is viewed as a fundamental human right. In other jurisdictions, especially the United States, the right to privacy is more often conceptualized as the right to be left alone from interference. Still, in other areas, including many Middle Eastern and some Asian countries, "privacy" in terms of commonly accepted Western conceptions is not often viewed as a matter of significant concern.

Generally, in most industrialized, Western nations, privacy rights developed slowly but somewhat steadily, at least until the latter part of the twentieth century. During the mid-to-late 1990s, privacy rights became the subject of increased focus and concern. One significant reason for this new focus was the advent of new technologies. Throughout this period, new technological developments were having a profound impact on the way in which we worked, played, and lived. They were enhancing our ability to exchange information, content, and data rapidly and across vast distances and national boundaries. Efforts to collect, process, and mine data, which were once extraordinarily time-consuming processes, could suddenly be accomplished almost instantaneously. As a result, there was increasing concern about how such technologies might have an adverse impact upon individual privacy rights. In essence, we wondered how to preserve this vague right to be left alone from interference, as the new technologies made it less and less likely that we would indeed be left alone.

Around the same period, a comprehensive data protection regime with elements of extraterritoriality was just coming into force in Europe. Europe's main data protection directive[1] (the Data Protection Directive), which was passed in 1995 and took effect in 1998, severely limited the ability of enterprises and organizations to transfer any personal data outside the European Economic Area (EEA) unless the country to which the data would be transferred provided *adequate* protection to such personal data. As a result, many jurisdictions were compelled to implement new privacy and data protection laws so as to ensure that entities within their national boundaries would be able to continue to receive personal data from within the EEA. The United States, of course, opted for a different approach and undertook efforts to negotiate a self-regulatory scheme as an alternative to comprehensive data privacy legislation.

All of the foregoing factors contributed to an increased demand for comprehensive privacy laws. And many jurisdictions responded. During this period, around the globe, many privacy laws were introduced and/or enacted.[2] At the same time, governmental and regulatory authorities in various jurisdictions directed attention toward launching investigations and commencing enforcement actions against companies that had been viewed as violating individual privacy rights.[3]

Back then, it seemed that, despite the lobbying efforts of some businesses, efforts to ensure the protection of individual privacy rights would only continue to grow and strengthen. There was even speculation that the United States would perhaps enact a broad, general federal privacy law, not too dissimilar from that of the EU data protection directive.

Then came the unspeakable and unexpected events of September 11—along with the additional attacks that were to follow. The terrorist attacks of September 11, 2001 were tragic, horrific events that changed the course of history on so many levels. While an in-depth analysis of all of the effects and repercussions of the terrorists attacks is clearly beyond the scope of this publication, this book will seek to examine one very significant side-effect of the attacks, that is, the general erosion of individual privacy rights in the United States and across the entire globe that accompanied the war against terrorism that followed 9/11. At the very least, the preoccupation with fighting terrorism and preventing the next terrorist attack reduced the focus on and concerns about individual privacy rights. Arguably, as this book will contend, the war on terror not only stalled the further advancement of privacy rights, but caused degradation in individual privacy rights in many different areas and on many different levels.

INITIAL RESPONSE TO THE TERRORIST ATTACKS OF 9/11

The attacks on America led to shock and horror around the world. World leaders responded immediately, expressing their collective outrage at the attacks, while extending their condolences and offers of assistance.[4] Likewise, citizens from all over the world expressed their sorrow, grief and solidarity with the United States. Not too long after this initial reaction, governments across the globe began to contemplate and eventually implement measures that they believed would be needed to prevent future tragedies from occurring anywhere in the world.

Still reeling from the horrific attacks and eager to prevent the occurrence of similar—or even worse—tragedies in the future, American legislators rushed to adopt and implement legal measures to prevent terrorism and capture terrorists. Given the nature of the current wave of terrorism and, specifically, the fact that many terrorists are organized in sleeper cells, striving to blend into society until it is time to attack, many of these measures included elements of enhanced powers of surveillance and investigation. At the time, it was maintained that many of these measures would be, in effect, temporary. But, now, more than five years after 9/11, all indications suggest that surveillance activity is still increasing, while efforts to protect privacy continue to decline.[5] In fact, it seems that each day brings more news reports revealing additional ways that the government has been infringing upon individual privacy rights in its "War on Terror."

The profound changes in privacy regulation were not limited to the United States. Since 2001, the privacy landscape has shifted enormously in many, if not most, countries around the world. The motivations behind such changes are varied, including pressure by and/or incentives from the United States government or other governments, the demands of their own citizens, and/or a concern about preventing horrific terrorist attacks from occurring within their own boundaries. Whatever the reasons may be, many countries have implemented legislative changes that are dramatically affecting the overall level of privacy enjoyed by their citizens.

A Rush to New Legislation

In the immediate aftermath of the September 11 attacks, international organizations responded swiftly, demanding that national governments undertake increased efforts to fight terror. Just a day after the attacks, the United Nations adopted Resolution 1368, calling on increased cooperation between countries to prevent and suppress terrorism.[6] Then on September 28, 2001, the United Nations Security Council adopted the more significant Resolution 1373.[7] Through this resolution, the Security Council called upon all States to take a very wide range of measures to fight terrorism. Specifically, UN member states were instructed to do the following:

- criminalize the willful provision or collection of funds by their nationals or in their territories with the intention that the funds should be used, or in the knowledge that they are to be used, to carry out terrorist acts;

- freeze without delay funds and other financial assets or economic resources of persons who commit, or attempt to commit, terrorist acts or participate in or facilitate the commission of terrorist acts; of entities owned or controlled directly or indirectly by such persons; and of persons and entities acting for, or at the direction of, such persons and entities, including funds derived or generated from property owned or controlled directly or indirectly by such persons and associated persons and entities;

- prohibit their nationals or any persons and entities within their territories from making any funds, financial assets or economic resources, or financial or other related services available, directly or indirectly, for the benefit of persons who commit or attempt to commit or facilitate or participate in the commission of terrorist acts, of entities owned or controlled, directly or indirectly, by such persons, and of persons and entities acting for or at the direction of such persons;

- refrain from providing any form of support, active or passive, to entities or persons involved in terrorist acts, including by suppressing recruitment of members of terrorist groups and eliminating the supply of weapons to terrorists;

- take the necessary steps to prevent the commission of terrorist acts, including by provision of early warning to other States by exchange of information;

- deny safe haven to those who finance, plan, support, or commit terrorist acts or provide safe havens;

- prevent those who finance, plan, facilitate, or commit terrorist acts from using their various territories for those purposes against other States or their citizens;

- ensure that any person who participates in the financing, planning, preparation, or perpetration of terrorist acts or in supporting terrorist acts is brought to justice and ensure that, in addition to any other measures against them, such terrorist acts are established as serious criminal offences in domestic laws and regulations and that the punishment duly reflects the seriousness of such terrorist acts;

- afford one another the greatest measure of assistance with criminal investigations or criminal proceedings relating to the financing or support of terrorist acts, including assistance in obtaining evidence in their possession necessary for the proceedings;

- prevent the movement of terrorists or terrorist groups by effective border controls and controls on issuance of identity papers and travel documents, and through measures for preventing counterfeiting, forgery, or fraudulent use of identity papers and travel documents;

- find ways of intensifying and accelerating the exchange of operational information, especially regarding actions or movements of terrorist persons or networks; forged or falsified travel documents; traffic in arms, explosives, or sensitive materials; use of communication technologies by terrorist groups; and the threat posed by the possession of weapons of mass destruction by terrorist groups;

- exchange information in accordance with international and domestic law and cooperate on administrative and judicial matters to prevent the commission of terrorist acts;

- cooperate, particularly through bilateral and multilateral arrangements and agreements, to prevent and suppress terrorist attacks and take action against perpetrators of such acts;

- become parties as soon as possible to the relevant international conventions and protocols relating to terrorism, including the International Convention for the Suppression of the Financing of Terrorism of December 9, 1999;

- increase cooperation and fully implement the relevant international conventions and protocols relating to terrorism and Security Council resolutions 1269 (1999) and 1368 (2001);

- take appropriate measures in conformity with the relevant provisions of national and international law, including international standards of human rights, before granting refugee status, for ensuring that the asylum seeker has not planned, facilitated, or participated in the commission of terrorist acts;

- ensure, in conformity with international law, that refugee status is not abused by the perpetrators, organizers, or facilitators of terrorist acts and that claims of political motivation are not recognized as grounds for refusing requests for the extradition of alleged terrorists.

Resolution 1373 was adopted under chapter VII of the United Nations Charter, since the Security Council determined that the attacks of September 11 were deemed to constitute "a threat to international peace and security."[8] Under the United Nations Charter, the Security Council is empowered to direct member states to comply with the program it has adopted, rather than merely suggesting or recommending courses of action.[9]

While the suggested United Nations program certainly seems to have been based on proper motivations, when one looks back in retrospect at the terms of the resolution, two issues are of particular concern. First, the resolution failed to include any precise definition of terrorism. Although it is true that it can be very difficult for a diverse group of parties to come to terms with a precise definition of terrorism, further efforts should have been directed toward this goal at the time the resolution was being adopted. When "terrorism" as a crime is defined without proper precision, there will be the risk that the actions of ordinary criminals—or, even worse, political protesters—will be considered terrorism, and result in subjecting the perpetrators of such acts to the harsh punishments that would apply under law to perpetrators of "terrorism." Subsequent chapters that examine the various national measures that have been adopted around the world will show how the lack of precision in defining terrorism can be a very serious problem.

A second major concern regarding Resolution 1373 is that it failed to require member states to address human rights considerations when implementing measures to counter the threat of terrorism. The subsequent discussion regarding national measures that have been adopted against terrorism will show that many laws and policies that have been adopted in the wake of September 11 infringe upon individual rights generally and privacy rights specifically. While it would not have avoided the problem entirely, it would have been useful if the Security Council resolution had required member states to include privacy and other human rights considerations in their counterterrorism initiatives. If nothing else, at the very least, doing so may have caused some leaders and legislators to keep such considerations in mind when developing their counterterrorism response.

The passage of Resolution 1373 appears to have been influential in motivating UN member states to modify their national laws to respond to the threat of terrorism. The UN Counter-Terrorism Committee maintains Web pages devoted to the national response to Resolution 1373, and the reports contained therein detail a lot of the responses that have been undertaken to date.[10] Even a cursory review of such pages demonstrates that countries have been taking the mandate put forth by the UN Security Council very seriously. While it is clearly beyond the scope of this publication to examine all of these measures in detail, the sheer volume of the measures proposed worldwide in the immediate aftermath of the attacks is certainly worth noting.

Of course, the immediate international response was not limited to the United Nations. Other international and regional organizations also responded quite rapidly. The Council of Europe condemned the attacks, urged solidarity among nations, and called upon national governments to cooperate more with other governments in efforts to prevent, investigate, and prosecute criminal matters.[11] About two weeks after the attacks, the Council of Europe Parliamentary Assembly asked countries to ratify conventions combating terrorism, lift any reservations in these agreements and extend the mandate of police working groups to include focus on "terrorist messages and the decoding thereof."[12] Such initial statements foreshadowed the more concrete and developed efforts to fight terror that would soon follow in many countries around the world.

In the weeks and months after the attacks and the immediate initial reaction thereto, many jurisdictions took concrete efforts to expand and enhance surveillance and investigative powers. A number of countries followed the directions of the Council of Europe and ratified international instruments, and numerous countries passed new laws to increase the ability of authorities to conduct communications surveillance. A great number of jurisdictions also increased search and seizure powers and expanded the ability of law enforcement authorities to detain suspects.

Unofficial actions of many governments also impacted privacy laws that had already been enacted prior to the 2001 attacks. For example, many of the privacy laws that were enacted prior to September 11, particularly those in Europe, had included comprehensive data subject access rights. However, the overall decline in privacy rights that occurred after the terrorist attacks also impacted this aspect of privacy rights. Justified by a need to ensure the protection of sensitive intelligence data, subject access requests are restricted as some databases are being exempted from both data protection and freedom of information laws.

The effects of the terrorist attacks on privacy have been profound and widespread. Not only have governments adopted measures to increase and enhance their surveillance and investigatory powers, in the wake of the terrorist attacks many governments have found increased support and new justification for continued study or even adoption of proposals for measures that had previously had little support (such as national identity cards). In many countries, legislative measures adopted to fight "terrorism" were drafted so broadly so as to permit an interpretation that would restrict virtually any kind of dissent.[13]

The general focus on the need to prevent terrorism has empowered police and judicial authorities to take actions that may have been deemed questionable before the terrorist attacks, for example, requiring the removal of veils for driver's license photographs,[14] placing restrictions on trainspotters and photographers[15] in a wide range of circumstances, and requiring law school administrators to turn over attendee lists from legal conferences concerning Islamic issues.[16] While in many cases such efforts may not have been motivated solely by concerns about terrorism, it has become much easier to establish a connection—either expressly or impliedly—between such efforts and the general war on terror.

Of course, upon initial consideration, preventing a hobbyist from viewing and photographing a train may not seem to be of great concern, especially if doing so may help prevent a terrorist attack against a train. However, all of these restrictions must be evaluated both in and of themselves and also in their totality. Such restrictions can have a chilling effect on all kinds of behaviors, as people become increasingly fearful of the prospects of being punished for engaging in ordinary behavior. And when taken in sum, such limitations detract people from the general culture of freedom and liberty upon which this country was based.

September 11 as a Rationale for Clamping Down on All "Terrorists" Worldwide

When examining the global impact of the war on terror, it is impossible to ignore the fact that around the world, governments have been using the September 11 attacks, as the resulting response thereto, as a rationale for enacting measures targeted at matters of particular concern to them within their own national boundaries. Various governments have become willing participants in the global war on terror, and some have used such participation as a means for equating separatists or other groups with political claims with the kinds of terrorists associated with the September 11 attacks on the United States. This phenomenon has been observed by a number of human rights groups and other organizations; for instance, a recent report published by Human Rights Watch substantiates this claim, contending that "[m]any countries—Uzbekistan, Russia and China among them—used the 'war on terrorism' to attack their political opponents, branding them as Islamic terrorists."[17]

The strongest example of this phenomenon, some may argue, may be Russia's attempts to clamp down on Chechen rebels. Some have contended that Russia has used the 9/11 attacks to bolster its own internal counterterrorism measures and to urge the United States to support and even participate in Russia's struggle against its own terrorists.[18]

Another example some may say may be witnessed in the Turkish government's increased efforts to control the political activities of the Kurdistan Workers' Party (PKK). Reports have suggested that the global war on terror has helped the government in Ankara in its struggle against the PKK, in that the global battle against al-Qaeda–type terrorists has helped create an environment that is inhospitable to all groups classified as terrorists by their own local governments.[19]

Arguably, similar activities have been occurring in Colombia as it struggles against various guerilla groups. Indeed, Colombian President Álvaro Uribe Vélez has not been timid in his attempts to link the global war on terror to the country's own internal struggles.

In his inauguration speech, for example, Uribe used terrorism to refer to "any violence against [a democratic state]". As the US prepared to invade Iraq and remove Saddam Hussein from power, the president added Colombia to the coalition of the willing"—the only South American nation to join—and explicitly linked Colombian violence to events in the Middle East.[20]

There have also been claims that "Chinese authorities now call the separatists in the western province of Xinjiang 'terrorists' to justify repression and shutting down publications."[21] Clearly, there is cause for great concern when these kinds of "side effects" of the U.S.-initiated war on terror are being felt worldwide.

Increased Information Sharing between Private Companies and the Government

Because of the global war on terror, there has also been a dramatic increase in information sharing between private entities and the government. In the United States, such information sharing has occurred within a number of industrial sectors, but the activity within the travel and communications sectors has been particularly heavy. There have been numerous reports of telecommunication companies and airlines sharing customer data and information with various governmental bodies, often in contravention of applicable privacy laws and the privacy promise they have made to their customers and almost always without advance notice to their customers.

Recent reports have emerged that during 2005 the Federal Bureau of Investigation (FBI) secretly sought information on more than "3,501 American citizens and legal residents from their banks and credit card, telephone and Internet companies without a court's approval."[22] Not long ago, dramatic reports of a comprehensive program to spy into Americans' telephone calling data have emerged and even more recently, details of a comprehensive data sharing program between educational institutions and the FBI came to light. Many experts feel that this is one of the most significant privacy issues of the future. Private companies have been able to amass huge amounts of data regarding individuals' purchasing habits, communications, travel, social networks, work history, finances, and more. Increasingly, the government may be looking to access, combine, mine, and otherwise process data from these databases concerning various initiatives, including its efforts to prevent future terrorist acts.

Against this backdrop, across the board and around the world, there has been a corresponding decline in efforts to protect privacy on the commercial side. With governments and individual citizens concerned about terrorism and focused on measures to prevent the same, efforts to place limitations on the ability of online retailers to use personal data for marketing purposes suddenly seemed less significant to legislators and regulators. This is ironic because evidence from around the world suggests that consumers remain concerned about the privacy and security of their online activities, especially given the slew of very public data breaches occurring in the United States and elsewhere throughout 2005 and 2006. Consider, for instance, a May 2006 global survey conducted by the UN International Telecommunication Union, which showed 44 percent of respondents claiming that privacy is poorly respected online and a startling 64 percent of respondents claiming that they avoided certain online activities because of security concerns.[23] Moreover, an April 2006 survey of 1,150 adults in the United States found that only 18 percent believed that existing laws are sufficient to protect them on the Internet.[24]

Furthermore, recognizing that many commercial entities have much valuable information concerning individuals, the governments of the United States and other countries have also exerted pressure on private industry, demanding the companies in the private sector to share certain information with the government. As noted above, this has been most visible in the travel industry. The governments of many countries, including, without limitation, the United Kingdom[25] and Canada,[26] have made proposals for increased sharing of airline passenger data with the government. Still, while widespread in the travel industry, such proposals for increased information sharing have not been limited to this industry. Clearly, there has been a dramatic increase in information sharing between financial institutions and governments.[27] Even charitable organizations have not been immune to such demands as governments increasingly examine charitable donations to investigate potential terrorist ties.

RISING CONCERNS

The various horrific terrorist attacks that have occurred during the past few years are still very fresh in the minds of most individuals. Many people remain of the view that the government should do everything within its power to prevent another possible terrorist attack, and they are comfortable with the notion that privacy rights and individual liberties will take a back seat to these efforts. At the same time, however, there is a rising chorus of voices that are beginning to call for greater focus on efforts to protect privacy rights. Such voices are beginning to clamor for more restraint and are calling upon the government to be more strategic and targeted concerning its data collection and data-mining efforts.

Survey results offer support for the notion that, slowly but surely, public concern over privacy rights within the context of the fight against terrorism is on the rise. In the time that immediately followed the terrorist attacks, many surveys demonstrated a high level of tolerance for privacy invasions, provided that such invasions were considered necessary or useful for fighting terrorism. For instance, a November 2001 survey conducted by National Public Radio, the Henry J. Kaiser Family Foundation, and the John F. Kennedy School of Government at Harvard University found that most respondents favored granting law enforcement broader powers in the following areas: (i) telephone wiretapping, (ii) interception of mail and email, (iii) examining an individual's Internet activity, (iv) tracking credit card purchases, and (v) examining banking records. In the same survey, 58 percent of respondents claimed that they believed that they would have to give up on some of their rights and liberties.[28]

More recent studies, however, have begun to demonstrate decreasing tolerance for invasion of privacy rights. For instance, a January 2006 poll conducted by ABC News revealed that three in ten Americans surveyed feel that the government had made unjustified intrusions into privacy as it investigates terrorism. While this is still less than a majority, it is double the level of concern that was expressed in similar surveys taken just a few years ago.[29]

In the same January 2006 survey conducted by ABC News, Americans were almost evenly divided with respect to their views on recent reports that the National Security Agency had engaged in wiretapping without warrants. Fifty-one percent of respondants called them acceptable in investigating terrorism, and 47 percent considered such activity unacceptable.[30] Interestingly, the results of the same survey tend to suggest that concerns about privacy are on the rise. In the most recent survey, 30 percent of respondents expressed a belief that the government is intruding on privacy without justification. In 2001, only 17 percent of the respondents expressed such a view. If the future brings new reports of additional and/or more egregious examples of the violation of privacy rights by governmental actions, it is likely that public concerns regarding privacy issues will continue to grow.

SUMMARY AND CONCLUSION

The quest to eradicate terrorism and apprehend terrorists is an essential mission. It is a crucial duty of all governments to provide for the safety of their citizens. It is certainly not the goal of this publication to assert that we should not be undertaking all necessary efforts reasonably designed to minimize the ability of terrorists to cause harm. It is, however, the purpose of this publication to urge that such efforts are undertaken with reasoned restraint and careful consideration. The theoretical question has been thrown around so much that it has become somewhat trite, but if we allow terrorists to cause us to change our society and to take away the freedoms and liberties that are so valuable to us, have they not already won?

One

Privacy in the United States Prior to September 11

INTRODUCTION

During the late 1990s, privacy was an important topic that was receiving much attention from governmental authorities and individuals alike. Because of the Internet and related technologies, individuals, companies, and governments had quickly become better equipped to transmit large amounts of data across great distances and to multiple geographic locations virtually instantaneously. At the same time, the ability of individuals, companies, and governmental entities to collect personal information from individuals, at times without the full knowledge and consent of these individuals, was also enhanced exponentially.

While considerations about privacy and the protection of personal data had been of particular concern to enterprises engaging in e-commerce with consumers, privacy concerns also arose in other areas and specifically targeted legislation often followed. Activities involving the transfer of personal data across national boundaries have led to particular concerns. As will be demonstrated herein, certain data privacy laws contain limitations on the ability of enterprises to transfer personal data across borders. Consequently, in the period of time preceding the terrorist attacks, in terms of privacy issues, many corporations were occupied with the challenges of addressing the goal of continuing to transfer a wide range of personal data across national borders in face of the new restrictions.

At least partly because of the perceptions that there were substantial new risks to the privacy of personal data, many jurisdictions The United States included, had enacted rules and regulations designed to protect individual privacy. The next section of this chapter will provide an overview of key legislative measures in the

United States applicable to data privacy. To emphasize trends that were developing prior to the terrorist attacks of September 11, this chapter will focus on developments arising at the close of the twentieth century.

LEGISLATIVE OVERVIEW

United States

As compared with other countries including, notably, the member states of the European Union, the United States has adopted an approach to data privacy that is rather piecemeal in nature. Instead of having a singular comprehensive data privacy law that applies across all industries, U.S. legislatures have opted for providing special protections to certain types of data, such as consumer credit information, medical records, and even video rental data. The following section will explore key legislative measures concerning data privacy that have been enacted in the United States with the goal of demonstrating the evolution of privacy rights in the period just prior to September 11.

While U.S. legislators have not elected to enact comprehensive data privacy legislation that applies to all types of personal data, lawmakers have passed significant federal laws that apply to particular types of personal data. Although these laws have a limited scope in that they are limited to certain sectors or types of data, generally they establish broad requirements and stringent restrictions with respect to the collection and use of the particular types of personal data to which they apply. The following sections shall examine several of these federal laws in closer detail. Although privacy requirements applicable to commercial entities are not the intended focus of this publication, they must be examined in some detail to set the stage and demonstrate the general trends in privacy rights just before the September 11 attacks. The reality is that there was not much activity concerning legal developments impacting the ability of governmental agencies to collect, use, and disclose the personal data of individual citizens.

The Health Insurance Portability and Accountability Act

During the 1990s, with a Democratic administration in place in the White House, there was much focus on health care, including patients' rights. It was during that period that legislators enacted the United States' first comprehensive rules regarding data privacy and security in the health sector. The Health Insurance Portability and Accountability Act of 1996, together with the regulations issued pursuant thereto (collectively HIPAA),[1] establishes many rules and requirements relative to the privacy and security of individually identifiable health information, which is defined as:

> [I]nformation that is a subset of health information, including demographic information collected from an individual, and: (1) Is created or received by a health care provider, health plan, employer, or health care clearinghouse; and (2) Relates to the past, present, or future physical or mental health or condition of an individual; the provision of health care to an individual; or the past, present, or future payment for the provision of health care to an individual; and (i) that identifies the individual; or (ii) with respect to which there is a reasonable basis to believe the information can be used to identify the individual.[2]

The data privacy and security requirements of HIPAA apply to health plans, health care providers, and health care clearinghouses (collectively, "Covered Entities"). Among its many requirements, HIPAA mandates the creation and distribution of privacy policies that explain how all individually identifiable health information is collected, used, and shared. HIPAA also establishes strict controls on the use and disclosure of individually identifiable health information. Entities that are subject to HIPAA's requirements are not permitted to use or disclose individually identifiable health information except as expressly permitted by the provisions of the HIPAA privacy rule.

While the requirements of HIPAA apply specifically to Covered Entities, other types of entities may be impacted by HIPAA because HIPAA requires Covered Entities to execute Business Associate Agreements with all third-party service providers that will be provided with access to individually identifiable health information by the Covered Entity. Accordingly, in addition to impacting Covered Entities directly, the law has indirect implications for a range of companies providing services to and / or otherwise involved in the activities of Covered Entities.

While the requirements of HIPAA are very comprehensive and have been posing incredible compliance challenges for many organizations, in light of the present discussion it is important to note that legislators had the foresight to ensure that national security concerns would supersede any nondisclosure requirements imposed by HIPAA. As noted above, the legislation does impose stringent nondisclosure restrictions on Covered Entities. Under the terms of HIPAA, one could not, for example, call the doctor of a family member to get information about that family member's medical condition unless the family member had previously executed a signed authorization allowing for the disclosure of his or her medical information to the particular family member making the inquiry. Nonetheless, HIPAA does authorize Covered Entities to disclose protected health information to authorized federal officials for the conduct of "lawful intelligence, counter-intelligence and other national security activities."[3]

The authority for disclosures related to national security activities is found in (i) the National Security Act[4] and applicable implementing authority[5] and (ii) the Foreign Intelligence Surveillance Act (FISA) [as amended by the Uniting and Strengthening America by Providing Appropriate Tools Required to Intercept and Obstruct Terrorism Act of 2001 (USA PATRIOT Act)].[6] As will be discussed in subsequent chapters, the USA PATRIOT Act permits FISA warrant searches of "any tangible thing" that could relate to "international terrorism or clandestine intelligence activities."

National security considerations can also impact another significant aspect of HIPAA, that is, the duty of Covered Entities to account for all disclosures of protected health information to third parties. Under HIPAA, Covered Entities may temporarily suspend their duty to account for disclosures because of law enforcement and/or national security reasons. All that is needed is a written or oral justification of the same. In a practical sense, all of the foregoing means that while HIPAA does provide for comprehensive privacy rights in the ordinary course, such rights can be overridden when "national security" concerns are at issue.

The Gramm–Leach–Bliley Act

Around this same period, lawmakers also enacted comprehensive provisions regarding financial privacy. While the Gramm–Leach–Bliley Act (GLB Act)[7] is a very broad measure, subtitle A of Title V focuses specifically on data privacy of financial institution consumers. Specifically, the GLB Act focuses upon privacy of the nonpublic information of individuals who are customers of financial institutions. The data privacy provisions of the GLB Act restrict the ability of financial institutions[8] to disclose a consumer's personal financial information to nonaffiliated third parties. Furthermore, the GLB Act also obliges financial institutions to provide notices about their information-collection and information-sharing practices to their customers and, subject to certain limited exceptions, to provide such individuals the opportunity to "opt out" if they do not wish for their information to be shared with nonaffiliated third parties.

Under the GLB Act there are specific exceptions under which a financial institution may share customer information with a third party without first granting an opt-out right to the customer. For example, the financial institution must provide notice but not the right to opt out when it gives nonpublic personal information to a third-party service provider that provides services for that financial institution or another financial institution(s) with which the financial institution has entered into a joint marketing agreement. A third-party service provider may market the financial institution's own products and services or the financial products or services offered under a "joint marketing agreement" between the financial institution and one or more other financial institutions. A joint marketing agreement with other financial institution(s) means a written contract pursuant to which those institutions jointly offer, endorse, or sponsor a financial product or service. However, to take advantage of this exception, the financial institution must (i) provide the initial notice as required to consumers and customers and (ii) enter into a contract with the third-party service provider or financial institution under a joint marketing agreement that prohibits the disclosure or use of the information other than for the purpose for which it was disclosed.

There are also certain exceptions to the notice and opt-out requirements.[9] The exceptions are as follows:

- disclosures necessary to effect, administer, or enforce a transaction that a consumer requests or authorizes;[10]

- disclosures made concerning servicing or processing a financial product or service that a consumer requests or authorizes; maintaining or servicing a consumer's account; or a proposed or actual securitization, secondary market sale (including the sale of servicing rights), or similar transactions;

- with consumer consent;

- to protect the confidentiality or security of records;

- to protect against or prevent actual or potential fraud;

- for required institutional risk control or for resolving consumer disputes or inquiries;

- to persons holding a legal or beneficial interest relating to the consumer;

- to persons acting in a fiduciary or representative capacity on behalf of the consumer (i.e., the consumer's attorney);

- to provide information to insurance rate advisory organizations, persons assessing compliance with industry standards, the financial institution's attorneys, accountants, or auditors;

- to law enforcement entities or self-regulatory groups (to the extent permitted or required by law);

- to comply with federal, state, or local laws;

- to comply with subpoena or other judicial process;

- to respond to summons or other requests from authorized government authorities;

- pursuant to the Fair Credit Reporting Act (FCRA), to a consumer reporting agency or from a consumer report generated by a consumer reporting agency;

- concerning a proposed or actual sale, merger, transfer, or exchange of all or a portion of a business or operating unit.

Like HIPAA, discussed in the previous section, the GLB Act contains exceptions for disclosures made to law enforcement authorities.

The GLB Act also contains significant security provisions. The GLB Act requires the Federal Trade Commission (FTC) and certain other federal agencies to establish standards with which financial institutions must comply to protect the security of their customers' nonpublic information. Furthermore, the FTC has issued a separate rule on Standards for Safeguarding Customer Information.[11] This rule requires financial institutions to develop, implement, and maintain a comprehensive information security program that contains administrative, technical, and physical safeguards. As part of such security program, each financial institution must (i) designate an employee or employees to coordinate the information security program; (ii) identify reasonably foreseeable internal and external risks to the security, confidentiality, and integrity of customer information that could result in the unauthorized disclosure, misuse, alteration, destruction, or other compromise of information and assess the sufficiency of any safeguards in place to control the risks; (iii) assure that contractors or service providers are capable of maintaining appropriate safeguards for the customer information and requiring them, by contract, to implement and maintain such safeguards; and (iv) adjust the information security program in light of developments that may materially affect the entity's safeguards.

Children's Online Privacy Protection Act

In the late 1990s, there was much concern regarding privacy on the Internet. There was even talk that the United States might enact a very broad law that would apply generally to privacy online. While U.S. legislators did not pass such a comprehensive measure, the country did enact a measure targeted toward a particular area of concern—that is, the privacy of children online.

The Children's Online Privacy Protection Act (hereinafter COPPA)[12] was signed into law on October 21, 1998. Its goals are (i) to enhance parental involvement to protect the privacy of children in the online environment; (ii) to help protect the safety of children in online forums such as chat rooms, home pages, and pen-pal services in which children may make public postings of identifying information collected online; and (iii) to limit the collection of personal information from children without parental consent.[13]

Pursuant to the act, operators of Web sites directed to children under 13 or that otherwise knowingly collect personal information from children under 13 on the Internet must provide parents notice of their information practices. Subject to certain very limited exception, such operators must also obtain prior, verifiable parental consent[14] for the collection, use, and/or disclosure[15] of personal information from children. Furthermore, upon request, operators must provide a parent with the ability to review the personal information collected from his/her child. The legislation also compels operators to provide parents with the opportunity to prevent the further use of personal information that has already been collected or the future collection of personal information from that child. In addition, Web site operators must also limit the collection of personal information for a child's online participation in a game, prize offer, or other activity to information that is reasonably necessary for the activity. Finally, the legislation mandates the establishment and maintenance of reasonable procedures to protect the confidentiality, security, and integrity of the personal information collected.[16]

The passage of COPPA is further evidence of the commitment on the part of U.S. legislators and regulators to afford protection to the privacy of children. The FTC has long demonstrated an interest in protecting children from unfair information-collection practices online. Even before the entry into force of COPPA, the FTC was active in investigating and even commencing enforcement actions against companies that were alleged to have engaged in unfair or deceptive information-collection practices involving children. For example, in 1998, the FTC commenced a proceeding against GeoCities for deceptive practices concerning GeoCities' collection and use of personal identifying information.[17] In addition, around the same time, the FTC also commenced an action against Liberty Financial Co. Inc. based upon allegations that the company was collecting data from children and using such data in a manner that was inconsistent with the company's stated policies.

Since the enactment of COPPA, the FTC has commenced several enforcement actions against entities alleged to have violated COPPA. On April 19, 2001, one year after the entry into force of COPPA, the FTC announced the settlement of the first three COPPA cases. These cases involved three companies—Monarch Services, Inc. and Girls Life, Inc., operators of www.girlslife.com; Bigmailbox.com, Inc. and

Nolan Quan, operators of www.bigmailbox.com; and Looksmart Ltd., operator of www.insidetheweb.com—with respect to alleged violations of COPPA.[18] The three companies were charged with illegally collecting personally identifying information from children under 13 years of age without parental consent.

In an aim to settle the FTC charges, the companies together agreed to pay $100,000 in civil penalties. Moreover, they also agreed to comply with COPPA concerning any future online collection of personally identifying information from children under 13 and to delete all personally identifying information collected from children online at any time since the effective date of COPPA.

Since the settlement of these three initial cases, the FTC has commenced several additional enforcement actions. In February 2003, the FTC received the largest COPPA civil penalties to date: a $100,000 from Mrs. Fields Cookies[19] and $85,000 from Hershey Foods.[20] While the cases settled thus far have been notable, all indications are that there will be additional enforcement actions. The FTC has demonstrated a tendency for being particularly vigilant insofar as the protection of children's privacy is concerned. Furthermore, the FTC recently sent notices to more than 50 Web site operators, warning them to bring their Web sites into compliance with COPPA.[21] The recent enforcement actions, along with the transmission of the warning letters, serve as a reminder of the importance of complying with the requirements of COPPA.

Electronic Communications Privacy Act

While the legislation is more dated than the previously discussed privacy measures, the Electronic Communications Privacy Act (ECPA)[22] is incredibly important within the context of the present discussion. This legislation places restrictions on the interception of electronic communications[23] and creates privacy protections for stored electronic communications. The ECPA was built on past law and was enacted to guard against potential abuses and constitutional violations in the area of electronic surveillance.

Prior to the ECPA, the key legislation applicable to communication surveillance was Title III of the Omnibus Crime Control and Safe Streets Act of 1968.[24] This measure codified rules regulating the use of wiretaps by law enforcement and provided that wiretaps may only be used in the investigation of certain identified categories of offenses (including counterfeiting, fraud, and offenses punishable by death) and only when the government can show probable cause that the suspect has committed, is committing, or is about to commit an allowable offense and there is probable cause that a wiretap will reveal communications concerning the offense. This measure also required that the government show that other means of obtaining the information have been exhausted. Under the terms of the law, court orders could authorize surveillance for a maximum of 30 days (with the possibility for a 30-day extension). Furthermore, authorities conducting surveillance were required to provide reports to the court every seven to ten days.

Generally, ECPA modifies Title III by imposing higher standards that must be met before the government is allowed to conduct electronic surveillance. To obtain a court order that would authorize electronic surveillance under Title III, the law enforcement agency must state the alleged offense being committed, the interception point for the communications, a description of the types of conversations to be intercepted, and the identity of the persons anticipated to be intercepted. Probable cause must be demonstrated with particularity, and it must be shown that normal investigative techniques are not effective in the investigation.

Once issued, court orders authorize surveillance for a maximum of 30 days (with the possibility of a 30-day extension) and require that reports are made to the court every seven to ten days.

The requirements for obtaining an order to allow the use of a pen register are less stringent: law enforcement need only show that the information likely to be obtained is relevant to an ongoing criminal investigation. Although the rules governing electronic surveillance were applied by the courts to Internet communications, the USA PATRIOT Act (which will be discussed in further detail in Chapter 3) amended the statutes governing electronic surveillance to explicitly extend to Internet communications.

ECPA is broken down into individual titles that cover different areas related to electronic communications. Title I of ECPA[25] concerns the acquisition and disclosure of communication streams. This title of the act is concerned with protecting both voice and data communications while in transit. The legislation's coverage of wire communications is limited to aural transfers made through cable, wire, and similar transmission media maintained by persons engaged in the business of providing or operating facilities for interstate or foreign communications.[26] ECPA prohibits the interception of oral, wire, and electronic communications by private and public parties unless specifically authorized by statute or by a court order.

Title II[27] of the act governs both the acquisition and the disclosure of stored information. The provisions of ECPA pertaining to stored communications prohibit the unauthorized access to or use of stored communications. These provisions also prohibit electronic communication service providers from disclosing the content of such stored communications except in certain limited circumstances.[28] Permissible disclosures include disclosures that are authorized by the sender or receiver of the message, disclosures that are necessary for the effective rendition of the service or system, and disclosures that pertain to the commission of a crime or law enforcement.[29]

Title III concerns the acquisition and disclosure of transactional information.[30] The provisions of this title contain restrictions on the use of mobile tracking devices, pen registers, and trap-and-trace devices. Such restrictions were modified by the USA PATRIOT Act.

The statute authorizes individuals or entities that are aggrieved by any intentional violation of ECPA to commence a civil action. Appropriate relief for individuals and/or entities damaged because of a violation of the statute may include preliminary, equitable or declaratory relief, as appropriate,[31] actual damages,[32] attorney's fees, and court costs.[33]

Video Privacy Protection Act

Also of potential interest concerning the present discussion of privacy rights in existence prior to 2001 is the Video Privacy Protection Act.[34] Subject to certain limited exceptions, this act prohibits video tape service providers[35] from disclosing personally identifiable information[36] about individuals who rent or buy videos to third parties.[37] The act provides that customers may bring an action against any video store that discloses personally identifiable information.[38] Actual damages are recoverable under the act but must not be less than liquidated damages in the amount of $2,500. In addition, punitive damages as well as reasonable attorney's fees and litigation costs and "preliminary and equitable" relief may be recoverable as deemed appropriate. There is a two-year statute of limitations on proceedings brought pursuant to the act.

State Laws

While the most significant data privacy laws in the United States have been enacted at the federal level, there is also a growing body of state privacy laws that have relevance to the present discussion. Many states have enacted legislation concerning specific matters of privacy protection such as the use of spyware, the protection of consumer credit information, school records, and financial data.[39] Other states have adopted more general privacy protection legislation. One example of the latter approach is California's Personal Information and Privacy Protection Act.[40] This legislation mandated the creation of an Office of Privacy Protection within the state's Department of Consumer Affairs and charged the office with protecting "the privacy of individuals' personal information in a manner consistent with the California Constitution by identifying consumer problems in the privacy area and facilitating development of fair information practices. . . "[41] The Personal Information and Privacy Protection Act contains many other notable provisions concerning privacy, including the requirement that all state governmental departments and agencies enact and maintain permanent privacy policies. California has clearly been the leader among the states in terms of enacting new privacy legislation; however, more recently a number of other states have begun to follow suit and regulate various aspects of privacy.

Representative Cases and Enforcement Actions

Overview

While enforcement actions involving data privacy violations are still relatively new, there have been many cases that show that entities that violate privacy laws may risk considerable penalties. To illustrate this point, this section shall examine several representative cases and enforcement actions.

FTC Enforcement of Privacy Policies

In addition to complying with requirements set forth in applicable data privacy laws and regulations, entities will also have to ensure that their data collection, use, and disclosure practices are conducted in accordance with their own stated policies. Many cases clearly demonstrate that companies will be bound by the terms of their stated policies. Such cases are of particular importance when one considers the kinds of demands for information that governmental authorities have been making on private entities, including requiring such companies to disclose customer data to the government, even where doing so would cause the companies to be in violation of their own policies.

In July 2000, the FTC commenced an enforcement action against bankrupt online toy store Toysmart.com, LLC and Toysmart.com, Inc. (collectively Toysmart). The FTC was alerted when, in conjunction with its dissolution, Toysmart attempted to sell personal data collected via the Internet, even though the privacy policy posted at the time the personal data were collected assured customers that the information that was collected from them would never be shared with third parties. Specifically, the privacy policy contained a provision which stated that "personal information, voluntarily submitted by visitors to our site, such as name, address, billing information and shopping preferences, is never shared with a third party." The policy continued, "[W]hen you register with toysmart.com, you can rest assured that your information will never be shared with a third party."

On May 22, 2000, Toysmart announced that it was closing its operations and selling its assets. Despite the assurances in Toysmart's privacy policy, Toysmart offered personal data collected via its Web site as part of the assets it was selling.

Because of Toysmart's actions, the FTC initiated an enforcement action against the company, charging that it had violated Section 5 of the FTC Act by misrepresenting to customers that personal data would never be shared with third parties and then disclosing, selling, and offering for sale that personal data in violation of the company's stated privacy policy.

This action eventually ended in a settlement, pursuant to which Toysmart was prohibited from selling its customer list as a stand-alone asset.[42] The settlement permitted Toysmart to sell such customer lists containing personal data only (i) as part of a package which included the entire Web site, (ii) to an entity that was in a related market, and (iii) to an entity that expressly agreed to be Toysmart's successor in interest as to the personal data. Under the terms of the settlement, the buyer of Toysmart's assets would have to agree to abide by Toysmart's privacy policy and to obtain the affirmative consent ("opt in") of the data subjects prior to using their personal data in any manner that was inconsistent with Toysmart's original privacy policy.[43]

Toysmart's difficulties with the FTC illustrate clearly the hazards of posting a privacy policy that is not completely accurate. For Toysmart, as well as many other similar companies, personal data are a major asset. By drafting a privacy policy in a very restrictive manner, Toysmart effectively limited its business plan and was not able to use one of its primary assets as it had intended. When the company attempted to transfer the personal data it had collected in contravention of its privacy policy, the FTC prevented it from doing so.

More recently, a series of FTC enforcement actions have suggested that the FTC is placing particular emphasis on enforcing data security assurances made in online privacy policies. First, in early 2001, pharmaceutical giant Eli Lilly became the subject of an FTC enforcement action because of the security guarantees made in its online privacy policy. Eli Lilly manufactures many pharmaceutical products, including the antidepressant Prozac. In marketing Prozac, Eli Lilly operates a Prozac Web site, through which it collects various personal data from visitors to the Web site. From March 2000 to June 2001, Eli Lilly offered a service called "Medi-Messenger" through its Prozac Web site. The Medi-Messenger service enabled registered users to receive individualized email reminders from Lilly concerning their Prozac medication or other matters. On June 27, 2001, Eli Lilly sent a form email message to subscribers to the service. The message included, in the "To:" entry line, the email addresses of every individual subscriber.

The FTC commenced an action against Eli Lilly, alleging that it made false or misleading representations in the privacy policy for the Medi-Messenger service.[44] The privacy policy that was posted on the Web site at the time the information was collected stated that Eli Lilly employed measures and took steps appropriate under the circumstances to maintain and protect the privacy and confidentiality of personal data obtained from or about consumers through the Prozac Web site. The FTC alleged that Eli Lilly had not employed such measures or taken such steps.

Further, it contended that Eli Lilly failed to provide appropriate training for its employees regarding consumer privacy and information security; failed to provide appropriate oversight and assistance for the employee who sent out the email, an individual who had no prior experience in creating, testing, or implementing the computer program used; and failed to implement appropriate checks and controls on the process, such as reviewing the computer program with experienced personnel and testing the program internally before broadcasting the email.

Eli Lilly eventually settled the matter with the FTC and signed a consent order containing provisions intended to prevent the company from engaging in similar acts and practices in the future.[45] The consent order applies broadly to the collection of personal data from or about consumers concerning the advertising, marketing, offering for sale, or sale of any pharmaceutical, medical, or other health-related product or service by Eli Lilly.[46] It consists of six parts, but the most significant to the current discussion are Parts I and II. Part I of the consent order prohibits misrepresentations regarding the extent to which Eli Lilly maintains and protects the privacy or confidentiality of any personal data collected from or about consumers.

Part II of the consent order requires Eli Lilly to implement a four-stage information security program designed to protect the confidentiality and security of consumers' personal data and to protect it against unauthorized access, use, or disclosure. The four stages require Eli Lilly to (i) designate appropriate personnel to coordinate and oversee the program; (ii) identify foreseeable risks to the security, confidentiality, and integrity of personal data and address these risks in each relevant area of its operations; (iii) conduct an annual written review by qualified persons that monitors and documents compliance with the program, evaluates its effectiveness, and recommends changes to it; and (iv) adjust the program in light of any findings and recommendations resulting from reviews or ongoing monitoring.

The FTC also commenced a similar enforcement action against Microsoft, and most recently, the FTC commenced an action against clothing manufacturer Guess.[47] The Guess action marked the third time that the FTC settled an enforcement action against a company that allegedly made false assurances regarding the level of security it provided to individuals' personal data. In this most recent case, the FTC alleged that clothing manufacturer Guess failed to use reasonable or appropriate measures to protect consumers' personal data and thereby exposed such consumers' information to commonly known attacks by hackers, all in contravention of Guess's assurances that the data collected through its Web site would be protected.

Guess has sold clothing and accessories through its Web site at www.guess.com since 1998. The FTC alleged that since October 2000, the company's Web site has been vulnerable to many commonly known Web-based application attacks. According to the FTC, despite these attacks, Guess's online statements assured consumers that their information would be protected. Specifically, according to the FTC, at the time the Guess Web site was attacked, it contained the following statements: "This site has security measures in place to protect the loss, misuse and alteration of information under our control" and "All of your personal information, including your credit card information and sign-in password, are stored in an unreadable, encrypted format at all times." The FTC alleged that, despite these assurances, Guess did not store consumers' information in an unreadable, encrypted format at all times and that the security measures implemented by Guess failed to protect against structured query language and other commonly known attacks.

The settlement agreement prohibits Guess from misrepresenting the degree to which it protects the security of personal information collected from consumers. It also requires Guess to establish and maintain a comprehensive data security program. Furthermore, Guess is required to have its security program certified annually by an independent security professional.

The Guess settlement marks the third case in which the FTC challenged the information security guarantees made by a company that has collected information from consumers online. This case, along with its predecessors, emphasizes that the FTC has become quite active in its efforts to ensure that companies are not making false or misleading promises about their data security measures.

Immediately after September 11, 2001, there was relatively little enforcement activity. However, more recently, there has been a slight resurgence in activity, particular with regard to data security. In terms of the more recent enforcement actions, the FTC has been active in commencing cases against companies that have failed to comply with their own promises regarding data security and, even more recently, has taken action against a company that has simply failed to have provided adequate security irrespective of any promises regarding the same.

PRIVACY DEVELOPMENTS AFTER SEPTEMBER 11

Legislative Development of Note

Since September 11, 2001, overall efforts to enact new privacy legislation in the United States have waned considerably. Efforts that have been taken have been centralized in certain limited areas. There have, for instance, been measures designed to protect credit card information and to impose restrictions upon (or, some would argue, to permit) the transmission of unsolicited commercial email.[48] Another area of much activity has been data security, with state legislators focusing on enacting legal measures to protect consumers from data security breaches. Such concerns have been justified, at least in part, by the numerous large-scale data security breaches that have been announced over the course of the past year and a half.[49]

Federal Level

On December 4, 2003, President George W. Bush signed into law the Fair and Accurate Credit Transactions Act of 2003[50] (FACTA). FACTA amends the FCRA, which created national credit reporting standards, but that was due to expire on January 1, 2004. The FCRA[51] placed duties on consumer reporting agencies.[52] Specifically, the law requires every consumer credit reporting agency to take appropriate measures to prevent any inappropriate disclosure of information. For their part, prospective users of information must identify themselves, certify the purposes for obtaining the information, and certify that the information will not be used for any unauthorized purposes. Under the FCRA, consumers have the right to opt out of receiving preapproved credit card offers in the mail.

FACTA contains many consumer protections, including new tools to improve the accuracy of credit information and to help fight identity theft. The act includes several notable provisions regarding general consumer rights, as summarized below:

- the legislation adds several responsibilities to companies that furnish information to the credit bureaus;
- FACTA provides more specific standards for accuracy of data maintained by reporting agencies;
- FACTA provides consumers with the right to correct inaccuracies in data profiles;
- it gives consumers the right to opt out of unsolicited offers.

Not surprisingly, given the emphasis placed on data security and the risks of identity theft during this period, FACTA includes several notable provisions regarding identity theft, including the following:

- procedures FACTA required credit bureaus to implement to handle fraud alerts will be required by December 1, 2004;
- consumers were given the right to place fraud alerts on credit report and block credit bureaus from reporting information in their credit files because of identity theft;
- credit bureaus were required to implement a 90-day alert on a consumer's credit file when customer's wallet or purse is lost or stolen;

- Consumers were empowered to request a 7-year alert where, in addition to the loss or theft of a wallet or purse, evidence exists that a thief opened credit accounts in the consumer's name;

- service members became able to request that a military duty alert be placed on their files since military personnel serving abroad would not be opening many new accounts during the time of service;

- consumers became entitled to obtain information about accounts or transactions in their name that result from identity theft.

While FACTA did establish certain important consumer protections, it has also been criticized on many grounds. Most significantly, it has been attached for preempting states from implementing more stringent—and perhaps more effective—laws concerning identity theft.

State Level

At the state level, much of the activity has focused upon addressing issues related to data security breaches. California was again a leader in this area, having enacted its own comprehensive data security breach notification law in 2002.[53] California's law, often referred to as "S.B. 1386," applies to any online business having customers in California—even if the business itself is not based in California. Pursuant to S.B. 1386, which was enacted in 2002 and entered into force on July 1, 2003, all agencies, persons, or businesses that conduct business in California and that own or license computerized data containing personal information will be required to report breaches in the security of such data to any resident of California whose unencrypted personal information has been compromised because of the breach.

To trigger the notification requirements under the law, the security breach must involve personal information, which is defined as an individual's first name or first initial and last name combined with one or more of the following pieces of data: (i) social security number; (ii) driver's license number or California Identification Card number; or (iii) account number, credit or debit card number, in combination with any required security code, access code, or password that would permit access to an individual's financial account.[54] Furthermore, the notification requirements will only be triggered in situations in which either the name or the additional data elements are not encrypted.

Where an agency, person, or business is processing such personal information and suffers a breach of the security of its systems, it must notify the affected customers in "the most expedient time possible and without unreasonable delay."[55] Significantly, the new law defines a breach of security broadly as an "unauthorized acquisition of computerized data that compromises the security, confidentiality, or integrity of personal information maintained by the agency, person or business."[56]

Individuals or entities required to provide such notice may do so in writing or electronically. However, all electronic notices must be in compliance with the federal Electronic Signatures in Global and National Commerce Act of 2000. Notwithstanding the foregoing, in instances where (i) the cost of providing the requisite notice would exceed $250,000, (ii) the number of people to be notified exceeds 500,000, or (iii) there is no sufficient contact information available, the affected individual or entity may provide substitute notice, which would consist of providing all of the following: (i) email notice if email addresses are available, (ii) Web site notice provided there is a Web site that can be used to post such notice, and (iii) notification to major statewide media.

After a series of high-profile data security breaches in early 2005, numerous states rushed to follow suit, enacting their own breach notification measures, the bulk of which are modeled closely after California's law.[57]

Among all states, California has certainly been the most active and, to date, has enacted numerous laws concerning the privacy of personal information. With respect to Web-related activity, one of the most notable measures is California's Online Privacy Protection Act of 2003[58], which became effective on July 1, 2004. The law requires all operators of commercial Web sites or online services ("Operators") that collect personally identifiable information from California residents through Web sites or other similar online service ("Web Sites") to post a privacy policy and to comply with the same.[59]

The Online Privacy Protection Act adopts a broad view of "personally identifiable information," defining it as any individually identifiable information about a person collected online including any of the following: (i) first and last name, (ii) a home or other physical address, (iii) an email address, (iv) a telephone number, (v) a social security number, (vi) any other identifier that permits the physical or online contacting of a specific individual, and/or (vii) information concerning a user that the Operator collects online from the user and combines with any of the identifiers described above.[60] The breadth of the definition of personally identifiable information ensures that the vast majority of Operators collecting information online will fall under the requirements of the new legislation.

In addition to requiring all Operators collecting personally identifiable information from California residents to post a privacy policy, the Online Privacy

Protection Act sets forth specific requirements about the content of such a privacy policy. Specifically, the privacy policy must:

- identify the categories of information that the Operator collects through the Internet and the categories of persons or entities with which the Operator may share the information;

- disclose whether or not the Operator maintains a process for an individual user of and/or visitor to the Operator's Web Sites to review and request changes to his or her personally identifiable information and, if so, provide a description of such process;

- disclose whether the Operator reserves the right to change its privacy policy without notice to the individual user of, or visitor to, the Web Sites;

- identify the effective date of the privacy policy.

Quite significantly, the legislation also establishes rules regarding the placement of privacy policies, requiring that they be posted conspicuously on the Operator's Web Site. While the law does include several examples of displays that would be considered conspicuously posted, it also contains a catch-all category. The Online Privacy Protection Act provides that an Operator will be considered in violation of the act if (i) the Operator fails to post a privacy policy within 30 days of being notified of that it is not in compliance with the requirements of the legislation and/or (ii) the Operator either knowingly and willfully or negligently and materially fails to comply with the provisions of its own privacy policy. The legislation will be enforced through California's unfair competition law,[61] which provides for civil fines and injunctive relief.[62]

Enforcement Actions of Note

In keeping with trends regarding legislative developments at the State level, in terms of enforcement actions in recent years, on the commercial side, much emphasis has been placed on data security issues. Indeed, most of the FTC enforcement actions to arise after 2001 have focused on data security issues. In 2004, the FTC entered into a consent agreement with Petco Animal Supplies, Inc. (Petco). The FTC alleged that Petco had engaged in deceptive trade practices by including various statements in its online privacy policy including:

At PETCO.com, protecting your information is our number one priority, and your personal information is strictly shielded from unauthorized access.

Entering your credit card number via our secure server is completely safe. The server encrypts all of your information; no one except you can access it.

The FTC alleged that these statements were a deceptive trade practice because Petco was unable to completely protect the data it received from its computer servers. The FTC settlement prohibits Petco from misrepresenting the extent to which it maintains and protects sensitive consumer information. It also requires Petco to establish and maintain a comprehensive information security program designed to protect the security, confidentiality, and integrity of personal information collected from or about consumers. It requires that Petco arrange biennial audits of its security program by an independent third party certifying that Petco's security program is sufficiently effective to provide reasonable assurance that the security, confidentiality, and integrity of consumers' personal information have been protected. The settlement also contains record-keeping provisions to allow the FTC to monitor compliance.[63]

In addition, the FTC targeted Gateway Learning Corporation (Gateway) in 2004 and entered into a consent agreement with Gateway. The FTC alleged that Gateway had engaged in unfair and deceptive trade practices by sharing customer information collected after explicitly promising on its Web site not to do so. Initially, the Gateway privacy policy stated that "[w]e do not sell, rent or loan any personally identifiable information regarding our consumers with any third party unless we receive customer's explicit consent." Gateway then decided to sell customer information collected on its Web site and altered its privacy policy to state that "from time to time" Gateway would provide consumers' personal information to "reputable companies" whose products or services consumers might find of interest.

The FTC charged that (i) Gateway's claims that it would not sell, rent, or loan to third parties consumers' personal information unless it received the consumers' consent and that it would never share information about children were false; (ii) Gateway's retroactive application of a materially changed privacy policy to information it had previously collected from consumers was an unfair practice; and (iii) Gateway's failure to notify consumers of the changes to its privacy policy and practices, as promised in the original policy, was a deceptive practice. The settlement bars misrepresentations about how Gateway will use data it collects from consumers. It prohibits Gateway from sharing any personal information collected from consumers on its Web site under the earlier privacy policy unless it first obtains express affirmative, or opt-in, consent from consumers and prohibits it from applying future material changes to its privacy policy retroactively without consumers' consent. It also requires Gateway to give up the $4,608 it earned from renting consumers' information.[64]

In April 2005, the FTC settled charges against BJ's Wholesale Club (BJ's). According to the complaint, the FTC alleged that BJ's use of a computer network to obtain bank authorization for credit and debit card purchases and to track inventory at that time, for credit and debit card purchases at its stores, BJ's collected information such as name, card number, and expiration date from the magnetic stripe on the back of the cards. The information was then sent from the computer network in the store to BJ's central datacenter computer network and from there through outside computer networks to the bank that issued the card. The FTC charged that BJ's engaged in many practices that, taken together, did not provide reasonable security for sensitive customer information.

These practices noted by the FTC as being deficient included (a) BJ's failure to encrypt consumer information when it was transmitted or stored on computers in its stores, (b) BJ's creation of unnecessary risks to the information by storing it for up to 30 days, and (c) storing the information in files that could be accessed using commonly known default user IDs and passwords. The settlement required BJ's to establish and maintain a comprehensive information security program that includes administrative, technical, and physical safeguards. The settlement also required BJ's to obtain an audit from a qualified, independent, third-party professional that its security program meets the standards of the order and to comply with standard book-keeping and record-keeping provisions.[65]

SUMMARY AND CONCLUSION

This chapter has focused on highlighting the general trends in the development of privacy law in the United States just prior to and immediately preceding the momentous attacks of 2001. During the late 1990s, under the Clinton administration, many laws concerning privacy rights in particular areas were enacted. Collectively, such laws elevated and increased the privacy rights enjoyed by individual citizens. For comparative purposes, this chapter then moved on to explore the relatively small amount of privacy measures that were introduced and enacted in the period just after September 11.

The next chapter will proceed to analyze how privacy rights unraveled and deteriorated in the United States in the months and years after the terrorist attacks. It will specifically examine the various measures that were introduced and undertaken by the U.S. government to respond to the new threat of terrorism that was upon the country. Efforts will be directed to showing how the breadth of such measures resulted in infringements upon fundamental human rights and liberties.

Two

War on Terrorism and
Privacy Rights in the United States

INTRODUCTION

Having introduced the privacy regime, as it existed prior to the terrorist attacks of September 11, in this chapter the focus will shift to examining how such attacks and our response thereto (including the legislation passed as a result thereof) have been eroding privacy rights in the United States. Significant focus will be placed on the Uniting and Strengthening America by Providing Appropriate Tools Required to Intercept and Obstruct Terrorism Act of 2001 (USA PATRIOT Act) and similar legislation. This chapter will also examine controversial data-mining programs and will show how the government has been calling upon private industry to participate in its counterterrorism efforts, including by requiring companies to share their customer data with various governmental agencies. This chapter will show how a lot of these measures were undertaken with great secrecy or, at the very least, a lack of full disclosure and will demonstrate why this is of great concern.

OVERVIEW OF SIGNIFICANT LEGISLATIVE DEVELOPMENTS AFTER SEPTEMBER 11

Generally

In the United States, laws and policies concerning terrorism (and impacting privacy) have undergone a dramatic change since September 11, 2001. The speed with which such measures have been proposed has been dramatic. By September 2002, just one year after the attacks, the Office of Management and Budget counted 58 new regulations responding to terrorism.[1] While it would exceed the scope of this publication to examine each of these measures as well as the numerous measures that have continued to have been proposed each year thereafter in detail, the following section shall examine some of the most significant counterterrorism legislation enacted in the United States subsequent to the terrorist attacks of September 11.

USA PATRIOT Act

Overview

One of the most important—and controversial—legislative developments to occur after September 11 is the USA PATRIOT Act[2] (Patriot Act). This extremely lengthy and comprehensive bill was passed in an extraordinarily fast manner. Once the legislation was introduced, former Attorney General Ashcroft was said to have given Congress one week in which to pass the measure. Vermont Democrat Patrick Leahy, chairman of the Senate Judiciary Committee, managed to convince the Justice Department to agree to some changes, and members of the House sought significant improvements. However, reportedly, the former Attorney General warned that new attacks were imminent, the legislation was needed right away, and cautioned that Congress could be to blame if the measures were not enacted and further attacks ensued.[3] Quick but extensive negotiations then ensued in the Senate, and a bill, stripped of many of the protections that Senator Leahy had worked to implement, resulted. Senator Thomas Daschle, the majority leader, sought unanimous consent to pass the proposal without debate or amendment; Senator Russ Feingold was the only member to object. Minor changes were made in the House, which passed the bill 357 to 66. The Senate and House versions were quickly reconciled, and the act was signed into law on October 26, 2001.

While the Patriot Act was long considered controversial by many, some took comfort in the fact that many of the provisions were intended to be of temporary effect. Many of the clauses of the Patriot Act were set to expire in 2005 if not renewed. After a massive public relations campaign in support of the legislation, the measure was renewed on March 2, 2006, with a vote of 89–11 in the Senate and on March 7, 2006, 280–138 in the House. The renewal was signed into law by President George W. Bush on March 9, 2006.

Significant Provisions of Note

The Patriot Act is extraordinarily complex and detailed legislation that made sweeping changes to many significant aspects of U.S. law. The Patriot Act amended several different federal laws, including (i) Wiretap Statute (Title III), (ii) Electronic Communications Privacy Act (ECPA), (iii) Computer Fraud and

Abuse Act, (iv) Foreign Intelligence Surveillance Act (FISA), (v) Family Education Rights and Privacy Act, (vi) Pen Register and Trap and Trace Statute, (vii) Money Laundering Act, (viii) Immigration and Nationality Act, (ix) Money Laundering Control Act, (x) Bank Secrecy Act, (xi) Right to Financial Privacy Act, and (xii) Fair Credit Reporting Act.

While it is beyond the scope of this publication to examine all of the changes brought on by the measure in close detail, it is useful to examine some of the main ways in which the Patriot Act enhanced the powers of the government to conduct surveillance and engage in related activities. First, the legislation made significant changes to the laws regarding wiretaps. Because of the Patriot Act, wiretap or interception orders can now be ordered for a larger number of suspected crimes (including acts related to terrorism and computer abuse).[4] In addition, a new exception to the general prohibition against wiretapping was created. This exception allows the interception of communications to or from a "computer trespasser" on a "protected computer."[5] The act allows for roving wiretaps[6] under the FISA.[7]

The Patriot Act also expanded the right of authorities to conduct searches and has increased the level of secrecy with which various searches may be conducted. Under the Patriot Act, authorities became authorized to obtain a nationwide search warrant when investigating domestic or international terrorism. The warrant can be authorized by a judge "in any district in which activities related to terrorism may have occurred . . ."[8] Nationwide authorizations may now be obtained for electronic evidence.[9] Prior to the Patriot Act, generally, law enforcement authorities were required to provide subjects of a search warrant with notice of the search warrant (for the purposes of allowing the individual subject to such warrant to evaluate the warrant for any deficiencies and invoke 4th Amendment rights). The Patriot Act has provided authorities with the ability to delay the notice of a search warrant.[10] Furthermore, under the legislative revisions brought upon by the Patriot Act, voice mails may be seized via a search warrant (rather than a wiretap order, which was previously the case).[11]

The Patriot Act also increased the ability of governmental agencies to share information with other governmental agencies. Under the act, a governmental attorney, investigator, or law enforcement officer with "knowledge of the contents of a wire, oral or electronic communication, or evidence derived therefrom, may disclose such contents to any other Federal law enforcement, intelligence, protective, immigration, national defense, or national security official to the extent that such contents include foreign intelligence or counterintelligence . . . or foreign intelligence information."[12] The disclosure must be made to assist the recipient officer "in the performance of his official duties," and the recipient is authorized to use the information "only as necessary."[13]

There are numerous troubling aspects to the Patriot Act that are beyond the specific substantive areas of concern noted briefly in the preceding paragraphs. The fact that such a detailed and comprehensive measure was passed so quickly and with such little debate is in and of itself a cause for concern. Many critics have also noted that the new powers introduced by the Patriot Act are overly broad in nature. In many respects, the legislation shifts the very well-established burden of proof.

INCREASED SURVEILLANCE ACTIVITY

In the aftermath of the September 11 terrorist attacks and those to follow, there has been a tremendous increase in surveillance activity in a great number of different areas. Around the country, vast amounts of public dollars are being poured into new surveillance initiatives, and many high-tech companies are discovering a new lucrative industry in which to specialize. One recent report suggests that the current video surveillance software market, while presently estimated at $153.7 million, is expected to witness a healthy compound annual growth rate of 23.4 percent to reach $670.7 million in 2011.[14] While these figures are impressive enough, it is important to remember that these particular figures apply only to the software component in the video surveillance systems. All indications suggest that surveillance will be a huge industry for years to come.

The examples of the surveillance systems being utilized and/or contemplated in the United States are virtually endless. Individuals seeking to take any form of transportation are subject to more frequent and more intense monitoring, and it has become difficult to identify any public area that lacks one or more closed-circuit televisions (CCTVs). More recently, news of President George W. Bush's reported actions in secretly authorizing the National Security Agency (NSA) to eavesdrop on Americans and others inside the United States to search for evidence of terrorist activity without the court-approved warrants ordinarily required for such activity causes concern among many and outrage among others, especially privacy advocates.[15]

Still, while the United States has been using surveillance methods, the country has not warmed up as quickly to the idea of widespread CCTV camera surveillance as certain other nations, notably the U.K. While private use of cameras is relatively widespread, the use of CCTV by law enforcement remains quite limited in the United States.[16]

New York City has a burgeoning network, and there are also cameras in New Orleans and on transportation systems around the country, but analysts say there is neither the depth nor coordination of coverage that there is in Britain.[17]

In addition to privacy concerns, costs have also prevented the widespread use of CCTV in a public manner within the United States. Some reports have asserted that in such systems, each camera could cost around $60,000, depending on each unit's capabilities.[18] With limited funds available, policymakers have been trying to determine where to best place available resources. While many agree that cameras can be useful in helping investigators piece together the elements of a terrorist attack, after the fact, there is less agreement on whether cameras can be as effective a deterrent as other mechanisms, such as bomb-sniffing dogs or explosive-detection machines.

While the use of CCTV remains relatively limited in the U.S. public transit system, certain cities have pursued other strategies to try and protect the security of buses and subways. Physical searches, for instance, have been utilized in many jurisdictions. However, in addition to raising privacy concerns, conducting physical searches assumes a large amount of police resources and can lead to delays in travel.[19]

DATA SHARING

In the wake of the terrorist attacks, a tremendous amount of effort has been directed toward developing and implementing new mechanisms and methods for data sharing and mining. The following section shall examine some of the most notable of those efforts.

Disclosure of Company Customer Data to the Government

Private enterprises are being put in the very difficult position of trying to respond to governmental demands while also honoring promises made to customers and clients. Proponents of such governmental efforts tend to argue that companies involved in the privacy industry have at their disposition a wide range of data that can be useful in the war on terror. But opponents have contended that, among other problems, such efforts allow the government to access and use information that it would not otherwise be permitted to access and use. The following sections will examine some of these measures and highlight some of the principle issues that are involved with this kind of information sharing.

The NSA and its Role in Data Collection

The NSA was created by President Harry Truman in 1952 during the Korean War. It is charged with protecting the United States from foreign security threats. Today, the NSA is considered to have significant expertise in data mining. While the NSA has been getting much press attention lately—even being the subject of frequent jokes on mainstream television programming, such as the Jay Leno and David Letterman shows—the agency has a long history of being associated with controversial privacy issues. Public concerns about the NSA were first raised in 1975 when a congressional investigation revealed that the NSA had been intercepting international communications for more than 20 years—in all instances without warrants. The widespread surveillance campaign—and the public outcry that followed—led to the enactment of the FISA in 1978, legislation designed to protect Americans from illegal eavesdropping.

FISA establishes procedures the government must follow to conduct electronic surveillance and physical searches of individuals believed to have been involved in espionage or international terrorism directed against the United States. FISA requests for warrants are considered by a special court of 11 members.

Notwithstanding the existence of FISA and other legal protections against surveillance activities within the domestic territory of the United States, recent reports have suggested that the government has been engaging in a range of questionable surveillance activities.

Collection of Telecommunication Data by the NSA

In May 2006, it was reported that various large telecommunication service providers had been providing telephone call records of tens of millions of Americans to the NSA.[20] The NSA has reportedly been using the data to analyze calling patterns in an effort to detect terrorist activity. The database of telephone calling records is the "largest database ever assembled in the world," according to one anonymous source quoted in a *USA Today* report.[21]

Anonymous sources quoted in various news outlets have claimed that AT&T, Verizon, and BellSouth have been working under contract with the NSA since shortly after September 11, 2001.[22] The program, as described by anonymous tipsters, is far more comprehensive and invasive than the program acknowledged by the White House in 2005. Previously, President George W. Bush had admitted that he had authorized the NSA to eavesdrop on international calls and emails of people suspected of having links to terrorism when one party to such communication is located in the United States. In defending the authorization of this previously disclosed program, the White House emphasized that its efforts were focused exclusively on international calls.[23] Therefore, while many individuals had concerns about such previously disclosed program, the assurances provided by the White House led many to believe that at least domestic communications (i.e., calls originating and terminating within the

U.S.) would remain private. The recent revelations regarding the nature and scope of the NSA's domestic surveillance program have caused many to rethink their assumptions about the privacy of domestic communications.

As another example of the secrecy with which the government has been carrying out many of its counterterrorism efforts, neither the NSA nor the White House has provided clear comment on the nature or extent of the program or even whether it actually exists as described. It is this very secrecy and lack of clear information that may be increasing public concern.

According to media reports, while the three major telecommunication companies did provide the requested data—without any warrants—Qwest refused to participate in the program because of concerns that complying with the request would result in a violation of federal privacy laws.[24] While Qwest is a much smaller company with 14 million customers in 14 states, the company has a significant base of users in the West and Northwest.

According to published news reports, the NSA approached the telecommunication companies soon after September 11, 2001, requesting that they provide their call-detail records, understood as a complete listing of the calling histories of all customers. Reportedly, the NSA was also requiring the carriers to provide regular updates on the provided data.

The program has raised grave concerns among many who are concerned with individual liberties and privacy rights. One reason for such alarm is the sheer size of the program. The three companies alleged to have participated in the program—Verizon, BellSouth, and AT&T—are the nation's three biggest telecommunication companies and collectively they provide telephone and wireless service to more than 200 million customers. Furthermore, in addition to traditional calling services, these companies provide a wide range of communication services to a very large body of American consumers and are therefore uniquely positioned to provide the government with a pool of data that will facilitate the government's ability to build a database that clearly outlines the communication activities of Americans. The breadth of the program is another obvious cause for concern. In amassing data from this immensely huge population of users, the government has cast an enormously large net around tens of millions of ordinary Americans, most of whom have never even been accused of a crime, let alone suspected of terrorism.

Of course, the program also raises significant legal concerns. Historically, telecommunication companies, such as those involved in this program, have required court orders before they would disclose any customer's calling data to governmental authorities. Such policies were based at least in part on law.

Pursuant to section 222 of the Communications Act,[25] carriers are prohibited from disclosing information regarding a customer's calling habits. The penalties for violating the Communications Act are far from inconsequential—even for large carriers. The Federal Communications Commission (FCC) has the power to levy fines up to $130,000 per day per violation, with a cap of $1.325 million per violation. Agreeing to participate and provide the government with the requested calling data may have also caused the carriers to be in violation of their own privacy policies, if such policies did not allow for the disclosure of data to governmental agencies in response to a request not involving a subpoena.

Public news of the NSA case has raised a tremendous amount of concern among the public and privacy advocates. The American public has previously demonstrated a relatively high level of tolerance for various governmental actions that infringed upon their privacy rights, provided that such actions appeared to be reasonably calculated toward preventing terrorism. However, reports of this particular program caused a significantly negative reaction among the public. An opinion poll reported in *USA Today* in May 2006 found that 51 percent of Americans polled disapproved of the program.[26] Similarly, a *Newsweek* poll conducted at the same time found 53 percent of Americans reporting that the surveillance program "goes too far in invading people's privacy."[27]

Reports of the NSA program have also led to numerous legal actions.[28] In May 2006, attorneys filed a class-action lawsuit against Verizon, BellSouth, and AT&T, alleging that each of the companies participated illegally in the NSA domestic spying program. The complaint is asking that the companies pay $200 billion in fines to their 200 million subscribers.

In another development, the Electronic Privacy Information Center (EPIC) filed a complaint with the FCC, asking the agency to investigate claims that telephone companies shared private customer data with the NSA as part of a domestic surveillance program.[29] The complaint focused on the requirements of the Communications Act and contended that if the media reports that accuse the telecommunication companies of sharing information with the NSA are accurate, then the carriers violated section 222 of the Communications Act.

In yet another development, on May 22, 2006, six prominent social and political leaders joined together with the American Civil Liberties Union (ACLU) to sue AT&T, accusing the carrier of violating the privacy of millions of customers in Illinois by disclosing telephone records to the NSA.[30] The suit alleges that AT&T violated the ECPA when it provided subscriber data to the NSA. The suit seeks a court order enjoining the telecommunication carrier from providing such records to the NSA or any other government agency, except as specifically authorized under law.

Veteran journalist Studs Terkel is a lead plaintiff in the action. He spoke out against the action of the NSA and the carriers, noting:

> Having been blacklisted from working in television during the McCarthy era, I know the harm of the government using private corporations to intrude into the lives of innocent Americans. When government uses the telephone companies to create massive databases of all our telephone calls it has gone too far.[31]

The FCC has asserted that it will not investigate whether telecommunication carriers violated the law by sharing subscriber data with the NSA. In a letter released on May 23, 2006, by Representative Edward MacKey (D-Mass.), FCC Chairman Kevin Martin contended that the FCC was unable to examine the NSA program because of its classified nature.

On May 26, 2006, a group of plaintiffs, including journalists, lawyers, ministers, psychiatrists, and a former Congressman, joined with the ACLU to file lawsuits against AT&T and Verizon, claiming that the companies violated their California privacy rights by allegedly providing telephone call information to the NSA.[32] In their lawsuit, the plaintiffs focused upon the constitutional rights to privacy afforded under article I, section 1 of the California Constitution as well as section 2891 of the California Public Utilities Code, which prohibits releasing telephone calling records without consent or a court order. The lawsuit seeks injunctions preventing Californians' personal telephone records from being turned over to the NSA.

The fall-out from this issue continues to develop. In June 2006, AT&T unveiled a new privacy policy. The company's new policy marked the first time that a telecommunication carrier asserted that records regarding customer calling and Internet usage constitute corporate property.

Under the revised privacy policy, AT&T restricted itself from sharing data with third-party marketing firms but clarified that it would share data with the government and law enforcement agencies under certain circumstances. Insofar as uses of its broadband Internet services are concerned, the company also clarified that it would collect information about which Web pages its users viewed, the time that is spent on each Web page, and what links are clicked. The new policy provides:

> While your account information may be personal to you, these records constitute business records that are owned by AT&T. As such, AT&T may disclose such records to protect its legitimate business interests, safeguard others, or respond to legal process.[33]

Critics have claimed that, in light of the recent debates regarding the disclosure of telecommunication data to the government, AT&T's actions mark a fundamental change in how the rights and information of online users are viewed.[34] They are, in essence, endeavoring to redefine information provided by a user (either directly or by virtue of the usage habits) as their information. This development is quite significant given the size and importance of AT&T, and it may set a precedent for other companies—both within and outside the telecommunication sector—to follow.

Travel Industry Data

Reports of data-sharing and data-mining efforts have also been particularly widespread and prominent within the travel industry and have resulted in many legal actions. Still, efforts to seek redress against companies that have disclosed personal information to various governmental bodies have not proven to be too fruitful. This is quite ironic as, unlike in other areas, such as where a company has shared data with other companies for marketing purposes and the customer has, at worst, received one or more undesired emails, this kind of information sharing, arguably, has the potential to be much more damaging.

It has been reported that in 2002 upon the instructions of officials for the Transportation Security Administration (TSA) and with the assistance of the private company Acxiom Corp., JetBlue Airways, Inc. (JetBlue) transferred approximately 5 million passenger name records to a Department of Defense (DOD) contractor studying data mining of personal characteristics to determine security threats posed to military bases. Because such a disclosure was contrary to commitments made by JetBlue in its own privacy policy, the action gave rise to many legal challenges.

In September 2003, EPIC filed a complaint with the Federal Trade Commission (FTC) regarding the information-sharing practices of JetBlue and Acxiom Corp.[35] In its complaint, EPIC alleged that JetBlue and Acxiom Corp. disclosed personal information of about 1.5 million passengers to Torch Concepts, an information mining company and DOD contractor. EPIC claimed that by sharing this passenger information, both JetBlue and Acxiom Corp. breached their own stated privacy policies, in which they each promised not to disclose such information without consumer consent. EPIC alleged that such a breach violated section 5(a) of the FTC Act, which prohibits unfair and deceptive acts or practices that affect commerce. The FTC investigated the complaint but chose not to take action. As outlined in the previous chapter, the FTC has, in many instances, commenced enforcement actions against companies for having engaged in unfair and deceptive trade practices by disclosing personal data when their privacy policies stated that they would not disclose data to third parties.

A class action also resulted from the JetBlue case, but in August 2005 a federal court in New York dismissed a multidistrict consolidated nationwide class-action suit against JetBlue that arose out of the company's alleged unauthorized disclosure of data to the government. The court ruled that the plaintiffs' claim that Jet-Blue committed a violation of the federal ECPA of 1986[36] could not be supported because JetBlue was not an "electronic communications service" or a "remote computing service" covered by the ECPA.

In January 2004, EPIC filed a complaint against Northwest Airlines with the Department of Transportation (DOT).[37] In its complaint, EPIC contended that the airline engaged in unfair and deceptive trade practices by disclosing millions of passenger records to the National Aeronautics and Space Administration (NASA) in violation of the terms of its own stated privacy policy. Later that year, in September 2004, the DOT concluded that Northwest's privacy policy did not prevent it from sharing customer data with NASA. They went even further, contending that even if Northwest's privacy policy contained such a restriction, the restriction would be unenforceable on public policy grounds. EPIC petitioned the DOT, requesting that it review its finding. However, the decision was upheld in March 2005.

There have been similar cases against other airlines. While none of the legal actions have brought success to the plaintiffs, it is undeniable that the airlines have suffered negative publicity as well as the financial cost of defending the various lawsuits.

International Banking Transaction Data

Even more recently, concerns were raised around the globe after it was revealed that the Society for Worldwide Interbank Financial Transactions (SWIFT), a Brussels-based organization, permitted U.S. officials to access banking records in connection with the efforts of such officials to track terrorist funding. According to the reports, the data-sharing initiative was established shortly after the September 11 terrorist attacks. However, the program did not come to public light until the story reporters from the *New York Times* broke the story on June 23, 2006.[38]

SWIFT is a huge source of information regarding a vast number of financial transactions. It handles financial transactions for about 8,000 institutions in 20 countries, routing transactions worth about $6 trillion per day through the global banking system.[39] Under the controversial and recently exposed program, the U.S. authorities have reportedly been tapping into this immense network in order to obtain information about terrorist funding.

Once again, the government has provided very little information regarding the scope of the program or, even, its existence. The Bush administration has, however, been very critical of the media's revelations of information about the program, contending that exposing the existence of the program would hamper counterterrorism efforts.[40] SWIFT, for its part, has asserted that it has "responded to compulsory subpoenas for limited sets of data from the Office of Foreign Assets Control of the United States Department of the Treasury."[41]

Other Examples

While the cases regarding telephone records, travel information, and financial transaction data were some of the most publicized, they were not the only cases in which the government obtained data from a commercial database without prior notice or consent of individuals whose data were involved. According to one report, ". . . since September 11, 2001, supermarket chains, home improvement stores and others have voluntarily handed over large databases of customer records to federal law enforcement agencies—almost always in violation of their stated privacy policies."[42]

It was recently disclosed that in May 2002 the Professional Association of Diving Instructors (PADI) voluntarily provided the Federal Bureau of Investigation (FBI) with data concerning people who had studied scuba-diving in the United States in the prior three years.[43] In sum, names, addresses, and other personal information of approximately 2 million people were disclosed to the law enforcement authorities.[44] PADI did not demand a warrant prior to making the data disclosure, and individuals were not informed that their data would be shared with the authorities.

There have also been reports of information sharing by colleges and universities. For instance, a 2001 survey revealed that 195 colleges and universities had turned over students' private information to the FBI. Of the 195 educational institutions, 172 of them did not wait for a subpoena.[45] Reports of such sharing are particularly surprising given the legislative framework that is in place to protect the privacy of educational records. Furthermore, a survey of travel and transportation companies found that 64 percent had provided customer or employee data to the government, even where their privacy policies provided otherwise.[46]

NEW GOVERNMENTAL SYSTEMS FOR DATA COLLECTION, SHARING, AND MINING

Overview

While there has been a general decline in the focus on privacy rights, there has been a simultaneous increase in the focus placed on developing and implementing new mechanisms for aggregating, mining, and sharing data. All of the data-sharing systems that will be discussed herein are based upon the underlying—and arguably faulty—premise that more is better. These systems assumed that the more data governmental authorities have regarding ordinary Americans, the better positioned the government will be to detect and apprehend terrorists. Many of these programs would involve centralizing and ultimately mining not only data and information available from the government, such as criminal histories and arrest records, but also a wide range of commercial and personal data, including medical and financial records, information about political and religious beliefs, travel histories, prescription data, purchasing habits, communications (telephone calls, emails, and Web surfing patterns), school records, personal and family associations, and other personal information.

Before diving further into this section, it is important to note that data mining is not new. In fact, a 2004 Report from the Government Accounting Office, undertaken at the request of Senator Daniel K. Akaka (D-Hawaii), details almost 200 data-mining activities, many of which were occurring outside the field of terrorism prevention and many of which predated the terrorist attacks.[47] Still despite the fact that governmental data mining did not originate with the terrorist attacks of 9/11, there is little doubt that the efforts taken by the government in response to the attacks have been particularly comprehensive and concerning. In fact, after the terrorist attacks and the public revelations that there was insufficient sharing of information among various governmental entities at the time of the attacks, it has been a clear mission of the government to increase and enhance the ability of various governmental agencies to access information collected and maintained by other entities.[48] This section will examine several of the most notable of these systems of data sharing that were either commenced or developed further after the terrorist attacks of September 11. Many of the systems that were commenced after the terrorist attacks have since been discontinued but not before the government had expended huge amounts of tax dollars in researching, developing, and implementing the programs.

Carnivore

Carnivore predates the terrorist attacks of September 11. The system was first used in 1999. Official notice of Carnivore's existence came to light in 1999 after U.S. marshals served Earthlink with a subpoena to install a monitoring device on its network for an investigation. Earthlink resisted the subpoena because of concerns about privacy and security and instead offered to create its own system that it would open to use by the government. The government insisted on installing

Carnivore and eventually won a court order, permitting it to do so.[49] However, reportedly, Carnivore slowed Earthlink's email service so much that shortly thereafter it was replaced by Earthlink's own proposed monitoring service.

Carnivore (later renamed to the more innocuous sounding DCS1000) can roughly be analogized to a kind of Internet wiretap. Through the technology, the FBI is able to segregate email messages from flagged addresses and capture the contents of the same.[50] Despite privacy concerns that were raised early on in the process in the weeks following the September 11 attacks, Congress gave initial approval to Carnivore.

Law enforcement officers were empowered to utilize Carnivore solely to the extent permitted by the applicable court orders. Such orders would identify the particular Internet service providers on which the FBI can install Carnivore on and for what period of time the installation would be authorized. When fully authorized, Carnivore was capable of capturing the entire text of emails as well as all Web sites a suspect visited. At a minimum level of authorization, Carnivore would be capable only of capturing the email address of messages sent to and from a particular account, along with the subject line and length of the message.

Many parties have expressed concern about the privacy implications of Carnivore.[51] Once again, governmental secrecy played a role in heightening fears about Carnivore. Concerns about Carnivore were:

> [C]ompounded by the FBI's reluctance to share information about Carnivore's true capabilities and their refusal to disclose the program's source code, even to computer programming experts who could critique it to ensure that it incorporates safety measures to prevent, among other things, inadvertent monitoring of non-suspects.[52]

Terrorism Information Awareness

The Terrorism Information Awareness (TIA) program is another initiative that is no longer operational; nonetheless, it is still worth mentioning as an example of the various mechanisms that were considered and implemented. The TIA was intended to scan enormous databases of personal information to detect terrorists. TIA's objectives were to:

> [I]magine, develop, apply, integrate, demonstrate and transition information technologies, components, and prototype closed-loop information systems that [would] counter asymmetric threats by achieving total information awareness useful for preemption, national security warning, and national security decision making.[53]

The TIA was renamed in May 2003 from its original and more frightening moniker of "Total Information Awareness" to Terrorism Information Awareness. However, given the scope of its coverage, the original name was probably much more appropriate.

TIA was operated by the Defense Advanced Research Projects Agency (DARPA), a branch of the DOD that works on military research. The operation was headed by John Poindexter, the former National Security Adviser under the Reagan administration.[54]

Congress acted to limit the project in February 2003 by requiring DARPA to submit a detailed report on TIA, and later in the year, the program was officially terminated when Congress eliminated funding for TIA on September 25, 2003, by a vote of 407–15 in the House and 95–0 in the Senate. While there were many objections to the TIA since its origin, such concerns were increased dramatically in July 2003, when it was disclosed that there were plans to use the TIA concerning the planned launch of an online trading market to test the theory that traders could help predict the probability of events like terror attacks, missile strikes, and assassinations of foreign leaders.[55] It was envisioned that such a program would cause terrorists or those aware of their plans to "show their hand," by using the system to profit off of acts they knew were planned.

Computer Assisted Passenger Profiling System

The Computer Assisted Passenger Profiling System (CAPPS) was a program developed by Northwest Airlines and utilized by airlines to check passenger names against a list of suspected terrorists. CAPPS assigns points to passengers whose actions are consistent with how authorities believe terrorists might behave. For instance, passengers who buy one-way tickets or pay for tickets at the last minute with cash score higher and therefore are subjected to more scrutiny. CAPPS was thought to be an insufficient mechanism for passenger screening because, among other reasons, over time, the experienced traveler learned about the criterion that was used for CAPPS screening and became aware of the fact that a particular sequence of numbers on their airline tickets indicated whether they have been picked for additional scrutiny.

CAPPS II

CAPPS was followed by CAPPS II—an expansion of CAPPS that involved more data. There are other differences as well. When the program was launched, CAPPS II was held out as a means to provide quick background checks of the more than 1.8 million people who fly each day.[56] Under the program, airlines were required to provide the TSA with a "passenger name record" for each passenger boarding a flight. The record would include the passenger's address, telephone number, and birth date. That information would be run through law enforcement databases to check for wanted criminals and suspected terrorists. Commercial databases also would be checked to see whether the passenger has a credit rating, an employment history, and a residence. The passenger's travel history was examined as well. Under the original CAPPS, all of the focus was placed upon the data provided by the passenger when he or she purchased a ticket. There was no comparison of that data with other databases.

Upon examination of the relevant data, passengers would then be rated using a color code. "Green" passengers would not be considered a risk and would be able to move through security quickly. "Yellow" passengers would receive additional screening at checkpoints. "Red" passengers would be stopped as soon as they were identified. According to reports, yellow and green passenger risk profiles would be destroyed when travel is completed.[57]

While the criteria for CAPPS were widely known, there was insufficient information available about the criteria used by CAPPS II. As was the case with other systems developed and described in this publication, such secrecy is one of the factors that alarmed privacy advocates. Also, like the other data-sharing developments that have been proposed and launched, CAPPS II was plagued by criticisms about the system's potential ability to infringe upon individual privacy rights and liberties. Concerns about CAPPS II were brought to the forefront when information about JetBlue's disclosure of passenger name data became public. While the use of commercial databases raised tremendous concerns, the TSA claimed that passenger names will be compared against commercial databases only to determine the likelihood that passengers are who they say they are and not for other purposes.[58]

As happens with many of these initiatives, in which private entities have been required to share a wide range of data with the government, CAPPS II has placed airline executives square in the middle of the delicate balance between security needs and privacy concerns. While airlines have a need and a desire to ensure that passenger safety is protected, they are also reluctant to share data with the government, where doing so might anger consumers and/or cause them to be in violation of privacy promises made to consumers.[59]

In addition to privacy concerns, the efficacy of the program in identifying terrorists and/or would-be terrorists was questionable. In this regard, some experts have suggested that the system would do more harm than good, in that it could lull people into a false sense of security.[60]

CAPPS II was terminated in August 2004[61] and replaced by a similar program called Secure Flight. The new program is relatively similar to CAPPS II. However, it does not involve comparing passenger name records against commercial databases.

National Security Entry–Exit Registration System

Another controversial data collection and aggregation program was the National Security Entry–Exit Registration System (NSEERS). NSEERS established a national registry for temporary foreign visitors (nonimmigrant aliens) arriving from certain countries or who meet a combination of intelligence-based criteria and are identified as presenting an elevated national security concern. The program involved the registration of nearly 82,000 male immigrants and visitors from predominantly Muslim countries. Specifically, the program included citizens or nationals from Afghanistan, Algeria, Bahrain, Bangladesh, Egypt, Eritrea, Indonesia, Iran, Iraq, Jordan, Kuwait, Libya, Lebanon, Morocco, North Korea, Oman, Pakistan, Qatar, Somalia, Saudi Arabia, Sudan, Syria, Tunisia, United Arab Emirates, and Yemen. However, according to documents from the Department of Homeland Security, individuals from more than 150 countries had registered with the program. The information collected through the program was to be held in a secure government database along with travel data and photographs and would be matched against other data held on potential terrorists.[62]

The Department of Homeland Security announced the suspension of NSEERS on December 1, 2003.[63] According to reports, the program is believed to have led to many deportations.[64] Table 2.1 presents the data that have been put forth by the Department of Homeland Security regarding the operation of the program from its origin through September 30, 2003.

Threat and Local Observation Notice

Another controversial program of information collection, sharing, and mining is a program called Threat and Local Observation Notice (TALON). There is very little information publicly available regarding TALON. Much of the information available regarding TALON has been through NBC News and the Public Broadcasting System (PBS).[65] While the program is believed to have been designed to record potential terrorist pre-attack activity, reports have suggested that the program was being used to monitor antiwar and antimilitary activity. According to media reports, late in 2005, the Pentagon ordered a review of the program after PBS displayed a DOD dossier allegedly showing that the military was already carrying

Table 2.1
NSEERS Statistics through September 30, 2003

Totals	
Total Number of Registrations	290,526
Total Number of Individuals Registered	177,260
Port-of-Entry Registration	
Total Port of Entry Registration	207,007
Number of Individuals	93,741
Domestic Registration	
Total Domestic Registrations	83,519
Referred to Investigation	
Notices to Appear Issued	13,799
Total Number Detained	2,870
Total Number In Custody	23
Total Number of Criminals	143

Source: Department of Homeland Security Press Release, "Fact Sheet: Changes to National Security Entry/Exit Registration System (NSEERS)," December 1, 2003, available at <http://www.dhs.gov/dhspublic/display?content=3020> (last visited August 2, 2006).

out surveillance and risk assessments of peaceful antiwar protests in the U.S. as part of the program. "The documents listed the license plate numbers of people attending anti-war rallies, and categorised the rallies as a 'threat.'"[66]

Just before the end of 2005, NBC News also revealed that the TALON database included information on dozens of antiwar protests and rallies including counter-military recruiting meetings held at a Quaker Meeting House in Lake Worth, Florida; antinuclear protests staged in Nebraska on the 50th anniversary of the U.S. atomic bombing of Nagasaki; an antiwar protest organized by military families outside Fort Bragg in North Carolina; and a rally in San Diego to support war resister Pablo Parades. According to reports, each of these activities was described in the government's database as a "threat."[67]

There has not yet been any official confirmation that the system has been used for this kind of tracking. If the system has been used for such tracking, it would not be the first time that such kinds of activities were undertaken by the government, but it would represent a significant departure from the policies of the past few decades. During the 1970s, army intelligence agents were believed to have been spying on antiwar protesters within the United States, and since then intelligence agencies have been required to operate under tight restrictions with respect to activities occurring inside the United States.[68]

Multi-State Anti-Terrorism Information Exchange

One of the most recent but least understood data-sharing initiatives is called the Multi-State Anti-Terrorism Information Exchange (MATRIX). As with other programs discussed herein, there was very little information made publicly available regarding MATRIX. Most of the limited information that is available regarding MATRIX has been obtained by the American Civil Liberties Union because of Freedom of Information Act (FOIA) requests made to state and federal agencies.

Reportedly, MATRIX was first used in Florida, shortly after the terrorist attacks. The database was hosted in the offices of Seisint, a private company based in Florida, and was purportedly developed by the founder of that company.[69] While it was started privately, it was supported by the government.[70] In 2003, for example, the U.S. Justice Department was reported to have provided $4 million and the Department of Homeland Security pledged another $8 million to expand the MATRIX program nationally.[71] Reportedly, the Department of Homeland Security also provided the computer equipment that allowed for information sharing among the different state entities.[72]

MATRIX was created by combining various information collected by the government, including data concerning criminal histories, driver license information, vehicle registrations, incarceration/corrections records, and similar data, with a vast collection of databases containing more than 20 billion records from private sources compiled by Accurint, a Seisint commercial subsidiary that helps creditors and other interested parties locate debtors. According to reports, MATRIX contained an "unprecedented amount of information: current and past addresses and telephone numbers, arrest records, real estate information, photographs of neighbors and business associates, car make, model and color, marriage and divorce records, voter registration records, hunting and fishing licenses, and more."[73] With the information assembled, many different manipulations could be performed. "For example, a user could identify all brown-haired divorced male residents of Minneapolis who drive a red Toyota Camry and are registered to vote."[74] MATRIX was believed to have brought together information on individuals from diverse sources—various government records as well as more than 20 billion commercial records. It would then use a computer data-mining tool to scan those records in a search for signs of terrorist activities or other wrongdoings.

Reportedly, MATRIX attempted to use its massive collection of "insignificant" data to identify individuals who may be terrorists. According to reports, slide presentation by Seisint listed some of the criteria for identifying potential terrorists, as the following:

- age and gender;
- information regarding driver's license usage;
- information regarding whether the data subject was a pilot and/or had an association with a pilot;
- the data subject's proximity to "dirty addresses/phone numbers";
- social security number anomalies;
- credit history;
- ethnicity, among other data.

Using such criteria, an initial search of the MATRIX database revealed 120,000 individuals with a "High Terrorist Factor" score. According to reports, Seisint then gave this list of names to various governmental entities, including the Immigration and Naturalization Service (INS) (now called the U.S. Citizenship and Immigration Services, a bureau of the Department of Homeland Security), the FBI, the Secret Service, and the Florida Department of Law Enforcement and several arrests followed. It is not clear who precisely were arrested and for what crimes.

There are many troubling aspects to MATRIX, and one of the most alarming is its sheer potential for abuse. While MATRIX has purportedly been created to assist in the fight against terrorism, there is reason to believe that the system will be used for other reasons. Indeed, according to the ACLU, a promotional pamphlet that they obtained from authorities in Florida sets forth 15 different examples of how MATRIX can be used, but only one of those examples relates to terrorism.[75] The potential for abuse has been noted by many civil libertarians. As Ari Schwartz, associate director of the Center for Democracy and Technology, warns, "It's going to make fishing expeditions so much more convenient. There's going to be a push to use it for many different kinds of purposes."[76]

The program was also very disturbing because of the volume of information that was at issue and the vast diversity of sources from which information was being consolidated. With the operation of MATRIX, state and federal officials would have access to an immense selection of data regarding individuals and their activities.

The secrecy surrounding MATRIX is also another very serious cause for concern. It has been difficult to get a firm understanding about the information that has been included in the database and how it was assembled. At the time the database was being created and used, Seisint had refused to open its operations for verifications after receiving requests from various parties including Senator Russ Feingold (D-WI) and the ACLU. Publicly, Seisint had asserted that its databases contain only "public data," but the full extent of that information and its origins have not been revealed in detail.

MATRIX and systems like it are also of great concern because of their potential chilling effects. If individuals know or even believe that the government is likely to track a slew of information about their private lives, they may be less likely to engage in innocuous activities (such as purchasing books online regarding Islamic issues or donating money to antiwar causes) for fear that the government will be monitoring and tracking such information. Over time, this chilling effect will eventually have a negative impact on the free exchange of information, upon which our democratic society is based.

There are also serious concerns about the security of the database and what that can mean for individuals' privacy and security. The potential security risks were amplified by the fact that MATRIX utilizes outside contractors. Significantly, such external contractors to a private company were not subject to the same type of controls employed by government agencies that share criminal information. The Web site for MATRIX asserted that the MATRIX databases were secured "in accordance with restrictions and conditions placed on it by the submitting state, pursuant to the submitting state's laws and regulations."[77] However, there continued to be serious questions on whether the security mechanisms would be sufficient given the risks. Consider, for example, the results if a hacker obtained access to the billions of records that comprise MATRIX. Clearly, the potential for abuse is without limit: a tremendous amount of unauthorized data sales, transactions, identity theft, and other problems could result.

In the beginning, it was announced that Alabama, Connecticut, Florida, Georgia, Kentucky, Louisiana, Michigan, New York, Oregon, Pennsylvania, South Carolina, Ohio, and Utah would participate. Shortly thereafter, however, California and Texas dropped out, citing privacy and security concerns. After the program was launched, more states began to drop out of participating because of concerns about privacy and individual liberties. The program was officially terminated in 2005.

Criticisms of Information-Sharing Programs

In addition to the specific concerns regarding each program, there are many reasons to be very wary of the use of the various data-mining and -sharing programs in general. This next section will examine some of the most significant criticisms regarding the use of such information-sharing programs within the context of the war on terror.

Mistakes and Errors

As is true with most technology, none of the proposed systems for data sharing are fool proof. The problem is that the consequences of a "mistake" in the context of the data-sharing programs used to fight terrorism can be quite severe: sometimes a question of freedom and liberty and/or of life and death.

Accuracy is also a very serious concern. Consider the example of the PADI scuba-diving records that were turned over to the government. While it is true that operators of dive shops, resorts, and similar facilities will maintain data on individuals who come in for scuba lessons, they are not likely to obtain and maintain their data with the same level of accuracy that one would expect of a government agency. Once such data, which may very well have been recorded inaccurately, are shared with the government, the consequences become much more significant. Clearly, having your name misspelled on a scuba catalog or vacation literature is quite different from having inaccuracies in government files.

Moreover, the discussion of mistakes and their consequences is not a consideration of something that is hypothetical and/or purely academic. Rather, the news media is replete with examples of how mistaken identity in this context has led to various serious problems for certain individuals. Consider, for example, the case of Brandon Mayfield. Reports have indicated that Mr. Mayfield, an attorney in Oregon, was arrested in connection with the 2004 terrorist bombings in Madrid. Mr. Mayfield's arrest was said to have resulted after the FBI used a computer database that matched a fingerprint from him with one found by Spanish authorities on a bag of detonating devices.[78] Mayfield was held in detention for 21 days before it was determined that the print at issue was in fact a match to an Algerian terrorist. "An FBI inspector general determined later that investigators ignored evidence of his innocence in favor of the databased fingerprint match."[79]

Regardless of the various checks and balances that are built in to these systems for data mining and data sharing, once personal information is used to make judgments about people, there will be a risk that a person who is guilty of no crime will be targeted by the government for the mere reason that he or she happens to share certain characteristics with individuals who are actually being pursued for the crime at issue.[80]

Of course, errors of mistaken identity are not the only types of errors about which concern is warranted. For instance, there is also the potential for incorrect inferences to be drawn from processed data. When, concerning anti-terrorism efforts, the government analyzes data, especially data collected for other purposes (such as the data residing in many commercial databases), there is the risk that governmental employees can make faulty inferences and draw an erroneous connection between a particular person and an act or event. For instance, reports demonstrate how, regarding the government's efforts to track down any individuals who had been associated with the hijackers who caused the horrendous destruction of 9/11, faulty inferences led to the arrest and detention of the wrong man. Shortly after September 11, authorities arrested a man who had obtained a driver's license at the same motor vehicle agency and within minutes of the time of which one of the actual hijackers had obtained his license. In this case, reports suggest that investigators had the proper information but made the wrong inference based upon the man's Arabic name and the time at which he happened to visit the motor vehicle office.[81]

Intrusion of Privacy

Information-sharing and data-mining programs can lead to a very serious erosion of privacy rights. Under the programs, there will be very few aspects of human life free from surveillance, inspection, and examination. When taken in sum, these different systems detract from the well-established right to be left alone.

A Potential for Abuse

All of these systems have demonstrated a tremendous potential for abuse. Arguably, such a large collection of data will, over time, prove to be too tempting for those who have legitimate access to it and/or for those who may obtain unauthorized access to the information. Human nature suggests that it would only be a matter of time before the databases would be used for political reasons and other purposes beyond terrorism prevention and terrorist apprehension.

Security Concerns

Of course, security issues are another major concern. Anytime there is such a large amount of valuable data maintained in a database, risks of security breach become an issue. The multitude of prominent security breaches occurring over the past few years clearly emphasizes the real potential for breaches of security. Where the data being maintained are highly sensitive and/or very detailed, the potential risks of security breaches become a greater concern.

A Presumption of Guilt

The systems are based upon massive dragnets instead of focused and individualized targeting. In this way, their use would represent a clear departure from the well-established tradition of actually conducting surveillance only on those individuals who are suspected of a crime or other wrongdoing. Under these systems, all individuals would be monitored, in hopes that such massive monitoring would eventually uncover some wrongdoing.

Is It Even Effective?

Another problem with the use of these proposed systems of data sharing is that it is truly questionable whether their use can and will be useful in preventing terrorism and/or apprehending terrorists. Given the negative effects that are inherent in such systems of data mining and given further that their results are largely unproven, the question then becomes: isn't it more logical to devote our resources to less controversial methods that are more likely to produce results in the battle against terrorism?

MANAGEMENT OF U.S. BORDERS

Overview

In the United States, some of the most dramatic changes that have accompanied the war on terror have occurred in the area of border control. Individuals wishing to travel to the United States have become subject to a host of additional requirements. The following section will examine some of the most notable developments in this area, with particular emphasis being placed on the border security measures that have implications for data sharing and other aspects of privacy rights.

Western Hemisphere Travel Initiative

While there have already been a number of notable changes, additional significant changes will come into play in 2007 and 2008 when new border security measures come into place. The Western Hemisphere Travel Initiative (WHTI) is a U.S. security initiative that was mandated by the Intelligence Reform and Terrorism Prevention Act of 2004. It will require all Americans and Canadians to have a passport or a roughly equivalent document to enter the United States. The requirement will become effective in early 2007 for travelers arriving by air and sea and by January 1, 2008, for travelers crossing the border by land. There are many concerns about how the new measure will impact cross-border travel, tourism, and commerce.

Plans

Recently, in January 2006, the Bush Administration announced many new measures designed to improve border security. Such planned measures include the following:

- reengineering the visa issuance process, including through expedited processing for business travelers and online applications;

- creating an "enhanced partnership with the private sector" to identify "best practices" and provide feedback on initiatives;

- encouraging students and academic study in the U.S.;

- implementing e-passports that will protect privacy;

- introducing a "[s]ecure, less expensive passport card for the U.S. land border" that will involve some use of biometrics, issued from late 2006, to satisfy the WHTI, that is, the requirement for passport documents for use at the land borders in the U.S.;

- developing and using "travel intelligence" before the arrival of travelers by the Terrorist Screening Center and the Human Smuggling and Trafficking Center;

- utilizing increased data sharing between the Department of Homeland Security and the Department of State.

The announcement of the new initiatives also included a statement regarding the functioning and efficacy of the US-VISIT to date. The announcement revealed that between January 2004 and December 2005 more than 45 million people have been processed, leading to 970 "interceptions" with prior or suspected criminal or immigration violations based solely on biometric data.

PRIVACY EFFORTS

Overview

It is undisputable that many of the measures undertaken by the government and discussed in this chapter have resulted in the diminishment of privacy rights and individual liberties. At the same time, however, proponents of the anti-terror measures adopted and implemented by the government have suggested that they are being undertaken in due consideration of and respect for individual privacy rights. The following section will examine some of the privacy considerations that are influencing the government's work.

Privacy Legislation

The government is subject to its own privacy requirements. The most significant of these measures is the Privacy Act of 1974.[82] This law was in effect since September 27, 1975, and can generally be characterized as an omnibus "code of fair information practices" that attempts to regulate the collection, maintenance, use, and dissemination of personal information by federal executive branch agencies.

The Privacy Act's imprecise language, limited legislative history, and somewhat outdated regulatory guidelines have rendered it a difficult statute to decipher and apply. Moreover, even after more than 25 years of administrative and judicial analysis, numerous Privacy Act issues remain unresolved or unexplored. Adding to these interpretational difficulties is the fact that many Privacy Act cases are unpublished district court decisions.

Designation of Privacy Officers

One of the ways in which the government has tried to ensure continued protection of privacy rights has been through attempting to ensure that certain government agencies have privacy officers who are responsible for addressing privacy issues of their particular agency. In fact, the Department of Homeland Security was the first agency to have a legally mandated privacy officer.[83] Within the Department of Homeland Security, the Privacy Office is responsible for integrating privacy consideration into the work and initiatives of the department. It also has oversight of policies regarding privacy and information disclosure, including review of the department's compliance with the Privacy Act of 1974 and the FOIA. It completes privacy impact assessments on all new programs launched by the department and evaluates new technologies proposed to be used by the department.[84]

SUMMARY AND CONCLUSION

This chapter has endeavored to outline the great number of changes that have occurred with respect to privacy rights and anti-terror measures after the September 11 terrorist attacks on the United States. In the wake of the terrorist attacks and in recognition of the nature of the threat that continued to face the United States, it was clear that something drastic needed to be done to prevent future attacks. However, it remains highly questionable whether some of the measures undertaken, including, specifically, the measures discussed in this chapter, were the most effective measures for uncovering terrorists and preventing terrorism. Indeed, many of the data-sharing programs discussed in this chapter were disbanded shortly after their creation but after significant expenditures had been made to develop them.

At the same time, even if the measures outlined in this chapter were the only or the most effective measures for preventing terrorism, can we honestly state that they were the proper course of action, considering the ways in which such measures affected individual liberties and privacy rights?

A Propaganda Campaign?

There have also been serious allegations that the government engaged in a carefully constructed plan of propaganda to keep citizens concerned about terrorism and willing to sacrifice privacy protections and other individual liberties to enjoy greater protections from the prospects of future terrorist attacks.

While there is really no way to confirm the accuracy of such allegations, there is support for the notion that such efforts could be effective. Social researchers have pointed out that "arguments over rights are arguments embedded in a context."[85] For ordinary citizens in ordinary times, civil liberties are likely to be relatively remote from everyday experiences. However, in certain contexts, civil liberty issues will have immediate implications for individuals' sense of freedom and well-being.[86] Furthermore, the vast majority of surveys that have been undertaken in this area (some of which are cited in *Introduction*) tend to demonstrate that individuals are much more likely to be supportive of measures that will be invasive of privacy rights when it is believed that such measures are needed to counteract the threat of terrorism.

What You Do Not Know Will Not Hurt You?

Many of the concerns regarding the data-mining, data-sharing, surveillance, and related activities of the present administration have been compounded by the extreme secrecy with which the government has conducted itself in this realm. Opponents of some of the current initiatives point to the secrecy with which the efforts have been carried out as one of the most troubling aspects of the efforts. While privacy advocates and public citizens alike have been outraged by many of the data-sharing and -mining efforts that have come to light, the more alarming aspect of such revelations is the prospect that they are just the tip of the iceberg. The more troubling question may be, What is it that we do not know? Of course, it is unlikely that it is merely a coincidence that many of these efforts have been carried out with great secrecy. After all, one cannot challenge a program about which there is no information. Put another way, you have no way of knowing what you do not know. Without sufficient information about the precise measures that are being undertaken by the government, individuals will simply not be able to assert their rights where such efforts exceed the scope of what is permissible under law.

In the next chapter, the examination on the global effects of the war on terror will continue. Specifically, our focus of the discussion will shift over to the Middle East and Africa. Privacy rights were not very well developed in this region prior to 2001, and today they remain underdeveloped as compared with other countries, especially European nations. Still the countries of the region were not immune to the effects of the September 11 attacks, and as will be shown in the next chapter, many countries of the region also undertook new anti-terrorism initiatives after the 2001 attacks.

Three

The Middle East and Africa

OVERVIEW

This chapter focuses on privacy issues in the Middle East and Africa. Generally, prior to the September 11 terrorist attacks, the vast majority of the countries in this region neither had, nor were undertaking, any concrete efforts to enact comprehensive privacy and/or data protection regulations. If the region followed some of the trends that developed in the rest of the world, it would be expected, however, that as societies in the region became more open and as the use of various technologies continued to grow, individual citizens would come to expect certain legislated protections of their privacy rights. In terms of counter-terrorism measures, prior to the 2001 attacks, many of the governments of the region were already very active in controlling the freedoms and liberties of their citizens.

The September 11 attacks on the United States had a significant impact on the counterterrorism measures undertaken by many countries in the region. Because individuals from many of the countries in the region were implicated in the attacks against the United States and with previous—and subsequent—terrorist attacks occurring throughout the Middle East and Africa, the region was placed under a microscope. Governments were pressured to take all necessary measures to detect and uncover terrorists and prevent future acts of terrorism. With such matters on their plates, privacy issues—if they were ever even a concern at all to local governments—fell sharply to the wayside. Subject to a few notable exceptions, there has been very little movement to advance privacy rights in the region in the past few years.

THE MIDDLE EAST

The Evolution of Privacy Rights prior to September 11

Overview

Privacy rights were not very well developed in the Middle East even before September 11. Generally, the region is well known for being a territory in which the government exercises great level of control over the conduct, including, without limitation, the Internet-related activity of their users. Cultural issues may also play a role in the stagnant development of privacy rights in the region. Indeed, Arabic has no equivalent to the English word "privacy"—some may say that the closest is the term *khususi* meaning "personal." According to one author, in the Arab world, the connotation of privacy does not relate to "personal" or "secret," as it does in other cultures. Rather, it concerns two specific spheres: women and the family.[1] Another author goes even further, claiming: "There is no concept of privacy among Arabs. In translation, the Arabic word that comes closest to 'privacy' means loneliness!"[2] Accordingly, the region lacks any real history of valuing privacy rights as fundamental human rights as other territories have, such as, quite notably, many European countries.

Select National Issues

Bahrain

Bahrain is a very prosperous, business-friendly country. It has a fairly large base of Internet users and, as compared with other countries in the region, has taken relatively limited steps to censor the Internet-related activity of its residents. There have, however, been reports of efforts to block Internet Web sites that are critical of the government.[3] The country did not have any comprehensive privacy and/or data protection laws in place prior to September 11. The country does, however, provide limited protection to individual privacy rights in its Constitution.[4] However, the U.S. State Department has observed that the government interferes with individual privacy rights.[5]

Egypt

Privacy rights are not well established or well protected in Egypt. The country has not enacted any comprehensive privacy and/or data protection legislation. The Constitution provides for the sanctity and secrecy of the home, correspondence, telephone calls, and other means of communication. Specifically, Article 45 of the Constitution provides:

> The law shall protect the inviolability of the private life of citizens. Correspondence, wires, telephone calls and other means of communication shall

have their own sanctity and their secrecy shall be guaranteed. They may not be confiscated or monitored except by a causal judicial warrant and for a definite period and according to the provisions of the law.[6]

However, such protections are overridden by the country's emergency laws. Egypt has been battling terrorism for years and has been under emergency rule— Emergency Law No. 162 of 1958 (the Emergency Law)—since 1967 (except for an 18-month break in 1980) and continuously since the assassination of President Anwar Sadat in October 1981.[7] According to reports, the government of Egypt has routinely used its authority under the Emergency Law to arrest individuals at will and detain them without trial for prolonged periods, refer civilians to military or exceptional state security courts, and prohibit strikes, demonstrations, and public meetings.[8]

Under the Constitution, police must obtain warrants before undertaking searches and wiretaps.[9] However, the Emergency Law empowers the Government to place wiretaps, intercept mail, and search persons or places without warrants. Security agencies have frequently placed political activists, suspected subversives, journalists, foreigners, and writers under surveillance, screened their correspondence (especially international mail), searched them and their homes, and confiscated personal property.

Iraq

Prior to 2001, Internet usage in Iraq was virtually nonexistent. Access to the public media, including the Internet, was tightly controlled by the ruling regime. Likewise, at the time, the country had not enacted any legislation concerning the protection of individual privacy rights.

Israel

Privacy rights are protected in many different ways in Israel. First, Israeli human rights laws afford some protections to privacy. Specifically, section 7 of the Basic Law on Human Dignity and Freedom, passed in 1992, provides:

(a) All persons have the right to privacy and to intimacy.

(b) There shall be no entry into the private premises of a person who has not consented thereto.

(c) No search shall be conducted on the private premises of a person, nor in the body or personal effects.

(d) There shall be no violation of the confidentiality of conversation, or of the writings or records of a person.[10]

The country also has enacted legislation specifically related to privacy of personal information in computer databases. The Protection of Privacy Law[11] establishes 11 categories of prohibited activities regarding personal data held in databases and provides for civil and criminal penalties for violations of an individual's privacy. Similar to the European approach, the law has certain registration requirements. Specifically, under the measure, holders of data banks containing more than 10,000 names or certain confidential information must register with the Registrar of Databases and report their purpose, use, means of data collection, and data security measures implemented. The Registrar maintains the register of databases and can deny registration if he or she believes that a database is used for illegal activities.

The law limits use of information in these databases to the purposes for which they were collected. In addition, controllers of databases are required to provide data subjects with access to their data. Significantly, under the Protection of Privacy Law, there are broad exemptions to certain privacy rules for police and security services.

The law was in existence well before the 2001 terrorist attacks and was last amended in 1996 to broaden the scope of databases covered and to increase penalties for certain breaches.

Jordan

Prior to the September 11 terrorist attacks on the United States, the legal right of privacy was still under development in Jordan.[12] At the time, the country had not enacted any specific privacy and/or data protection laws. Nonetheless, the country's Constitution did long include recognition of the protection of privacy rights. Article 10 of the Constitution, for example, stipulates, "[d]welling houses shall be inviolable and shall not be entered except in the circumstances and in the manner prescribed by law."[13] Additionally, article 18 provides: "[a]ll postal, telegraphic and telephonic communications shall be treated as secret and as such shall not be subject to censorship or suspension except in circumstances prescribed by law."[14]

Tunisia

Tunisia has had a relatively large base of Internet users. However, in the time prior to September 11, it had not enacted any privacy and/or data protection laws. In addition, at the time, the country's constitution only addressed privacy issues in a limited way. Specifically, Article 9 (Home, Secrecy of Correspondence) provides: "The inviolability of the home and the secrecy of correspondence are guaranteed, save in exceptional cases established by the law."[15] However, Tunisia took a huge step forward when it recently became the first Arab country to enact a comprehensive data privacy law.

United Arab Emirates

The United Arab Emirates (UAE) is a relatively modern and technologically advanced society. It has numerous Internet cafés and a large number of Internet users. Freedom of expression is protected in articles 30 and 31 of the country's Constitution.[16] The country did not enact privacy laws prior to September 11.

Privacy Rights and Anti-Terror Measures After September 11

Overview

Generally, following the terrorist attacks of 2001, in the Middle East, there was very little progress in the enactment of new privacy legislation. For the most part, after the attacks, the countries of the region only stepped up their efforts to increase surveillance and censorship. The sole exception was Tunisia, which, as noted earlier, recently became the first Arab country to enact comprehensive data protection legislation. At the same time, most of the countries in the region either enacted new anti-terrorism legislation or increased their enforcement of existing measures. The next section shall examine some of the important national developments to result after 2001.

Select National Issues

Egypt

Egypt has a long and established history of having and utilizing comprehensive anti-terrorism decrees and declarations of emergency rule, including by relying upon the permanent use of the Emergency Law. Reports suggest that such repressive measures have intensified since the September 11 attacks.[17] Since September 11, 2001, Egypt has arrested hundreds of suspected government opponents, many for alleged membership in the Muslim Brotherhood, a banned but nonviolent group, and others for the possession of so-called suspicious literature. According to reports, many of those individuals who were arrested (some of whom included professors, physicians, lawyers, and other professionals) have been referred to military courts or to emergency and regular state security courts, whose procedures often fail to be in line with accepted international standards for trial procedure. Such activities continued in early 2003, when security forces used provisions of the Emergency Law to detain without charge or trial persons involved in peaceful demonstrations opposing military intervention in Iraq and in support of the Palestinian uprising against Israeli military occupation.

On February 23, 2003, without prior notice, the government introduced a bill in the People's Assembly to extend the Emergency Law for another three years and rushed its passage the same day. Prime Minister Atif Ubayd cited the "war on terrorism" and new security laws passed in the United States and elsewhere since September 11, 2001, to justify the extension of the country's Emergency Law.

This major legislative development is, of course, only one example of how Egyptian governmental officials have relied upon the events of September 11, 2001 to justify their repressive policies. Since the attacks, the government has been active in pointing to the events of September 11 to emphasize the need to adopt more restrictive anti-terrorism measures. Quite remarkably, President Hosni Mubarak was quoted in 2001 as saying: "There is no doubt that the events of September 11 created a new concept of democracy that differs from the concept that Western states defended before these events, especially in regard to the freedom of the individual."[18] He further added that the U.S. decision to authorize military tribunals "proves that we were right from the beginning in using all means, including military tribunals."[19] Reports of such comments should cause all in America to take pause. Are these truly the types of lessons and examples the United States wishes to give to the rest of the world?

Jordan

Since the 2001 attacks on the United States, there has been a noticeable crackdown on privacy rights and individual liberties in Jordan. Despite the Constitutional protections, there continue to be concerns regarding the government's infringement on certain aspects of citizens' private lives, especially as regards the government's role in conducting surveillance, monitoring communications, and apprehending suspects.

> Security officers officially monitored telephone conversations and Internet communication, read private correspondence, and engaged in surveillance of persons considered to pose a threat to the government or national security.[20]

While the government did not enact any broad-based privacy laws after the 2001 attacks, in December 2001 the country did enact the Electronic Transactions Act (ETA).[21] A provision of this law prohibits authentication institutions from disclosing the secrets of any client.[22] While not a broad-based data protection measure, it is an interesting development, especially because it was enacted when much of the legislative focus was placed upon anti-terrorism measures, as opposed to privacy protection initiatives.

Tunisia

While there was very limited activity designed to increase privacy rights in the post–9/11 period, Tunisia did actually take steps to increase privacy rights after September 11. In fact, Tunisia recently became the first Arab country to enact a comprehensive privacy law. On July 28, 2004, Tunisian President Ben Ali promulgated the Data Protection Act ("Loi organique relative à la protection des données personnelles").[23] The law is based on the EU Data Protection Directive. It created a Data Protection Commission selected by the president to enforce it. However, quite significantly, unlike the EU Directive, there is no exemption for journalistic uses. As the legislation is very new, time is needed to see how the law will be implemented and enforced in actual practice.

UAE

There have been a few notable changes in the UAE since the 2001 attacks on the U.S. Most notably, in 2004, there were reports that the country passed a new anti-terrorism law. One of the most significant aspects of the law concerns its imposition of new, stricter sentences, including the possibility of the death penalty, for terrorism-related offenses. The new measure also allows prosecutors to hold suspects in cases involving terrorism for six months without being charged, a substantial increase over the previous time frame of three weeks.[24] Furthermore, once suspects are charged in a terrorism case, their cases are handled by the Supreme Court and such court may extend the detention period indefinitely.

There have not been significant developments in the area of privacy rights. In 2002, Dubai enacted its own local measure entitled the Electronic Transactions and Commerce Law.[25] The main purpose of this law is to give effect to electronic signatures. However, it does also prohibit Internet service providers from disclosing information gathered in providing services.

AFRICA

Privacy Rights and Anti-Terror Measures prior to September 11

Overview

Similar to the Middle East, privacy rights were not very well developed in Africa at the time of the 2001 attacks. While legislative proposals were being considered in many countries before 2001, there was not much movement toward actually legislating privacy rights. In the next section, the efforts of several countries in the region to enact privacy legislation shall be examined in further detail.

Select National Issues

Nigeria

There are limited protections for privacy in the Constitution of Nigeria. Specially, chapter IV, ß37 of the country's Constitution provides that "the privacy of citizens, their homes, correspondence, telephone conversations, and telegraphic communications is hereby guaranteed and protected."[26] Aside from the limited Constitutional protections, there are no specific laws concerning privacy and/or data protection in Nigeria.

South Africa

Privacy is protected generally by the Constitution of South Africa. Specifically, section 14 of the South African Constitution of 1996 provides: "Everyone has the right to privacy, which includes the right not to have – (a) their person or home searched; (b) their property searched; (c) their possessions seized; or (d) the privacy of their communications infringed."[27] Also notable is section 32, which provides:

> (1) Everyone has the right of access to – (a) any information held by the state, and; (b) any information that is held by another person and that is required for the exercise or protection of any rights; (2) National legislation must be enacted to give effect to this right, and may provide for reasonable measures to alleviate the administrative and financial burden on the state.[28]

While the country did have such Constitutional protections in place during the late 1990s, it did not have comprehensive privacy or data protection legislation prior to the 2001 attacks on the United States. Efforts to enact a comprehensive data privacy law have since continued and are examined in further detail below in the section on developments in Africa after 2001.

Uganda

Uganda has had its own problems with terrorism that predated the attacks on the United States. During the late 1990s, the country suffered from a wave of terrorism that included bombings in public places. The activity during this period was blamed on a dissident group known as the Allied Democratic Front (ADF) with bases in Congo. The violence that occurred during that time resulted in the deaths of more than 50 people and injuries to over 160.

At the time, the country did not have specific legislation concerning terrorism. The official response of authorities during this period generally consisted of placing individuals suspected of terrorist activity in illegal detention facilities known as safe houses. The country was criticized by many groups including the Uganda Human Rights Commission (UHRC) for its activities in detaining suspects without due legal process. UHRC has noted particular concern about the safe houses and has contended that:

> While the constitution of the Republic of Uganda prohibits torture, inhuman and degrading treatment or punishment, FHRI [the Foundation

for Human Rights Initiative, a local human rights group] reports that it has received reports of systematic and widespread use of torture against victims especially in "safe house". It says suspects were physically tortured by severe beatings or psychologically and mentally tortured through interrogation, threats to their lives and the presentation of other persons who had already been tortured. They were also held incommunicado during detention, "which added to their mental anguish and anxiety about their lives."[29]

On the basis of its concerns about the manner in which the government was responding to suspected terrorists, including by using the controversial safe houses, the UHRC advised the government of Uganda to enact a law to control and eliminate terrorism.[30] Specific legislation was not prepared until after the 2001 attacks on the United States. The legislation that was eventually enacted in the country was highly controversial and is discussed in further detail in the following section.

Privacy Rights and Anti-Terror Measures After September 11

Overview

Like in other areas, in the wake of September 11, many countries in Africa undertook efforts to respond to the risks of terrorism through legislation and other measures. The countries that comprise the African continent are not nearly as unified as the countries of other regions, including, most notably, those of Europe. Therefore, not too surprisingly, there was not a cohesive, organized response to terrorism across the country. Nonetheless, there were many significant national initiatives. The following section shall explore several of the most notable national initiatives to emerge in the post–September 11 period.

Select National Issues

Kenya

Because Kenya has been identified as an area of terrorist activities, including, most notably, the terrorist attacks against U.S. facilities and the USS Cole, Kenya has been a particular focus in the global war on terror. The government has responded by proposing new legal measures to respond to terrorism. In 2003, the government introduced a draft Suppression of Terrorism Bill.[31] The draft drew heavy criticism from lawyers and human rights activists. The main objection to the draft legislation was that it negated the fundamental rights and freedom of Kenyans.[32]

One critic contended that the bill:

purports to set up a different criminal justice system for persons charged under the Bill separate from the other Criminal justice system which applies to other accused persons. It severely limits the rights of the accused person as guaranteed in the Constitution and International fair trial standards. It shifts the burden of proof and assumes that any person or organisation charged under this Act is guilty until proved innocent.[33]

Kenya's proposal has been sharply criticized as being overly influenced by the United States and United Kingdom. "The public believe the Americans and the British are its architects. The similarity between it and the US Patriot Act is disconcerting. The fact that the Americans support it lends credence to this perception. It intensifies Kenyans' resentment against official America over its handling of the war on terror," observed one commentator.[34]

Parliament overwhelmingly voted the Bill out. Kenya has, however, acceded to the International Convention for the Suppression of Terrorism Bombings and ratified both the International Convention for the Suppression of the Financing of Terrorism and the OAU Convention on the Prevention and Combating of Terrorism.

South Africa

South Africa has also pursued efforts to regulate further the surveillance powers of the government. Notably, some of these efforts were commenced prior to the September 11 attacks. They are mentioned here because while initiated prior to the 2001 attacks on the United States, they were generally developed further and finalized after such attacks. For one, a new Interception and Monitoring Bill was introduced into Parliament on July 18, 2001. The bill proposed amendments to the Interception and Monitoring [Prohibition] Act of 1992.[35] After its initial introduction, the bill was subject to consultations, which continued for approximately 18 months. The new measure—the Regulation of Interception of Communications and Provision of Communication-related Information Act—became operational in December 2002 (the SA Interception Act).[36]

The passage of the new measure had been delayed because of South Africa's involvement with the Council of Europe. South Africa is one of four nonmember signatories to the Council of Europe Convention on Cybercrime. Under the Convention, member states and nonmember signatories were required to enact measures consistent with the Convention. The new legislation in South Africa conforms to the requirements of the Cybercrime Convention.

The SA Interception Act generally prohibits wiretaps and surveillance, except where necessary for law enforcement purposes. While generally limiting surveillance, the law does require that all telecommunication service providers, including Internet service providers, make their services capable of being intercepted before being made available to the public. The law provides that service providers may be subject to criminal penalties should they refuse to make their services capable of being intercepted and/or fail to assist law enforcement. Furthermore, repeat offenders may also face the revocation of their service license granted under the Telecommunications Act.[37]

The SA Interception Act contains many other provisions of note. First, it gives the country's National Intelligence Agency (NIA) the authority to intercept all postal, telephone, and Internet communications under the auspices of crime control and national security, actual or potential threats to public health and safety, and to assist foreign law enforcement agencies with interception regarding organized crime or terrorism, under a mutual assistance agreement.[38] The new measure also expanded the litany of grounds for obtaining a wiretap order, including a wiretap to find a person in an emergency.[39]

Surveillance has been a sticky issue in the country for some time. The public disclosure of a few very public cases of government surveillance and monitoring has led to significant backlash. Back in 1996, it was revealed that the South Africa Police Service was monitoring thousands of international and domestic telephone calls without a warrant.[40] Then, in early 2000, the government apologized to the German government after it was found that an intelligence operative had placed spy cameras outside the Germany Embassy.[41]

One significant development to occur after the 2001 attacks was the promulgation of the Electronic Communications and Transactions Act (ECTA).[42] The goal of the law was to facilitate e-commerce by promoting trust and confidence in electronic transactions, including by providing legal effect to electronic signatures and documents.[43] While it does not address privacy and/or data protection specifically, it does create several offences related to computer crimes, including unauthorized access to data, interception of or interference with data.[44] The ECTA also permits the government to declare certain public and private databases critical in "national interest" or "economic and social well-being" of the country. If a database has been subject to such a declaration, the government can require the database, along with information about its location and its contents, to be registered. Under the ECTA, the government is also authorized to determine technical standards and set procedures for the general management of critical databases, their security, and disaster recovery procedures.[45]

More recently, in May 2006, the government introduced a bill for an amendment that would require providers of cellular phone services to record the personal data of customers who utilize prepaid cellular phones. Individuals using these prepaid cellular phones often pay for minutes of service in cash and in advance; therefore, the use of prepaid cellular service is usually anonymous. The proposed measure, the Regulation of Interception of Communication and Provision of Communication-Related Information Amendment Bill,[46] would require providers of prepaid cellular phone services to collect and store the following information for each subscriber identity module (SIM) card:

- the mobile subscriber integrated service digital network number of the SIM card;

- the international mobile equipment identity number of the cellular phone;

- the name, identity number , and address of the SIM card user.

The cellular service provider would be required to verify and store the above-described information in a secure manner. The proposed measure would impose fines of R100,000 (approximately $14,800) per day upon service providers that fail to maintain the required information on their clients. Furthermore, cellular phone users could face imprisonment of up to 12 months for giving away their cellular phones and/or SIM cards to others without proper notification to their service providers.

The proposed measure has been sharply criticized. Companies have contended that the costs and challenge of compliance will be too burdensome, while individuals and privacy advocates have spoken out about the invasive nature of the legislation. Indeed, the potential penalties for the mere act of providing one's cellular phone or SIM card to another without prior notice to the cellular carrier appear to be extremely harsh. The impact of the proposed legislation, should it be passed, is likely to be particularly strong in South Africa, where many of the country's residents, particularly those living in rural areas, rely upon prepaid cellular phones for their communication needs.

In terms of specific anti-terror measures, the country had commenced efforts to revise its existing anti-terrorism measures even prior to the September 11 attacks. The proposed bill, which has still not been passed, has been criticized for many reasons, including the very broad way in which it defines terrorism and terrorists, the way it impacts personal freedoms, as well as its provisions regarding detention, bail, and wide police search and seizure powers. Many commentators have suggested a link between the 2001 attacks on the United States and the proposal for tough new legislation in South Africa, one commentator even suggesting that "[t]he South African government has used the September 11 attacks in the US in order to push through new anti-terrorism legislation reminiscent of the draconian laws of the apartheid era."[47] After the 2001 attacks, South Africa has continued its very slow efforts to enact a privacy law. In 2002, the Law Commission of South Africa provided notice of its plans to undertake efforts to work on drafting a comprehensive privacy law. In 2003, the government generated an Issue Paper on the draft law on privacy and data protection.[48] Under South African law, an Issue Paper generally lays out the issues to be covered by the proposed legislation and requests public comment on the issues. Thereafter, the second stage is achieved when a Discussion Paper, which will contain the draft legislation, will be published. When the draft legislation is published, the Law Commission seeks comments on the draft. The process then culminates in the publication of a Report which contains the Commission's recommendations to the Cabinet on draft legislation. The country recently issued a discussion paper on the proposed privacy law and such discussion paper closed for public comments on February 28, 2006.[49]

Uganda

In the aftermath of the terrorist attacks on the United States, Uganda enacted the Anti-Terrorism Act, 2002, a comprehensive piece of legislation regarding terrorism. The Anti-Terrorism Act, 2002 was assented to by the president on May 21, 2002, and came into force on June 7, 2002.

The new legislation adopts a very broad definition of terrorism, defining it as:

> any act which involves serious violence against a person or serious, damage to property, endangers a person's life (but not just the life of the person committing the act), creates a serious risk to the health or safety of the public. Any such act must furthermore be designed to influence the Government or to intimidate the public or a section of the public and to further the advancement of a "political, religious, social or economic aim" indiscriminately without due regard to the safety of others or property.[50]

The legislation then includes examples of acts that can constitute terrorism:

(a) intentional and unlawful manufacture, delivery, placement, discharge or detonation of an explosive or other lethal device, whether attempted or actual, in, into or against a place of public use, a State or Government facility, a public transportation system or an infrastructure facility, with the intent to cause death or serious bodily injury, or extensive destruction likely to or actually resulting in major economic loss;

(b) direct involvement or complicity in the murder, kidnapping, maiming or attack, whether actual, attempted or threatened, on a person or groups of persons, in public or private institutions;

(c) direct involvement or complicity in the murder, kidnapping, abducting, maiming or attack, whether actual, attempted or threatened on the person, official premises, private accommodation, or means of transport or diplomatic agents or other internationally;

(d) intentional and unlawful provision or collection of funds, whether attempted or actual, with the intention or knowledge that any part of the funds may be used to carry out any of the terrorist activities under this Act;

(e) direct involvement or complicity in the seizure or detention of and threat to kill, injure or continue to detain a hostage, whether actual or attempted in order to compel a State, an international intergovernmental organisation, a person or group of persons, to do or abstain from doing any act as an explicit or implicit condition for the release of the hostage;

(f) unlawful seizure of an aircraft or public transport or the hijacking of passengers or group of persons for ransom;

(g) serious interference with or disruption of an electronic system;

(h) unlawful importation, sale, making, manufacture or distribution of any firearms, explosive, ammunition or bomb;

(i) intentional development or production or use of, or complicity in the development or production or use of a biological weapon;

(j) unlawful possession of explosives, ammunition, bomb or any materials for making of any of the foregoing.

The legislation establishes very serious penalties for individuals who engage in terrorism. Section 7(1) provides that the offence of terrorism is "an offence punishable, on conviction, by death if the offence directly results in the death of any person." Other terrorist offences, including aiding, abetting, financing, harboring, or rendering support to any person, knowing or having reason to believe that the support will be applied or used for or in connection with terrorism, also carry a potential death penalty.[51] Other crimes involve lesser penalties. For example, being a member of a terrorist organization is an offense punishable by up to 10 years' imprisonment.[52]

The legislation provides authorities with new powers to investigate and prevent terrorism, including extraordinarily broad surveillance powers and stop and search powers.[53]

The new act has been criticized on many bases. First, there is great concern about the very broad definition of terrorism. As drafted, the term can include a wide range of actions. Moreover, most of the terms and concepts that are utilized in the definition are not defined. The act has also been criticized for the wide range of offences that are being tied to prescribed terrorist organizations. By focusing on the individual's ties to a particular terrorist group as opposed to his or her actions regarding the same, the law imposes guilt by association as opposed to guilt on the basis of an individual's particular acts. Critics have also pointed out that while the law permits extradition in cases of terrorist crimes, it does not include any safeguards in relation to the surrender of individuals for extradition.

The law could—and has been—used to restrict and intimidate journalists and news outlets. David Ouma Balikowa, an editor at the independent daily newspaper, *The Monitor*, has observed:

> The state or individuals within the state can use this law to victimise the media for publishing news or any other material about rebel activities. This law can also be used to censor news about rebel activities and deny the public truthful information on how the government's counter-insurgency operations are progressing in the country. This fear is exacerbated by the fact that the truth is often the first casualty in a situation of war. Government, as our unending wars have demonstrated, is often at pains to try to underplay the magnitude of rebellion even when human casualty figures are increasing. The state often plays hide and seek when the media and public demand to know more about the war with rebels.[54]

Indeed since the enactment of the legislation, news reports have alleged that the law has been used to clamp down on the free expression of journalists. According to one report, "[I]n Uganda, the Anti-terrorism Act, 2002, has been used to repress political dissent and strictly limit freedom of expression, especially by the media. Radio stations were last year warned against airing interviews with exiled opposition leader, Col Kizza Besigye and threatened with prosecution under the Act."[55]

The situation of Uganda is somewhat ironic. Human rights groups called upon the country to enact legislation to improve how the government was attempting to reign in the activities of its own domestic terrorists. However, the terms of the legislation are so problematic that it appears to have worsened the situation within the country.

SUMMARY AND CONCLUSION

Privacy rights were not well developed in either the Middle East or Africa prior to 2001. While some African and Middle Eastern countries have recognized some form of privacy rights, such countries have generally had a different concept of privacy than the notion of privacy that is commonly accepted in Western nations. By and large, privacy rights have not advanced substantially in the region since the attacks on the United States.

On the other hand, since the terrorist attacks of 9/11, many countries in the region have been undertaking new initiatives to clamp down on terrorism. In several countries, such efforts have included the enactment of new anti-terror legislation that has generally expanded the governments' rights to conduct surveillance and confiscate evidence, while decreasing the individual liberties of citizens.

In the next chapter, our focus will shift to Europe. Europe is an extraordinarily interesting region within the context of the present discussion. The region is an area which has elected to place a very high value on privacy rights. In addition, given the jurisdictions' own challenges in facing terrorism as well as pressures from the U.S. government to participate in the war on terror, European countries have been particularly challenged in trying to find an appropriate balance between efforts to ensure citizens' safety from terrorism and measures to protect individual privacy rights.

Four

Europe

OVERVIEW

This chapter will examine the impact of the war on terrorism on privacy rights in Europe, with a particular focus upon the European Union (EU). Privacy rights have long been respected in the EU. In fact, privacy is considered a fundamental human right in the EU. The EU has also enacted the Data Protection Directive, very broad legislation that provides individuals with comprehensive privacy rights and places restrictions on the export of personal data outside the EU.

Even though privacy rights have long been respected in the EU, this jurisdiction has not been immune to the effects of the war on terrorism on privacy rights. The EU has been under increasing pressure from U.S. authorities to participate in efforts to combat terrorism by disclosing personal data regarding European citizens. At the same time, European authorities' efforts to prevent terrorism within the EU have also had a negative effect on the privacy rights of European citizens. While the European legal regime regarding privacy and data protection continues to be one of the most stringent in the world, especially as it has been implemented on the commercial side, on the public side there has been continuous erosion in individual privacy rights. This chapter will explore European privacy rights, both as they have existed prior to September 11 and as they have evolved after the terrorist attacks.

After examining EU-specific issues, a few words will be said about the situation in Russia. Given the importance of the country's relationship with the United States, the nature of the country's legal system, and the country's own very forceful responses to terrorism, the country merits its own discussion.

PRIVACY RIGHTS BEFORE SEPTEMBER 11

Overview

European Privacy Rights

Privacy rights have been afforded a high value in Europe for some time now. New concerns about privacy rights began to emerge in earnest after World War II. Just before and during the war, Socialist governments in several countries were using census data to identify households of certain ethnic, religious, or other targeted groups. Around the same time, the U.S. government was also using census data to identify Japanese-Americans for relocation. In the years following World War II, in light of the horrors raised by the holocaust, governments were sensitive to the importance of respecting their citizens' right to maintain the privacy of certain personal information.

Years later, as concerns about the significance of privacy rights and shame about past actions began to swell, nations began to propose and enact privacy laws. The first emerged in the German province of Hesse in 1970 in reaction to the computerization and centralization of personal information. Three years later, in 1973, Sweden passed the first national data protection law at a time when concern about the adoption of national identity cards was beginning to grow. Generally, the process continued as such, with each country enacting its own measures designed to respond to its particular domestic issue.

With a growing body of legislation emerging in different countries, it was only a matter of time before trade disputes arose. Companies based in countries with strict data protection laws were increasingly reluctant to transmit data to other European countries without any privacy or data protection laws or with less stringent mandates. To curtail such disputes, data protection laws were harmonized across Europe, first with the Council of Europe Convention for the Protection of Individuals with regard to Automatic Processing of Personal Data and then with the EU Data Protection Directive.

The EU Data Protection Directive

The European Data Protection Directive (hereinafter Data Protection Directive or Directive)[1] was passed on October 24, 1995, and came into effect on October 25, 1998. It is extremely comprehensive legislation that concerns all aspects of personal data processing. It treats the protection of personal data from a very broad perspective. Indeed, "personal data" is defined under the Directive as "any information relating to an identified or identifiable natural person."[2]

The Data Protection Directive, as other European Community directives, is not a law directed at individual entities. Instead, it serves as a set of directions to the EU member states, requiring them to implement certain requirements in their own national laws. The result of this is that while the laws of each member state must be consistent with the Directive, they will often differ from each other in certain, potentially significant ways. This is an important detail because entities in control of operations involving the processing of personal data (also called "controllers") must comply with the data protection laws of the country in which they are established as well as the laws of the particular member state(s) in which they process personal data.[3] While the Data Protection Directive is intended to ensure that the free market functions correctly, the liberty that individual member states have in implementing the Data Protection Directive means that there will be varying compliance obligations from state to state.

Basic Principles

The Directive addresses the protection of personal data from many different perspectives. At its most basic level, the Directive establishes certain conditions that must be met to process personal data. The Directive specifies that there are only six situations pursuant to which entities can process personal data:

(i) the individual has provided his or her unambiguous consent to such processing;[4]

(ii) the individual has entered into a contract which provides for, or anticipates, the processing of the data;[5]

(iii) the processing is necessary to fulfill a legal obligation of the individual;[6]

(iv) the processing is necessary to protect the individual's "vital interests";[7]

(v) the processing is in the public interest or is being done at the behest of an official authority;[8]

(vi) the processing is necessary to pursue the legitimate interests of the party collecting or using the data, except to the extent those interests may be overridden by the rights of the individual to the privacy of the information about himself/herself.[9]

In addition to these general preconditions that are applicable to all kinds of personal data, the Data Protection Directive places heightened restrictions on the collection and use of "special categories" of personal data which consist of "personal data revealing racial or ethnic origin, political opinions, religious or philosophical beliefs, trade union membership, and . . . data concerning health or sex life."[10] These special categories of data may only be processed if:

- the individual has provided his or her consent, provided that the laws of the particular member states recognize it;[11]

- the party collecting or using the information is doing so in fulfillment of its legal employment law-related obligations;[12]

- the individual is unable to give consent, and his or her vital interests are at stake;[13]

- the party collecting or using the information is a nonprofit organization with a political, philosophical, religious, or trade union aim of which the individual is a member or is regularly associated;[14]

- the information is the subject of legal claims or has otherwise been made public;[15]

- the information concerns health care, provided it is collected or used by a professional under a legal or professional obligation of confidentiality;[16]

- such use or collection of data is in the interest of substantial public interest, in accordance with national law.[17]

Notice Requirements

The Data Protection Directive also has significant notice requirements. Under the terms of the Directive, entities processing personal data must notify the applicable data protection supervisory authorities of the details of their data processing operations[18] of the member state in which they are operating. The supervisory authorities of each member state tend to have their own procedural and notice requirements. However, generally, the notice that is made to the supervisory authorities must indicate the following:[19]

- the name and address of the controller and of his representative(s);

- the purpose(s) of processing;

- a description of the category or categories of the data subject and of the data or categories of data relating to him;

- the recipients of categories of recipient to whom the data might be disclosed;

- proposed transfers of data to third countries;

- a general description allowing a preliminary assessment to be made of the appropriateness of the measures taken pursuant to article 17 to ensure the security of personal data processing.

In many countries, failing to act in accordance with the notice requirements can leave the controller subject to serious penalties. The notice requirements play a very important role in the overall scheme of personal data protection. The intent of the comprehensive notice requirements appears to be to ensure that the individual who is the subject of data processing operations can effectively monitor the movement of his or her personal data as they move between different data processors and data controllers.

The Rights of the Data Subject

The Directive provides individuals who are data subjects with several rights to ensure that the entity that is controlling the processing of their data is not processing more personal data than is necessary and is processing the correct data. Specifically, pursuant to the Directive terms, data subjects have the right to obtain the following information from the data controller:[20]

- whether the controller has any data about the individual;

- the purpose for which the data are being used, if any;

- the categories of data that have been obtained;

- the recipients or categories of recipients of the data;

- the actual data undergoing processing, in a readable form;

- the source of the data, if known;

- to the extent the data are being used in any "automated decision making" capacity, the logic by which such decisions are being made.

The Directive requires that such information be provided to the data subject "without constraint" and "without excessive delay or expense."[21] Such rights of access and rectification, not generally available in the United States, appear to be a very important part of ensuring that personal data are used properly and in compliance with applicable law. If access and rectification rights are truly available and are used by data subjects, the likelihood that incorrect data will linger in organizations' systems diminishes substantially.

Data Security

The Directive also requires data controllers and processors to implement appropriate security measures to protect personal data. This obligation to ensure that personal data are afforded adequate security is a requirement that is appearing in an increasing number of laws and regulations both in the United States and abroad. When analyzed, the requirement is very logical. In reality, entities' promises concerning the limitations on the use and transfer of personal data that they collect are only as useful as the security measures that they implement to protect such data.

The Data Protection Directive establishes a relatively broad and rule concerning the security of personal data. The Directive provides that:

> Member States shall provide that the controller must implement appropriate technical and organizational measures to protect personal data against accidental or unlawful destruction or accidental loss, alteration, unauthorized disclosure or access, in particular where the processing involves the transmission of data over a network and against all other unlawful forms of processing.[22]

Further, in determining what security measures would be "appropriate," the Directive calls upon data controllers to consider the state of the art, the cost of implementing the security measures, the risks represented by the processing, and the nature of the data to be protected.[23]

The result of the use of such general language in the Directive is that there are considerable differences in the security requirements—and the penalties for violating those requirements—from member state to member state. Many member states have implemented stringent requirements, which may vary somewhat based upon the kind of processing that is being undertaken. Spain, for instance, requires entities to implement very high security measures for processing operations involving personal data revealing racial or ethnic origin, political opinions, religious or philosophical beliefs, trade union membership, or data concerning health or sex life, and data for police purposes, whenever there is no consent of the data subjects.[24] Entities that fail to implement such high-level security requirements when processing these types of data may face fines from €60,100 to €601,000.

It is also notable that the European approach to data security seeks to hold the controller accountable for the security measures that are implemented by any third-party data processors involved with the processing of personal data. Under the terms of the Directive, controllers are not able to simply delegate their security obligations to the processing entities. Instead, the Directive compels controllers that rely on data processors to "choose a processor providing sufficient guarantees in respect of the technical security measures and organizational measures governing the processing to be carried out."[25] Furthermore, the Directive requires the controller and processor to enter into an agreement that binds the processor to the controller and stipulates that the processor may only act upon the instructions of the controller and that the processor must act in compliance with the security requirements of the Directive as they are implemented in the laws of the relevant member state(s).[26]

Cross-Border Data Transfers

One of the most notable aspects of the Data Protection Directive is the section concerning transfers of personal data to countries outside the European Economic Area. Article 25 of the Directive prohibits the transfer of personal data to third countries that do not provide adequate protection to personal data unless one of several limited exceptions applies.

Article 25(2) of the Directive sets forth a list of factors to be taken into account when judging the adequacy of protection in third countries. In determining whether a particular jurisdiction provides adequate protection to personal data, European authorities are required to assess not only the actual privacy laws in place in the country at issue but also the efficacy of those laws.

Significant in relation to making adequacy assessments is the working party that was established pursuant to article 29 of the Data Protection Directive (the "Working Party") and which is composed of Data Protection Commissioners from each EU member state along with European Commission officials. The Working Party has produced useful guidance documents on the approaches that are to be taken when evaluating whether the level of protection provided in a third country is adequate. The proposal put forth by the Working Party focuses on six principles. The first principle is the purpose limitation principle. According to this principle, personal data should be processed for a specific purpose and subsequently used or further communicated only insofar as this process is compatible with the purpose of the transfer.

The second principle is the data quality and proportionality principle. According to this principle, data should be accurate and, where necessary, kept up to date. Furthermore, personal data should be adequate and relevant and should not be excessive in relation to the purposes for which they are transferred or further processed.

The transparency principle is the third principle. According to this principle, individuals should be provided with information on the purpose of the processing and the identity of the data controller in the third country and other information insofar as this information is necessary to ensure fairness.

The fourth is the security principle. According to this principle, technical and organizational security measures should be taken that are appropriate to the risks presented by the processing. Any person acting under the authority of the data controller must not process data except on instructions from the data controller.

The fifth is individual's rights to access, rectification, and opposition. According to this principle, the data subject should have a right to obtain a copy of all data relating to him or her that are processed and a right to rectification of those data where they are shown to be inaccurate. In certain situations, he or she should also be able to object to the processing of the data relating to him or her.

Lastly, restrictions on onward transfers must also be considered. Generally, the receiving party should not be permitted to transfer the personal data on to another third party, unless such third party is contractually bound to maintain same data protection guarantees that the data subjects would possess in the home territory. This principle is intended to advance the European regulators' goal of prohibiting countries providing "adequate" protection to personal data from being used as intermediaries for exporting data to third-party countries that fail to provide adequate protection to personal data.

To date, the European Commission has approved only few jurisdictions, including Hungary, Switzerland, Canada, Argentina, and Guernsey, as providing adequate protection to personal data. Of course, the U.S. Safe Harbors program has also been deemed to constitute adequate protection of personal data. Entities that desire to participate in the Safe Harbors program must certify that they comply with the seven major principles of the initiative, which are as follows: notice, choice, onward transfer, access, security, data integrity, and enforcement. These principles are summarized in Appendix 1.[27]

While Safe Harbors may not be the perfect solution to the differences in data protection requirements found in the EU and the United States, it does offer many advantages for entities that process personal data. For instance, entities engaging in frequent transfers of data between the EU and the United States are likely to appreciate the predictability and continuity offered by the Safe Harbors program. Instead of having to analyze each and every proposed transfer of data to determine whether it complies with one of the exceptions contained in the Data Protection Directive, entities participating in Safe Harbors will simply have to comply with the Safe Harbor principles and the certifications made to the U.S. Department of Commerce. In addition, the Safe Harbors program provides for a comparative flexible approach that many small and medium enterprises are likely to welcome.

Although the negotiation of the Safe Harbors initiative is something that was long anticipated, there has not been a very large response rate to the program. There are many possible reasons for this relatively lackluster response. One is that many entities are simply not aware of the requirements of the Data Protection Directive and the possibility of enrolling in Safe Harbors as a means for achieving compliance. Other companies, while aware of the issue, may not believe that achieving compliance in Europe is worth the time and expense or risks of assuming additional legal obligations and potential liabilities in the United States. Still other companies may have determined that other compliance solutions better fit their needs and business models. It will be interesting to monitor this situation and analyze whether any increase in enforcement actions on the part of the Europeans leads to increased enrollment in Safe Harbors in the United States.

The Safe Harbors accord was very controversial when negotiated. There were many European constituencies that contended that the accord did not afford sufficient privacy protections. The controversial nature of the Safe Harbor accord has not died down. In early 2005, the Commission issued a working document[28] (the "Report") concerning the implementation and efficacy of Safe Harbors. The Report was quite significant in that it observed that many companies participating in Safe Harbors were not acting in compliance with its requirements. It also described various ways in which Safe Harbors, generally, was not functioning properly. The Report was based upon the Commission's experiences and a study which the Commission assigned to a group of third-party contractors.[29] The Commission and its contractors examined many materials, including (i) the Safe Harbors pages of the U.S. Department of Commerce's Web site, (ii) the privacy policies of 10 percent of the organizations that have signed up with Safe Harbors, and (iii) the privacy policies of eight independent dispute resolution mechanisms.

In the Report, the Commission noted that there were two main ways in which the efficacy of Safe Harbors could have been evaluated: (i) by auditing the organizations' behavior and (ii) by analyzing participating organizations' publicly available privacy policies. Owing to the expense and the legal difficulties involved with the first option, the Commission opted for the second option. In its Report, the Commission contended that it was appropriate to focus the review on the organization's publicly available privacy policies because the Federal Trade Commission's authority to enforce the Safe Harbor principles upon a given organization is triggered by such organization's public commitment to comply with the Safe Harbor principles, as set forth in the organization's privacy policy.

The Report highlighted many important observations about the way in which Safe Harbors has been implemented. Most notably, the Commission expressed concern that many participating companies have not published a privacy policy or have published a policy that is not compliant with the Safe Harbor requirements. To be compliant with the Safe Harbor principles, an organization's privacy policy must address all seven Safe Harbor principles. In its Report, the Commission expressed concern that relatively few of the participating organizations had posted privacy polices that addressed all seven mandates.

The Commission noted that four principles in particular appeared to have been most problematic for participating organizations: (i) the notice principle, (ii) the principle of choice, (iii) the access principle, and (iv) the enforcement principle. The Commission noted that, of the organizations studied, many failed to correctly translate the foregoing four principles into their privacy policies.

Also of note were the critical observations that the Commission made about some of the alternative recourse mechanisms that are being utilized by companies participating in Safe Harbors. Participants involved in Safe Harbors can comply with the enforcement principle by adhering to independent resource mechanisms that have publicly stated their competence for hearing individual complaints for noncompliance with the terms of the Safe Harbors accord. Safe Harbors imposes certain rules on the alternative recourse mechanisms: (i) they should be readily available, independent, and affordable; (ii) they should provide individuals with information about how the dispute resolution procedures work when filing a compliant; (iii) they must undertake to remedy problems arising out of organizations' failure to abide by the Safe Harbors principles; and (iv) they must include rigorous sanctions that would deter companies from committing further violations. The Report observed that many of the alternative recourse mechanisms failed to comply fully with requirements (ii), (iii) and (iv).

While the Report did not call for the termination of Safe Harbors, it did put forth some very serious criticisms about how the program has been implemented and raises the likelihood that the effectiveness of the program will be revisited in the near future. In considering the transfer of personal data to third countries, one must also consider the exemptions that are included in the Data Protection Directive. Article 26(1) of the Directive provides certain exemptions from the requirement for adequate protection. The first exemption concerns situations in which the data subject provides his or her unambiguous consent to the proposed transfer. While it is likely that many enterprises will attempt to rely upon this exemption when making transfers of personal data to third countries, it is important that the particular facts of the proposed transfers as well as the relevant national laws be reviewed very carefully before attempting to rely on this exemption. Generally, to be valid, consent must be freely given, specific, and informed. However, the various national laws implementing the Directive may differ on the interpretation of consent. Accordingly, when attempting to implement a mechanism for obtaining user consent for a data transfer, it will be necessary to examine specific national interpretations of the meaning of consent. It is also not practical to obtain consent for very large, bulk transfers such as the kinds that have been requested by U.S. authorities in many contexts.

The second and third exemptions are somewhat related in that they both concern the performance of a contract. Article 26(2)(b) of the Directive provides that a transfer of personal data can proceed to a third country regardless of whether there has been a finding of adequacy in that country if "the transfer is necessary for the performance of a contract between the data subject and the controller or the implementation of pre-contractual measures taken in response to the data subject's request."[30]

Similarly, Article 26(2)(c) provides that such transfers may proceed where "necessary for the conclusion of performance of a contract concluded in the interest of the data subject between the controller and a third party." While these exemptions are relatively broad, it is once again necessary to caution against taking the exemptions at face value. Instead, national law must be examined to understand the precise interpretation of the exemption at issue under the law of the member states(s) from which one is attempting to transfer personal data.

The next exemption provides that transfers of data may proceed where "necessary or legally required on important public interest grounds, or for the establishment, exercise or defense of legal claims."[31] This category of exemption might be used where personal data are being transferred between various public administrations or concerning litigation.

The fifth exemption under article 26 of the Directive applies when the "transfer is necessary in order to protect the vital interests of the data subject." When analyzing the potential use of this exemption, it is necessary to also give consideration to recital 31 of the Directive, which defines vital interest narrowly, as interests "essential for the data subject's life."[32] On the basis of such definition, it would appear that this exemption would be limited to situations such as when the transfer of data would be necessary to provide urgent medical care to an individual.

The final exemption is somewhat of a catch-all, providing that transfers of data may proceed if the "transfer is made from a register which according to laws or regulations is intended to provide information to the public and which is open to consultation either by the public in general or by any person who can demonstrate legitimate interest, to the extent that the conditions laid down in law for consultation are fulfilled in the particular case."[33]

When viewed facially, this list of derogations from the requirements of article 25 of the Directive does appear rather broad. However, the actual utility of any of the foregoing options will depend to a great extent on how they are interpreted and implemented under the relevant national law. While one or more of the derogations listed above may be useful for certain transfers of data, it may not always be possible to rely upon one of the aforementioned categories. One method that may be utilized to transfer personal data when such a transfer would not otherwise be authorized in accordance with one of the exceptions is by contracts. Article 26(3) of the Directive provides that member states may authorize transfers of personal data to countries that do not provide adequate protection to personal data where the controller "adduces adequate safeguards with respect to the protection of the privacy and fundamental rights and freedoms of individuals."[34] This section goes on further to indicate that the "adequate safeguards" may result from the use of appropriate contractual clauses. Placing reliance upon this approach is probably one of the most palatable options for the business community, which is well accustomed to using contracts for many purposes, including the achievement of regulatory compliance. However, once again, some level of caution is necessary. In practice, European regulators may desire and expect much more burdensome contractual clauses than many American companies receiving data would generally be willing to accept.

Another potential option for ensuring the continued free flow of data from Europe to third countries such as the United States is through the development and implementation of various self-regulatory initiatives. Thus far, the opinions issued by the Working Party appear to have left open the option of using industry self-regulation as a means of ensuring adequacy of data protection. The approval of specific self-regulatory initiatives at the European Community level would be particularly attractive to American companies, which are accustomed to working within the confines of self-regulatory initiatives in many different areas including, notably, the advertising sector. At the same time, however, while self-regulation remains at least a theoretical possibility, it may be difficult to convince European regulators that a self-regulatory plan would in fact offer effective data protection. The recent approval of use of binding corporate rules as a measure for achieving adequacy is a particularly notable advancement in this regard.

Select National Issues

Overview

Because of the Data Protection Directive and similar measures, issues regarding privacy rights and data protection, especially in the commercial sense, were largely harmonized in Europe before 2001. Even non-EU member states such as Switzerland had enacted privacy measures similar to those in place throughout the EU. In addition, many Central and Eastern European countries were enacting new privacy laws and/or reusing existing legislation to prepare for possible ascension into the EU. As a result, subject to many minor differences and few larger, more significant differences, legislation in Europe concerning privacy was largely harmonized.

It is a substantially different story insofar as anti-terrorism legislation is concerned. There were and continue to be distinct differences in the countries' legislation concerning terrorism-related issues. Given the history of terrorism in Europe, it is not surprising to note that many European countries, including United Kingdom,

France, Italy, Portugal, Greece, and Spain, already had detailed counterterrorism laws on the books prior to the September 11 terrorist attacks in the United States.[35] The following section shall explore some of the most significant national measures that were in place before the 2001 terrorist attacks. Because much of the national legislation concerning privacy and data protection was harmonized, the exclusive focus will be on anti-terrorism measures.

Spain

Like other European countries, prior to the attacks against the United States, Spain had already been dealing with its own battles against domestic terrorism. Over the years, Spain's problems have mainly arisen concerning the efforts of a protracted conflict with the armed Basque separatists, Euskadi ta Askatasuna (ETA). ETA uses violent means to seek the creation of an independent Basque state in parts of northern Spain and southern France.[36] The group is believed to have been responsible for more than 800 deaths since the 1960s. In recent years, it has targeted civilians, including academics and journalists.

Because of its domestic threats, Spain had anti-terrorism measures in place before the September 11 attacks. Spain's anti-terror laws permit the use of incommunicado detention, secret legal proceedings, and pretrial detention for up to four years. The investigating magistrate of the Audiencia Nacional, a special court that oversees terrorist cases, can request *causa secreta* status for 30 days, consecutively renewable for the duration of the four-year pretrial detention period. Secret proceedings bar the defense access to the prosecutor's evidence, except for information contained in the initial detention order. Prior to the September 11 attacks, Spain had enacted a range of laws that, while not targeted at issues of terrorism, proved to be of value in the fight against terrorists.

Article 54(1), together with article 57(1) of the Law on Foreigners, for example, allows the government to expel from the territory of Spain those foreign nationals who are considered to have participated in acts against the national security of Spain or that might prejudice Spain's relations with other countries.[37]

United Kingdom

Overview

Like Spain, the United Kingdom was well acquainted with terrorism by the time of the 2001 attacks against the United States. Given the history of the United Kingdom, it is not surprising that the country had already implemented legislation to counter the threat of terrorism prior to 2001. The following sections shall examine some of the main legislation that had already been enacted in the country at the time that the 2001 attacks occurred.

Terrorism Act

The primary anti-terrorism legislation in the United Kingdom had long been the Terrorism Act 2000[38] (the "2000 Act"). The legislation was passed by Parliament on July 20, 2000, and entered into force on February 19, 2001. The legislation was a response to the changing threat posed by international terrorism. It replaced the previous temporary anti-terrorism legislation that dealt primarily with Northern Ireland.

Among other significant provisions, the 2000 Act outlawed certain terrorist groups and made it illegal for them to operate in the United Kingdom. The act also provided police with enhanced powers to investigate terrorism, including wider stop and search powers and the power to detain suspects after arrest for up to 14 days (a period which can be extended upon the approval of a magistrate). The 2000 Act also created new criminal offences, including the following:

- inciting terrorist acts;

- seeking or providing training for terrorist purposes at home or overseas;

- providing instruction or training in the use of firearms, explosives, or chemical, biological, or nuclear weapons.

Regulation of Investigatory Powers Act 2000

Another significant piece of legislation that was in place prior to the 2001 terrorist attacks in the United States was the Regulation of Investigatory Powers Act 2000[39] (RIPA). RIPA provides for, and regulates the use of, a range of investigative powers, by a variety of public authorities. Among other significant features:

- RIPA updated existing legislation that had governed the interception of communications to address technological developments, including the increasingly widespread use of the internet and related technologies;

- RIPA placed other intrusive investigative techniques on a statutory footing for the first time;

- RIPA provided new powers to authorities to counteract threats posed by the use of strong encryption;

- In accomplishing the foregoing, RIPA also included clauses providing for independent judicial oversight of the powers in the act.

PRIVACY RIGHTS AND ANTI-TERROR MEASURES AFTER SEPTEMBER 11

European Issues

Overview

Prior to the terrorist attacks against the United States, the EU was not only working very diligently to ensure that its citizenry enjoyed a high level of privacy protection, because of the extraterritorial approach taken by its main data privacy instruments, but was in fact having a very positive influence on the development of privacy rights worldwide. The terrorist attacks on America and those that followed in Europe did not appear to change the European view on the fundamental nature of privacy. It did, however, in certain areas and during certain times, place privacy rights on a lower priority.

The situation concerning anti-terrorism efforts was quite different in that at the time of the terrorist attacks against the United States the EU did not have a comprehensive, integrated policy for responding to terrorism, or addressing other criminal activity, for that matter. Within the EU, criminal matters were and are a responsibility of Justice and Home Affairs, which falls under the "third pillar" within the EU's "three pillar" framework.[40] Accordingly, terrorism and other criminal matters were not subjects for lawmaking at the level of European community law. Instead, such matters were to be addressed in EU terms only within a framework of mutual agreement among the different member states. The integration of the member states of the EU has been progressing slowly but surely, with certain matters being harmonized before others. The three-pillar framework is an essential part of this staggered transition. In the "first pillar," areas like economic regulation, and other areas explicitly outlined by the set of treaties that make up EU law, EU law is superior to and binding on the member states and is enforceable by the European Court of Justice (ECJ). In the "second pillar," area of foreign and security policy, as well as in the "third pillar," area of Justice and Home Affairs, the EU may only act by cooperation and consensus among all of the member states through their adjustments of national laws and policy.

Despite the existence of this three-pillar framework, over the years, there have been calls for great cooperation on matters related to Justice and Home Affairs. Such calls have become more frequent and more vocal in recent years. The attacks of September 11 appear to have been a factor that is contributing to the current push for greater integration and cooperation on such matters. Shortly after the September 11 attacks, the Council of Justice and Home Affairs Ministers met and agreed on a variety of concrete proposals that would result in more coordination and cooperation between police and intelligence services throughout the EU.[41] Then, in the following month, the General Affairs Council adopted an anti-terrorism "roadmap" that included proposals for cooperation in many areas including a European arrest warrant.[42] There has already been concrete progress on many of the proposals outlined in the roadmap.

One of the most significant steps toward integration taken thus far occurred in June 2002 when a Framework on Combating Terrorism that was proposed by the European Commission in 2001 was adopted.[43] This framework decision provided a common definition of terrorist acts that EU member states were committed to adopting as part of their domestic, substantive criminal law. In this regard, it was an incredible significant development toward greater cooperation. It is likely that cooperation will continue to increase in the days ahead.

Immediate Response to the Terrorist Attacks

As in other jurisdictions, the EU responded rapidly to the 2001 terrorist attacks against the United States. In the immediate aftermath of the attacks, EU authorities initiated efforts for a European arrest warrant, common legislative frameworks for terrorism, increasing intelligence and police cooperation, freezing assets, and ensuring passage of the Money Laundering Directive.[44]

U.S. pressure on EU authorities for greater cooperation on counterterrorism initiatives was swift and strong. Shortly after the occurrence of the attacks, in October 2001, President George W. Bush sent a letter to the president of the European Commission requesting that the EU "[c]onsider data protection issues in the context of law enforcement and counterterrorism imperatives" and to "[r]evise draft privacy directives that call for mandatory destruction to permit the retention of critical data for a reasonable period."[45] U.S. authorities already aware of the ways in which European data protection laws could impede transfers of data on the commercial side did not wish to witness similar obstacles as it sought data for its counterterrorism efforts.

Such pressure continued steadily. In November 2001, the U.S. Department of Justice submitted several recommendations to the European Commission working group on cybercrime. Such recommendations included the suggestion that any data protection regime should strike an appropriate balance among the protection of personal privacy, the legitimate needs of service providers to secure their networks and prevent fraud, and the promotion of public safety.[46] Similar pressure was exerted at international fora. For instance, at a May 2002 meeting of the G8 Justice and Interior Ministers, U.S. representatives requested that countries ensure that data protection legislation, as implemented, takes into account public safety and other social values, in particular by allowing retention and preservation of data important for network security requirements, law enforcement investigations or prosecutions, and particularly with respect to the Internet and other emerging technologies.[47]

Airline Passenger Data Transfers

In the aftermath of the attacks, as U.S. and EU authorities began to cooperate more closely on counterterrorism issues, key areas of discord began to emerge. One of the most notable examples of U.S. authorities pressuring authorities of other jurisdictions to lessen their privacy standards to provide the United States with information concerning the war on terror has arisen with U.S. demands for detailed information regarding all individuals traveling to the United States by air, as required under the Aviation and Transportation Security Act 2001.[48] The legislation called for the transfer of "passenger name records" from "foreign carriers" to combat terrorism and maintain national security.[49] The exact details of these transfers were to be left for subsequent regulations and agreements. Over time, the U.S. government commenced demands for very broad rights, including the ability to access the reservation systems of foreign carriers to review the personal data on individuals planning to travel to the United States.

The ability of European authorities and European airlines to comply with such demands were limited by European privacy laws, including, most notably, the European Data Protection Directive. Therefore, the EU was placed in the untenable position of upholding its privacy law and facing sanctions of the U.S. Government, where the U.S. Government could fine airlines up to US$3000 per passenger; or granting the U.S. Government access to these data and breaching fundamental privacy guarantees and facing penalties and sanctions back home. In addition, European citizens were protesting vociferously to the proposed data transfers, thereby adding to the mix of concerns, a potential public relations nightmare.

Many of the European concerns about the measure were summarized in a 2003 opinion of the Article 29 Data Protection Working Party (the "Working Party").[50] Among the chief concerns expressed by the Working Party were the retention time (the original proposed period of seven to eight years was considered unjustified) and the excessive amount of data being requested.

The discord between European and American offices eventually led to lengthy negotiations that continued throughout most of 2003 and the early part of 2004. European authorities eventually caved in to U.S. demands, agreeing in early 2004 to permit the transfer of customer information from European airlines to the Department of Homeland Security. For its part, the Department of Homeland Security has promised that it would retain such passenger data only for 3.5 years, about one-half of the originally requested retention period. U.S. authorities also agreed to reduce the amount of information required, down to 34 data fields from the originally requested 60, and a reduced set of processing purposes, modifying from "any purpose" to purposes related to "combating serious crime and terrorism" in addition to other key components.

Because of such concessions and despite a significant amount of protests from the public and the European parliament, on May 14, 2004, the Commission released a decision on adequacy finding that the U.S. program provided adequate protection to the passenger name record data, and on May 16, 2004, the Council adopted a decision approving the agreement. The decision came into force on May 28, 2004.

The European parliament remained unconvinced that the accord was appropriate and elected to seek a halt to the transfer of data on legal grounds. As a result, the Parliament took the Commission and the Council to the ECJ over this agreement. In bringing the suit, the European parliament asked the court to determine the following:

- whether the Commission could adopt the decision on adequacy on the basis of the Data Protection Directive considering that Directive's scope excludes data that are processed for public security, defense, state security, and criminal law;

- whether article 95 of the Treaty of the European Council (EC) allows for the EU to conclude an agreement with the United States to preserve the internal market.

In a very significant turn of events, on May 30, 2006, the ECJ decided to annul the deal between the EU and the United States to transfer passenger reservation data from EU carriers to the U.S. Department of Homeland Security.[51] In accordance with the decision of the ECJ, the previously negotiated accord will be annulled as of September 30, 2006.

In considering the first issue identified above, the ECJ determined that because the transfer of passenger name record data to the United States constitutes processing operations concerning public security, and because private operators must operate within a framework established by public authorities, the European Commission was acting beyond its remit by establishing an agreement in an area in which it has no jurisdiction (i.e., public security). The court then stated that the Commission was not competent to conclude the agreement. With regard to the second point, the ECJ determined that the EU did not have sufficient jurisdiction to conclude the agreement. As the agreement relates to the transfer of data that are excluded from the scope of the Directive, there is no legal basis for the agreement.

While the immediate results of the decision in annulling the accord that allowed for transfers of data to the United States were a victory for privacy advocates, it is interesting to note that it was not based upon privacy considerations. Instead, the decision was founded in the court's rejection of the underlying legal basis of the agreement, a legal technicality. Specifically, the court determined that (i) when the Commission declared that the data would be adequately protected by the United States it was in fact acting beyond the confines of European law and (ii) when the EC approved the agreement it did not do so on an appropriate legal basis. Therefore, there continue to be concerns among privacy proponents that the original legal accord can be tweaked to address the technical legal issues identified by the court, without resolving the underlying differences in privacy. Now, it appears that this is precisely what will occur. On June 19, 2006, just two weeks after the decision, the European Commission announced that it would create a "legally sound framework" to ensure the continued transfer of passenger name record data to the United States.[52] Such a framework, it appears, would essentially alter the underlying legal basis upon which the original accord was based, but would not address specific privacy-based concerns. The Commission's actions are not likely to be viewed favorably by European data protection regulators, who have made demands for specific changes to the accord, nor by members of the European Parliament, the body that launched the legal challenge against the accord in the first place. This is, however, far from the final word in this ongoing debate. It will be very interesting to see how U.S. authorities on both sides of the Atlantic will grapple with the challenges presented by the court's decision in the weeks and months to come.

At first glance, the ECJ ruling would appear to be a positive development for privacy rights, in that it could serve as an obstacle to continued transfers of passenger name record data to the United States. However, privacy advocates are very concerned about the precise basis of the ruling and the very serious loophole potentially caused by the decision. Recall that in making its ruling the court opined that although the Data Protection Directive does apply to the transfer of personal data for commercial reasons, it does not apply to transfers in the context of criminal offenses or state security. The European Data Protection Supervisor (EDPS) has expressed grave concerns about the ruling for these reasons. A statement issued by the EDPS indicated: "[The decision] seems to create a loophole in the protection of the European citizen since it is no longer assured that data collected for commercial purposes but used by police are protected by the data protection directive."[53] Clearly, that would be a huge and immensely significant loophole. In essence, it would appear to sanction much of the highly controversial mining of commercial databases by the government that has been occurring in the United States.

There has been a proposal for a framework for data protection in the third pillar[54] that would address privacy and data protection in the areas of Justice and Home

Affairs. However, such a proposal appears to have been stalled in the Council. Until that proposed framework or other alternative measures to allow for the continued transfer of these kinds of data across borders are finally adopted, it will be interesting to see how the loophole will play out.

Data Retention

A notable development to consider concerning the struggle with balancing privacy rights and anti-terrorism concerns was the recent approval of a new European directive concerning data retention (known as the "Data Retention Directive"). On December 14, 2005, the European parliament approved new measures that will require providers at publicly available electronic communication service and/or public communication networks (collectively, service providers) to comply with new requirements regarding the retention of traffic and location data. In imposing new retention requirements, the Data Retention Directive will amend Directive 2002/58/EC, also referred to as the Directive on Privacy and Electronic Communications.

The Data Retention Directive will cover traffic and location data transmitted through a wide range of communication services, including short message service, which are text messages sent via cellular phones, voice mail, call forwarding, call transfer, and messaging. Under the terms of the new Directive, covered service providers will be required to retain traffic data and location from 6 to 24 months, depending on the local law of the applicable member state. Furthermore, the Data Retention Directive also will afford the governments of individual member states to exceed that range and impose even longer retention requirements. There has been some speculation that at least one member state was considering the adoption of a rule that would require enterprises to retain such data for as long as 15 years. Many industry groups have expressed grave concerns about the flexibility that will be afforded to individual member states, arguing that it will result in compliance challenges as well as distortions in competition in the marketplace.

The Directive also raises the thorny issue of cost. For the most part, service providers will have to bear the financial burdens of the new requirements. Observers also have noted that costs will vary from state to state. The Data Retention Directive will provide individual member states the freedom to determine what—if any—financial assistance they will give to service providers to offset the costs of setting up data retention systems.

Member states must transpose the Directive into national law by August 2007. In the meantime, member states have the authority to postpone the implementation of local data retention measures related to Internet access, Internet telephone services, and email. However, the states must apply general requirements of the Directive, including rules controlling data access and criminalization of illicit access.

Privacy advocates have been critical of the new measures. Before the Data Retention Directive was approved, opponents' objections were detailed in an October 2005 Opinion of the Article 29 Working Party. The Opinion questioned whether the justification for the data retention requirements were based on clear evidence and challenged the proposed retention periods. It also identified 20 specific safeguards that member states should establish to minimize the interference with individual privacy rights. The safeguards can be summarized as follows:

(i) Data should only be retained to fight terrorism and organized crime.

(ii) The Directive should provide that the data will only be given to specifically designated law enforcement authorities (and a list of those authorities should be made publicly available).

(iii) Large-scale mining of the data covered by the Directive should not be permitted.

(iv) Any further processing of the data should be prohibited or limited stringently by appropriate safeguards. Further, access to the data by other governmental bodies should be prohibited.

(v) Any retrieval of the data should be recorded; but access to the records would be limited and must be destroyed within one year.

(vi) Access to data should be authorized only on a case-by-case basis by a judicial authority, without prejudice to countries that allow a specific possibility of access, subject to independent oversight.

(vii) The Directive should clearly define which service providers are specifically covered by the retention requirements.

(viii) It should be clear that there is no need to identify the customer unless it is necessary for billing purposes or some other reason to fulfill the contract with the service provider.

(ix) Providers should not be allowed to process data for their own purposes or any other reasons not specifically required by the directive.

(x) The systems for storage of data for public-order purposes should be logically separated from systems used for the providers' business purposes and protected by more stringent security measures.

(xi) The Directive should provide for minimum standards for technical and organizational security measures to be taken by the providers, specifying the general security measures established by the Directive on Privacy in Electronic Communications.

(xii) The Directive should specify that third parties are not allowed to access retained data.

(xiii) There should be a clear definition of the data categories covered by the retention requirements and a limitation on traffic data.

(xiv) The Directive must specify the list of personal data to be retained.

(xv) Specific guarantees should be introduced to ensure a stringent, effective distinction between content and traffic data.

(xvi) The different categories of traffic data related to unsuccessful communication attempts should not be included.

(xvii) There should be limitations on the location data that can be stored.

(xviii) There should be effective controls on the original and any further compatible use of the data by judicial authorities.

(xix) The Directive should include an obligation to provide citizens with information regarding all processing operations undertaken under the directive.

(xx) The Directive's provisions regarding costs should be modified to clarify that providers would be reimbursed for investments in the adaptation of communication systems and for responding to law enforcement demands for data.

Efforts were made to address many of the issues identified above in the final version of the Data Retention Directive. However, privacy issues still remain a concern and were further highlighted on December 19, 2005, when the office of the EDPS issued an opinion criticizing certain aspects of the Directive and calling for enhanced privacy protection measures. Specifically, the EDPS called for the following steps with regard to the protection of data used by law enforcement officials:

- The main data protection rules should cover all police and judicial data (not just data exchanged between member states, but also data used within one country).

- Data on different categories of individuals (such as criminal suspects, convicted persons, victims, witnesses, and contacts) should be processed with appropriate conditions and safeguards.

- The principles of necessity and proportionality should reflect the case law of the European Court on Human Rights.

- The quality of data received from a third country would need to be assessed carefully (in light of human rights and data protection standards) before used in any manner.

- Specific provisions on automated individual decisions (similar to those in the main Data Protection Directive) should be introduced.

Surveillance

Across Europe, many countries have been undertaking efforts to enhance and increase the ability of governments to conduct surveillance activities. Such efforts were stepped up considerably after the London transportation bombings, once it was demonstrated that London's complex system of cameras had allowed for the identification of the bombing suspects. For the most part, such surveillance efforts have been done on an ad-hoc basis, in accordance with national laws. Therefore, the issue of surveillance shall be examined more closely in subsequent paragraphs regarding select national issues.

International Cooperation

Council of Europe Cybercrime Convention

There were also many interesting developments in the area of international cooperation. One of these was the development of the Council of Europe's Convention on Cybercrime[55] (the "Cybercrime Convention" or "Convention"), which was adopted by the foreign ministers of the Council of Europe on November 8, 2001, and opened for signature on November 23, 2001. At the opening ceremony, the Convention was signed by 26 of the 43 member states of the Council of Europe, along with Canada, Japan, South Africa and the United States, who participated in the drafting of the Convention but who are not member states of the Council of Europe. The Cybercrime Convention may be opened for signature by additional nonmember states in the future.

The Cybercrime Convention is a lengthy endeavor, the main aim of which is to pursue "a common criminal policy aimed at the protection of society against cybercrime, inter alai by adopting appropriate legislation and fostering international co-operation."[56] The Convention seeks to do this by establishing international agreement on the kinds of offences that will be considered as cybercrimes, harmonizing various procedures for detecting and responding to international cybercrime, and setting forth rules concerning mutual assistance in the detection, investigation, and prosecution of cybercrime. In this regard, it is viewed as an instrument with potential utility in preventing cyberterrorism and apprehending cyberterrorists.

The Cybercrime Convention calls upon participating states to consider specific acts involving computers as crimes.[57] These acts are divided into four main categories:

(i) offences against the confidentiality, integrity, and availability of computer data and systems,[58] including illegal access, illegal interception, data interference, system interference, and misuse of devices;

(ii) computer-related offences[59] including forgery and computer fraud;

(iii) content-related offences[60] including production, dissemination, and possession of child pornography;

(iv) offences related to infringement of copyright and related rights,[61] including the wide-scale distribution of pirated works.

Interestingly, the Cybercrime Convention does not call upon participating states to classify the violation of data protection rules or other violations of privacy protections as criminal behavior.

The Convention also seeks to harmonize certain procedural measures related to cybercrime.[62] Specifically, it requires parties to ensure that the following measures are available under their national law: expedited preservation of stored data; expedited preservation and disclosure of traffic data; the ability to order a person to provide computer data under his or her control and to order a service provider to provide subscriber information under its control; search and seizure of stored computer data; real-time collection of traffic data and interception of content data. Currently, such procedures are extremely important in detecting, investigating, and prosecuting international cybercrime, and such significance is only likely to grow in the future.

Of the provisions, those pertaining to international cooperation are particularly notable.[63] The obligations pertaining to mutual assistance contained in the Cybercrime Convention are broad and cover many areas including extradition, spontaneous information, preservation of computer data and traffic data, disclosure of and access to computer and traffic data, transborder access to stored data, and real-time collection of traffic data and interception of communications. The Cybercrime Convention also allows parties to make requests for mutual assistance by expedited means, such as fax or email.

The Convention provides that participating nations must establish jurisdiction for offences committed on their territory, on ships flying their national flag, on aircrafts which they have registered, or by their nationals (unless another nation has territorial jurisdiction for such crimes).[64] It further provides that when one party claims jurisdiction over an alleged offense established in accordance with the Convention, the parties shall, where appropriate, consult with each other in an effort to determine the most appropriate jurisdiction for the prosecution.

Although the Cybercrime Convention is intended to foster international cooperation in the growing area of cybercrime, there are also justifiable concerns about the potential effects of the Cybercrime Convention on individual privacy. At a very basic level, individuals may have concerns about the collection of their personal information and the monitoring of their use of information systems. Such concerns may become magnified because of the mutual assistance provisions contained in the Convention. In practice, the mutual assistance provisions of the Cybercrime Convention would result in the exchange of a large amount of very sensitive data between participating countries, some of which have lesser standards of privacy and data protection standards than others.

Interestingly, the preamble of the Cybercrime Convention makes references to many international instruments that provide protection to personal data, including, without limitation, the 1966 United Nations Convention on Civil and Political Rights, the 1981 Council of Europe Convention for the Protection or Individuals with Regard to Automatic Processing of Personal Data (Data Protection Convention), and Recommendation No. (87) 15 regulating the use of personal data in the police sector [Recommendation No. (87) 15]. It does not, however, harmonize the safeguards that will apply to the obligations contained in the Cybercrime Convention based upon reference to the text of the instruments. While the Cybercrime Convention does note that the "establishment, implementation and application of the powers and procedures [provided for in the section pertaining to procedural measures] shall be subject to the conditions and safeguards provided under the domestic law of each Party concerned," it does not require that any such safeguards actually be in place.

Council of Europe countries are required to provide certain protections to personal data in accordance with the Data Protection Convention, Recommendation No. (87) 15, and other instruments. However, the Cybercrime Convention is intended to be open to countries from outside the Council of Europe and has been signed by Canada, Japan, South Africa, and the United States, countries which arguably have less protective personal data protection legislation. The Convention does not require such countries that are not Council of Europe member states to meet the privacy standards set forth in the Data Protection Convention, Recommendation No. (87) 15, and other relevant instruments. This may create the risk that personal data from individuals within a country that is highly protective of the privacy of personal data would be transferred, pursuant to the mutual assistance obligations contained in the Cybercrime Convention, to a country that is not as protective of the privacy of personal data.

The risks of the transfers of data that are required by the Cybercrime Convention are of such concern that they were even recognized in a special opinion of the Data Protection Working Group that was established by the Data Protection Directive.[65] The Working Party recommended that "the draft Convention should contain data protection provisions outlining the protections that must be afforded to individuals who are subject of the information to be processed in connection with all the measures envisaged in the draft Convention."[66] Nonetheless, the final version of the Cybercrime Convention does not contain such data protection provisions. In fact, except for a recital referencing the need to be mindful of the protection of personal data and relatively vague language concerning confidentiality and limitation of use obligations related to mutual assistance requests, the Convention provides very little protection to the privacy and integrity of personal data.

Select National Issues

Overview

The 2001 terrorist attacks in the United States, combined with the more recent attacks occurring throughout Europe, including, most significantly, the transit bombings in London and Madrid, prompted many governments to begin taking specific national efforts against terrorism. Specific measures have arisen in a great number of different areas. For example, many states have increased their surveillance activity. The efforts of France and the United Kingdom will be discussed in greater detail below. Germany's parliament has called for increased surveillance of airports, train stations, and underground networks. Other states have opted to implement broad packages of measures. In Italy, for example, the government recently approved a package of new anti-terror measures, including taking saliva samples from suspects for DNA tests, the power to detain suspects for up to 24 hours without charges and to expel terrorist suspects from Italy rapidly. There has also been heightened security at Italy's ports and on its railway and underground networks.[67] The following sections shall explore in further details some of the more significant measures undertaken in key European countries.

France

France has had to deal with its own matters of domestic terrorism for many years. While, as noted in the beginning of this publication, terrorism actually has its roots in France, when considering contemporary acts of terrorism one must focus mainly on the past few decades. During the 1980s and 1990s, France suffered from two major waves of bombings linked to terrorism. During the first wave, which occurred between 1985 and 1986, there were eight bombings in Paris, which resulted in 13 deaths and 281 injuries. The second wave of bombings occurred between 1995 and 1996. During this time, there were six bombings in Paris and Lyon, killing 10 and injuring 262.

Given its history, France has been sensitive to the problem of terrorism and has been fairly active in undertaking new measures to prevent terrorism and apprehend terrorists. Such efforts received new attention and focus after the recent attacks on the transportation systems of Madrid and London.

One measure of particular note is a new anti-terrorism law that was drafted after the July 2005 transit bombings in London.[68] Certain individuals in France, including, most notably, Interior Minister Nicolas Sarkozy, author of the legislation, have been pushing for legislation that would allow for the dramatic increase in surveillance throughout the country. For many individuals, the need for increased surveillance was highlighted by the London bombings and the fact that authorities were able to rapidly identify the bombers based in large part upon the surveillance footage that was captured at the train stations. While there are more than 3 million video surveillance cameras already operating in Britain, there are less than 50,000 in France. Supporters of the measure have contended that it might help enable France to be better prepared to counter a potential terrorist attack.

On December 15, 2005, France's upper house of Parliament approved the framework for anti-terrorism legislation, and on December 22, 2005, the French Senate gave their final approval to the bill.[69] It will increase dramatically the ability of public authorities to use video surveillance, particularly at high-risk sites including airports, train stations, and nuclear power plants. It will also allow automatic surveillance and photography of vehicles on freeways or at toll booths and permit greater identity controls on cross-border rail services. It will also offer business owners wider leeway to use video surveillance cameras for antitheft operations and open access to images in these cameras to law enforcement. Furthermore, it will require firms in the transportation industry, including airlines, ferry operators, rail networks, and travel agents, to provide law enforcement with extensive passenger data upon request.[70]

It also reinforces existing data retention standards for Internet service providers (ISPs), cybercafé operators, and telecommunication firms.[71] In addition to imposing data retention standards on private entities, the measures will grant law enforcement new, sweeping authority to access a wide variety of information from government and private sector databases, while limiting judicial oversight of terrorism investigations. Specifically, the proposed law would force cybercafé operators to retain certain data for a minimum one-year period and make this information available, upon request, to law enforcement authorities working on terrorism investigations. Framework legislation dating to 2001 already requires ISPs and telecom firms to retain various types of "traffic" data on the source, destination, and time of a communication, including user Internet protocol (IP) addresses, sites visited, and length of connection, for Internet users, and numbers dialed, for mobile phone users. However, France has yet to publish the administrative decrees that would force firms to apply these measures.

There has been some resistance to these new measures in France. For instance, Senators from the Socialist and Communist Party bloc attempted, unsuccessfully, to amend the measure to create a new oversight role for the Commission Nationale de l'Informatique et des Libertes (CNIL) over the anti-terror legislation. For its own part, the CNIL has previously claimed that the proposed anti-terror legislation threatens essential freedoms and has urged the government to limit its application to a three-year period, subject to future review. The CNIL has also expressed concern that the government has yet to "list precisely the entities that must conserve technical data relating to Internet use" and worries that the lack of judicial oversight could eventually allow government new de facto rights to spy on citizens.

The new law was also subject to criticism from human rights groups. Human Rights Watch even prepared a transmitted letter addressed to the French senators, cautioning them against undertaking the measure. Human Rights Watch expressed particular concern about the provisions that would increase the maximum duration of police custody for terrorism suspects without improving safeguards with respect to access to counsel and judicial supervision. The group contended that such provisions were inconsistent with the country's obligations under international human rights law.[72]

Italy

Italy has also taken steps to clamp down on terrorists. In the immediate aftermath of the 2001 attacks on America, the government passed a decree concerning emergency measures against terrorism.[73] More recently, in 2005, the government approved a package of comprehensive and controversial anti-terror measures. Among other changes, such measures allow the government to take saliva samples from terrorism suspects, to process DNA tests; to detain suspects of terrorism for up to 24 hours without charge;[74] and to expel terrorists from Italy very rapidly.[75]

The legislation is reaching into many aspects of citizens' private lives. After the passage of the legislation, authorities ordered managers offering public communication services to make photocopies of the passport of every customer seeking to use services such as the Internet, telephone, or fax. In practical terms, this means that operators of cybercafés and similar facilities have suddenly become foot soldiers in the war on terror.[76] Such measures have come at a cost to local businesses, all of which now have the added responsibility of checking in and documenting all individuals who come into use the services, and most of which have had to purchase expensive computer monitoring software. Such "software saves a list of all sites visited by clients, and Internet café operators must periodically turn this list into their local police headquarters."[77] Many Internet cafÈ operators have reported witnessing a drop in business since the new measures were implemented.

Of course, the increase in surveillance activity is not limited to Internet cafés and communication facilities. Reportedly, the country has also increased surveillance activities, principally at the country's ports, trains, and other transportation hubs.[78]

Spain

Spain has had its own difficulties with terrorism since well before the 2001 attacks on America. In addition to the nation's protracted battles with ETA, in March 2004 the country was the site of a deadly and horrific bombing attack. Ten virtually simultaneous explosions on four different commuter trains caused the loss of 191 lives and resulted in more than 1,400 injuries. While there was some initial speculation that ETA may have played a role in the attacks, it soon became clear that they were carried out by al-Qaeda operatives. In the aftermath of the 2001 attacks in the United States and the 2004 attacks in Madrid, Spain applied its existing forceful body of anti-terrorism legislation to the investigation, apprehension, and detention of suspected al-Qaeda operatives. Reportedly, since September 11, Spain has also been using its anti-terror laws to clamp down on the activities of ETA. Since the 2001 attacks, various members of ETA have been detained and held under Spain's anti-terror laws.

United Kingdom

Overview

There have been many extraordinary developments occurring in the United Kingdom in the past few years. This is not too surprising given the cooperation that the country has generously extended to the United States prior to the 9/11 attacks and the country's own unfortunate experience with transit bombings as well as its long history in battling terrorism. "Londoners have lived under the threat of random acts of terror since the '70s when the Irish Republican Army extended its bombing campaign to the British mainland. Each new attack – massive explosions at Harrods department store (1983), Bishopsgate (1993) and Canary Wharf office complex (1996) – prompted new measures."[79] More recently, the attacks of July 7, 2005 claimed 52 lives and caused fear and panic. They also led to increased efforts to detect terrorists and clamp down on terrorism. The following section shall examine some of the more significant developments that have occurred within the United Kingdom since 2001.

Notable Legislative Developments

Terrorism Act 2006

The United Kingdom has been very active in proposing new legislation to respond to the threat of terrorism. Most recently, the Terrorism Act 2006[80] (the "Terrorism Act") received Royal Assent on March 30, 2006. The Terrorism Act contains a comprehensive package of measures designed to provide police, intelligence agencies, and courts with the tools they require to tackle terrorism and bring terrorists to justice. The act creates many new offences. Once it is brought into force, it will be a criminal offence to commit the following:

- *Acts preparatory to terrorism*: This aims to capture those planning serious acts of terrorism.

- *Encouragement to terrorism*: This makes it a criminal offence to directly or indirectly incite or encourage others to commit acts of terrorism. This will include the glorification of terrorism, where this may be understood as encouraging the emulation of terrorism.

- *Dissemination of terrorist publications*: This will cover the sale, loan, or other dissemination of terrorist publications. This will include those publications that encourage terrorism and those that provide assistance to terrorists.

- *Terrorist training offences*: This makes sure that anyone who gives or receives training in terrorist techniques can be prosecuted. The Terrorism Act also criminalizes attendance at a place of terrorist training.

The Terrorism Act also makes amendments to existing legislation, including by

- introducing warrants to enable the police to search any property owned or controlled by a terrorist suspect;

- extending terrorism stop and search powers to cover bays and estuaries;

- extending police powers to detain suspects after arrest for up to 28 days (though periods of more than two days must be approved by a judicial authority);

- improved search powers at ports;

- increased flexibility of the proscription regime, including the power to proscribe groups that glorify terrorism.

One clearly controversial aspect of the law is the fact that it makes it illegal to sell, loan, or otherwise disseminate publications concerning terrorism. Clearly, such a prohibition could have a dramatically negative effect on individuals' freedom of expression. Even before the enactment of this most recent legislation, human rights and educational groups have expressed grave concerns about the ability of the government to monitor the kinds of materials that people access and read.[81]

Anti-Terrorism, Crime and Security Act
The Terrorism Act follows a slew of legislative changes that had been occurring within the United Kingdom since the 2001 attacks on America. First, shortly after the September 11 attacks, the government proposed the Anti-terrorism, Crime and Security Act 2001[82] (ATCS Act), which was then approved by Parliament in December 2001. The measure built upon the Terrorism Act 2000, which had been the primary piece of anti-terrorism legislation in the country.

The law deals with many issues relating to terrorism prevention, but one of the most notable aspects of the law is its protections regarding data retention. The ATCS Act permitted the Home Secretary to issue codes of conduct for the voluntary retention of communication data by service providers. It applied only to communication data already being held by the service providers for business purposes. The Code of Practice was approved in December 2003. Pursuant to such Code of Practice, some communication data can be retained for up to one year.[83]

There have been frictions between privacy officials and the government on the issue of data retention. Notably, an opinion commissioned by the Office of the Information Commissioner found that the access to information retained under the act for non-national security purposes would violate human rights and would be unlawful.[84] Notwithstanding such privacy concerns, there is little indication that the government will undertake efforts to limit its anti-terror powers. In fact, most recent proposals have included an expansion of powers.

The ATCS Act also contained very significant provisions regarding the detention of suspects. Specifically, the measures permitted the detention, subject to ensuing review and appeal, of foreign nationals who were suspected of being international terrorists. In addition, it also contained measures designed to (i) cut off terrorist funding, (ii) ensure that government departments and agencies can collect and share information required for countering the terrorist threat, (iii) streamline relevant immigration procedures, (iv) ensure the security of the nuclear and aviation industries, (v) improve security of dangerous substances that may be targeted/used by terrorists, (vi) extend police powers available to relevant forces, and (vii) enable the United Kingdom to meet its European obligations in the area of police and judicial cooperation and the international obligations to counter bribery and corruption.

The ATCS Act was sharply criticized by many groups including, in particular, Human Rights Watch. Prior to the parliamentary reading of the bill back in November 2001, the group called upon lawmakers to reject the bill's broad definition of "terrorism."[85] Specifically, the group was concerned that terrorism would be defined so broadly that individuals could result in being found "guilty by association." The group also criticized the bill's provision regarding detention periods.

The Prevention of Terrorism Act 2005

In March 2005, the country approved the Prevention of Terrorism Act 2005[86] after a compromise was reached to resolve a remarkable conflict between the House of Commons and the House of Lords. Through this law, Parliament repealed the powers of detention of terrorism suspects that had been established by the ATCS Act and replaced such powers with a system of control orders. The Prevention of Terrorism Act allows for control orders to be made against any suspected terrorist, whether a U.K. national or a non-U.K. national, whatever the nature of the terrorist activity (international or domestic).

A few explanatory words about control orders are necessary. Control orders are essentially preventative orders that impose one or more obligations upon an individual which are designed to prevent, restrict, or disrupt his or her involvement in terrorism-related activity. This could include measures ranging from a ban on the use of communication equipment to a restriction on an individual's movement. Specific conditions imposed under a control order are tailored to each case to ensure effective disruption and prevention of terrorist activity.

The Home Secretary must normally apply to the courts to impose a control order based on an assessment of the intelligence information. If the court allows the order to be made, the case will be automatically referred to the court for a judicial review of the decision. In emergency cases, the Home Secretary may impose a provisional order which must then be reviewed by the court within seven days. A court may consider the case in open or closed session—depending on the nature and sensitivity of the information under consideration. Special Advocates will be used to represent the interests of the controlled individuals in closed sessions. Control orders will be time limited and may be imposed for a period of up to 12 months at a time. A fresh application for renewal has to be made thereafter.

A control order and its conditions can be challenged. Breach of any of the obligations of the control order without reasonable excuse is a criminal offence punishable with a prison sentence of up to five years and/or an unlimited fine.

Individuals who are subject to control order provisions have the option of applying for an anonymity order.

The kinds of obligations that can be covered by a control order are extraordinarily broad. The act states that the "obligations that may be imposed by a control order made against an individual are any obligations that the Secretary of State or (as the case may be) the court considers necessary for purposes connected with preventing or restricting involvement by that individual in terrorism-related activity."[87] The act then further lists the following examples of the kinds of obligations that may be covered by control orders:[88]

(a) a prohibition or restriction on his possession or use of specified articles or substances;

(b) a prohibition or restriction on his use of specified services or specified facilities, or on his carrying on specified activities;

(c) a restriction in respect of his work or other occupation, or in respect of his business;

(d) a restriction on his association or communications with specified persons or with other persons generally;

(e) a restriction in respect of his place of residence or on the persons to whom he gives access to his place of residence;

(f) a prohibition on his being at specified places or within a specified area at specified times or on specified days;

(g) a prohibition or restriction on his movements to, from or within the United Kingdom, a specified part of the United Kingdom or a specified place or area within the United Kingdom;

(h) a requirement on him to comply with such other prohibitions or restrictions on his movements as may be imposed, for a period not exceeding 24 hours, by directions given to him in the specified manner, by a specified person and for the purpose of securing compliance with other obligations imposed by or under the order;

(i) a requirement on him to surrender his passport, or anything in his possession to which a prohibition or restriction imposed by the order relates, to a specified person for a period not exceeding the period for which the order remains in force;

(j)   a requirement on him to give access to specified persons to his place of residence or to other premises to which he has power to grant access;

(k)   a requirement on him to allow specified persons to search that place or any such premises for the purpose of ascertaining whether obligations imposed by or under the order have been, are being or are about to be contravened;

(l)   a requirement on him to allow specified persons, either for that purpose or for the purpose of securing that the order is complied with, to remove anything found in that place or on any such premises and to subject it to tests or to retain it for a period not exceeding the period for which the order remains in force;

(m)   a requirement on him to allow himself to be photographed;

(n)   a requirement on him to co-operate with specified arrangements for enabling his movements, communications or other activities to be monitored by electronic or other means;

(o)   a requirement on him to comply with a demand made in the specified manner to provide information to a specified person in accordance with the demand;

(p)   a requirement on him to report to a specified person at specified times and places.

Surveillance

Communication Surveillance

Given the history of the country and its experiences with terrorism, it is not surprising that the law of the United Kingdom contained many anti-terrorism measures even before the 2001 attacks on the United States and/or the subsequent attacks on London. In terms of communication surveillance and wiretapping, it is interesting to note that the RIPA[89] governs the interception of communications. Part I of the RIPA is one of the most significant components of the law. It authorizes the Home Secretary to issue warrants for the interception of communications. It also requires providers of communication services to configure their networks so as to provide for reasonable interception capability. Significantly, the act also authorizes any public authority designated by the Home Secretary to access communication data (including source, destination, and type of any communication) without a warrant.

Part II sets rules on other types of "human intelligence" powers that had not been previously regulated under U.K. law. Key provisions of Part III address encryption issues. Specifically, it allows senior members of the civilian and military police, customs, and members of the judiciary to demand that users hand over the plain text of encrypted material or, in certain circumstances, decryption keys themselves.

Video Surveillance

In recent years, there has been a dramatic increase in the use of video surveillance in the country. While the use of video surveillance has been particularly prevalent in London, it has not been limited to London. In fact, a recent report noted that there are more than 4 million cameras in Britain, one for every 14 residents.[90] For the most part, such cameras tend to be funded, at least in part, by Home Office grants and are operated by police, local authorities, or private companies. There have been reports that some of the cameras that were purportedly installed for crime prevention and/or traffic control were subsequently outfitted with facial recognition technology and used for other purposes.[91] The widespread nature of closed-circuit television (CCTV) surveillance in the United Kingdom has been noted by many commentators:

> [N]o place rivals the United Kingdom for use of surveillance cameras, whose role as a crime-fighting tool increased as part of the move to counter bombings by the Irish Republican Army. So pervasive are the devices, visible on many building corners, that one study estimated a Briton could be filmed 300 times a day while waiting for a bus, parking in a public garage, riding a train or strolling along the Thames. There are some 4.2 million cameras around the country, with at least 500,000 in London. London's Underground subway network is watched by more than 6,000 cameras.[92]

Much of the surveillance has been focused on the transportation system. The possibility of utilizing explosive scanning within the transportation system has also been discussed.[93]

Physical Surveillance of Suspects

In recent years, especially in the wake of the London transit bombings, there have been many reports of increased monitoring of individuals suspected of being involved in terrorist activities in the country.[94] In a report issued soon after the July attacks, Home Secretary Charles Clarke disclosed that hundreds of suspected British terrorists were being tracked by police and MI5. In a special hearing on the bombings, he noted: "There are certainly hundreds of people who we believe need to be very closely surveilled because of the threat they offer."[95]

Summary and Conclusion

Britain has had to face its own struggle of trying to balance the needs and goals of preventing terrorism while also protecting fundamental rights and freedoms, including privacy rights.[96] While there was much focus being placed upon these kinds of issues after the attacks on the United States, the emphasis became magnified after the horrific attacks on the country's own transit system.

RUSSIA

Overview

Before closing this chapter on European developments, a few words must be said about Russia. With its own significant history with terrorism of a different nature, Russia has had an interesting and important role to play in the current war on terror as well as the ensuing war on privacy. While Russian leaders have long struggled to develop effective mechanisms for addressing the risks posed by its own domestic terrorists, the country has frequently been criticized for the way in which it has trampled on human rights in its efforts to curtail terrorism.

Privacy Rights before September 11

Privacy and Data Protection Laws

Russia has not had comprehensive data protection or privacy legislation that is analogous to the Data Protection Directive. There are, however, constitutional protections for privacy as well as laws that protect certain aspects of privacy.[97] Consider, first, the constitutional protections. Many clauses within the country's constitution protect different aspects of privacy. For instance, article 23 of the Constitution of Russian Federation,[98] which was adopted by national voting on December 12, 1993, provides the following:

1. Everyone shall have the right to privacy, to personal and family secrets, and to protection of one's honor and good name.

2. Everyone shall have the right to privacy of correspondence, telephone communications, mail, cables and other communications. Any restriction of this right shall be allowed only under an order of a court of law.

In addition, article 24 goes a bit further than many constitutional provisions of this nature do. Part of it provides that data cannot be collected without the data subject's consent. Article 24 provides the following:

1. It shall be forbidden to gather, store, use and disseminate information on the private life of any person without his/her consent.

2. The bodies of state authority and the bodies of local self-government and the officials thereof shall provide to each citizen access to any documents and materials directly affecting his/her rights and liberties unless otherwise stipulated under the law.

An additional protection is found in article 25, which states, "The home shall be inviolable. No one shall have the right to enter the home against the will of persons residing in it except in cases stipulated by the federal law or under an order of a court of law." Such a protection can have important implications for the discussion regarding the kinds of searches and surveillance that are often carried out for anti-terrorism efforts.

Legislation in place prior to the 2001 attacks on the United States placed limitations on the ability of the government to collect information regarding individuals. Federal legislation entitled the Law on Information, Informatisation and the Protection of Information[99] (LIIPI) places limitations on the collection, storage, use, and distribution (processing) of information pertaining to the private life of a person without his or her permission, except where judicial warrant is issued.[100] Interestingly, articles 11 and 21 of the LIIPI[101] provide that special federal law is to list the kinds of personal data that are to be protected and how they are to be protected. While there have been many bills for legislation that would further specify how personal data are to be protected, there has not been much movement in that regard.

Existing legislation criminalizes certain privacy violations. The Criminal Code provides a penalty for violation of the immunity of private life,[102] violation of secrecy of communications,[103] and infringement of home inviolability.[104]

The Criminal Code also provides liability for unauthorized access to legally protected computer information.[105] The Criminal Code provides with sentences ranging from fines, forced labor, arrest, to a ban on the right to hold certain positions or to be engaged in a certain activity and, in some cases, imprisonment for a period of up to five years.[106] Violations can also result in fines, which, in certain cases, can be based upon the perpetrator's income, being based upon the " . . . income of the convicted person for a period of five to eight months . . . "[107]

There are also relevant provisions in the Civil Code. According to the Civil Code,[108] privacy is a legally protected non-property right. Attached to this right are personal dignity, personal immunity, honor and good name, business name, personal secret, and family secret. If an individual suffers physical or moral damages by violation of his or her personal non-property rights or some other nonmaterial welfare rights as well as in other cases provided by the law, a court can force the person invading privacy to provide financial compensation.[109]

The existence of constitutional protections for privacy as well as limited legislative protections has not allowed Russia to be immune from criticism. Indeed, the United Nations Human Rights Committee has expressed concerns over the state of privacy in Russia. Consider a report from 1995 during which time the committee recommended the enactment of additional privacy laws: "The Committee is concerned that actions may continue which violate the right to protection from unlawful or arbitrary interference with privacy, family, home or correspondence. It is concerned that the mechanisms to intrude into private telephone communication continue to exist, without a clear legislation setting out the conditions of legitimate interference with privacy and providing for safeguards against unlawful interference. The Committee urges that legislation be passed on the protection of privacy, as well as strict and positive action be taken, to prevent violations of the right to protection from unlawful or arbitrary interference with privacy, family, home or correspondence."[110]

Anti-Terror Measures

Russia also had many provisions regarding anti-terror measures before the 2001 attacks. Significant among these measures were the Law on Operational Investigation Activity. This law, which regulates surveillance methods used by secret services, generally requires a court-issued warrant for most surveillance activity.[111] Significantly, article 5 of the Law provides that an investigative structure must secure people's privacy. The Law also provides: "If one believes that some actions of bodies conducting operational investigation have infringed on an individual's rights or freedoms, the individual has the right to appeal to a court, a prosecutor, or to a higher body that carries out investigative activities."[112]

Privacy Rights and Anti-Terror Measures after September 11

Overview

Russian law and policy underwent significant transformation after the September 11 terrorist attacks in the United States. While some of these changes were undoubtedly prompted by pressures or incentives to participate in the U.S.-prompted global war on terror, it is likely that others were because of the country's own battle with domestic terrorism. For many years now, rebels from Chechnya have been opposing the rule of the Russian government and undertaken various acts of terrorism against the Russian government and the Russian people.

In 1999, Russian authorities launched a military operation in Chechnya. Since the launch of such operations, the government has characterized its efforts as a fight against terrorism. When the severity of its actions against Chechen rebels has been called into question by the international community, Russian leaders have often emphasized that they were fighting a terrorist battle. Such efforts have been stepped up exponentially since the 2001 attacks. On September 12, 2001, for example, just one day after the attacks on America, Russian President Vladimir Putin declared that America and Russia had a "common foe" because "Bin Laden's people are connected with the events currently taking place in our Chechnya."[113]

After September 11, the battles between the Russian military and the Chechen rebels increased in vigor. On October 23, 2002, a group of Chechen terrorists captured about 800 hostages in one of Moscow's theaters. Their demand to the Russian government was to withdraw their troops from the territory of Chechnya. The terrorist attack ended with the death of all terrorists and 129 of the hostages.

The following sections shall examine some of the more significant changes to have occurred within Russia after the attacks.

International Cooperation

The Russian Federation has been taking many steps to increase its commitment to cooperating with other countries in the war on terror. President Vladimir Putin recently signed a federal law to ratify the Council of Europe Convention on the Prevention of Terrorism. The law was adopted by the State Duma on March 24, 2006, and approved by the Federation Council on April 7, 2006. On November 8, 2001, the Russian Federation signed the Convention of Council of Europe 1981 for the Protection of Individuals with regard to Automatic Processing of Personal Data but has not ratified the document.[114] In the fall of 2001, the Council of Europe adopted the Convention on Cybercrime. This Convention comprises, in particular, provisions that critics say are threats to privacy. Although Russian representatives participated in the elaboration of the Convention, Russia has neither signed nor ratified the Convention by the end of 2002.[115]

Legislative Developments

On April 30, 2002, President Vladimir Putin announced a bill on Counteraction to Extremist Activities. The bill contained broad definitions of "extremist activities"[116] and, some critics argued, enabled a wide range of public protest actions to be viewed as extremism. The first draft contained an article relevant to the Internet. Specifically, under the terms of the draft, ISPs were forced to censor materials on their servers and remove/block "extremist sites." That clause was later replaced with the indistinct reference to other legislation, and the controversial procedure of Internet monitoring and censorship was dropped.[117]

After the terrorist attacks in Moscow of October 2002, the State Duma quickly adopted several amendments to many laws, including the Law on Mass Media,[118] banning any distribution of information that could impede anti-terrorist actions.

While enacted prior to the 2001 attacks, the 1995 Law on Communications[119] underwent a significant revision, and a new version of this law came into force on January 1, 2004. Under the law, the tapping of telephone conversations, scrutiny of electronic communications, delay, inspection, and seizure of postal mailings and documentary correspondence, receipt of information therein, and other restriction of communication secrets are allowed only with a court order.[120]

More recently, on March 6, 2006, President Vladimir Putin signed Federal Law No. 35-FZ on Counteraction of Terrorism.[121] The measure has been severely criticized to be overly broad and too vague. Among other measures, the legislation empowers Russian secret services to tap telephone conversations and control electronic communications in areas where counterterrorism operations are carried out. It also enables air-defense forces to shoot down hijacked planes to prevent attacks on strategic facilities or public places. The law also bans organizations whose purposes and actions include propaganda, justification, and support of terrorism.

Proposed Legislation

It is very likely that more changes will follow as the country has been considering many proposals on a pretty regular basis. On March 28, 2006, members of the State Duma and the Federation Council proposed several amendments to the Criminal Code,[122] the Criminal-Procedural Code,[123] and other laws that can have implications for issues related to terrorism, including the Law on the Media,[124] all concerning the recently adopted law on countering terrorism and the Council of Europe's Convention on the Suppression of Terrorism, which was recently signed into law by President Vladimir Putin.

The main proposed amendment would permit courts to hear a case regarding a criminal defendant *in absentia* when the defendant is not located within the territory of the Russian Federation and would not be summoned to return, provided that the matter for which the defendant is being tried concerned a grave crime and provided further that the trial would not interfere with the establishment of the truth.

Changes that are being proposed to the Criminal-Procedural Code would allow the confiscation of property with regard to persons convicted *in absentia*. In addition, a parallel amendment of the Criminal Code will allow the trial of Russian citizens for crimes committed abroad. The new counterterrorism package would also penalize public calls for terrorism or public justification of terrorism as well as the financing of terrorism. In emergency situations, the Federal Security Service will be permitted to restrict the constitutional rights and freedoms of citizens without a court warrant for two days and send special forces to combat terrorists and their bases abroad. The headquarters of a counterterrorism operation will decide how the operation may be covered by the media.

SUMMARY AND CONCLUSION

Europe is an extraordinarily interesting jurisdiction to consider when examining the ongoing battle to balance the needs to protect society from the threat of terrorism while also preserving fundamental human rights and liberties. The region has a longer history and greater experience with both efforts to protect privacy rights and efforts to counteract the threat of terrorism. Therefore, the jurisdiction may be able to offer some points of guidance for other countries that are dealing with these challenges.

Nonetheless, there are certainly many areas in which European authorities and legislators do appear to cross the line and encroach upon individual privacy rights and freedoms in its quest to protect citizens from the threat of terrorism. Indeed, quite remarkably, a December 2005 report from Privacy International contends that "on every policy involving mass surveillance of its citizens, the EU is prepared to go well beyond what the U.S. Government find[s] acceptable and palatable, and violate the privacy of its citizens."[125] In commenting on the report, Gus Hosein, the study's author said:

> It is no surprise that governments introduce harsh laws after terrorist attacks. But what is surprising when you compare the surveillance laws in Europe and the U.S. you find that the EU always goes further. The EU plans to fingerprint all of its citizens, monitor all communications transactions, surveil all movement and travel. All these policies have been rejected by the U.S. but are now law in Europe. The EU and some of its member states may paint the U.S. as a monster when it comes to anti-terror powers and civil liberties but they need to look into the mirror every now and then.[126]

Clearly, the quest to find an appropriate balance between what measures are necessary to fight terrorism and what protections are needed to preserve individual liberties is an ongoing challenge. Quite clearly, such challenge is not something that is unique to the United States but is instead something that is being faced by all countries around the world. The successes—and failures—of other jurisdictions in confronting these issues can be very instructive to us all as we consider the proper balance that must be struck and proper measures that should be taken in this area.

Five

Northern and Southern Neighbors

OVERVIEW

This chapter will focus on the northern and southern neighbors of the United States. Owing to their extreme proximity to the United States as well as their role as very important trading partners of the United States, Canada and Mexico have been particularly impacted by U.S. efforts to combat terrorism. Like the European Union (EU), Canada has comprehensive privacy legislation and a relatively long history of undertaking efforts to protect privacy rights and individual liberties. Therefore, Canada has been trying to balance the need to collect, disclose, and use personal data to prevent terrorism with the need to protect the privacy rights of its citizenry. In Mexico, privacy rights were really just beginning to emerge prior to the events of September 11. The attacks and struggle against terrorism that followed seemed to stall this process. As governmental officials and legislators in the country began to focus on other areas that were deemed to be more important, concerns about taking further steps to protect individual privacy rights received much less focus.

CANADA

Privacy Rights prior to September 11

Like Europe, Canada has comprehensive data privacy laws. Also similar to the European approach, Canada's main federal legislation applies cross-sectors and is not, as is the case with much of the U.S. legislation, limited to particular sectors. Unlike the case of many other jurisdictions, including, notably, the United States, the legislation in Canada has been deemed by European data protection authorities to provide an "adequate" level of protection to privacy.

In Canada, data privacy is regulated at the state and federal levels. The Personal Information Protection and Electronic Documents Act[1] (the "Canadian Act" or "Act") is comprehensive federal legislation that is intended to "govern the collection, use and disclosure of personal information to protect the privacy of individuals" while recognizing "the need of organizations to collect, use or disclose personal information for purposes that a reasonable person would consider appropriate in the circumstances."[2]

The Canadian Act adopts a broad view of "personal information." Under the Act, "personal information" consists of "information about an identifiable individual, but does not include the name, title or business address or telephone number of an employee of an organization."[3] Therefore, because it excludes basic identifiable information such as name, title, and business address, the definition of "personal information" in Canada is slightly narrower than the definition of "personal data" under the EU regime. Under the Canadian Act, "personal information" will consist of a wide range of information concerning an identifiable person including, by way of example, information about an identifiable individual's race, ethnic origin, color, age, marital status, religion, education, medical, criminal, employment, or financial history, address and telephone number, numerical identifiers such as the Social Insurance Number, fingerprints, blood type, and so forth.

The Canadian Act has been implemented in three phases. The first phase, which became effective on January 1, 2001, applies to certain data collected for the operation of a "federal work, undertaking or business" as well as to organizations that, over the course of commercial activity, disclose the personal information outside the province in exchange for consideration. During phase II, which commenced in 2002, the health care sector was required to comply with the terms of the Act. Lastly, phase III, which commenced on January 1, 2004, broadened the reach of the Act to regulate all personal information collected, used, or disclosed in the course of all commercial activity, which, according to the Act, consists of any particular transaction, act, or conduct or any regular course of conduct that is of commercial character, including the selling, bartering, or leasing, or donor membership or other fundraising lists.[4] With the Canadian Act entering into force in these different phases, it is significant to note that the legislation does not have any "grandfather clause." Therefore, if entities collect personal information prior to the effective date of the Act, they will not be able to use or disclose such information unless such data at issue were collected and will be used in accordance with the requirements of the Canadian Act.

The Canadian Act incorporates[5] the Canadian Standards Association Model Code for the Protection of Personal Information (the "Code"),[6] a model code that was approved as a National Standard of Canada by the Standards Council of Canada in 1996. Although these principles are described in the Act as recommendations, an entity's failure to comply with such recommendations can constitute grounds for a complaint. The Code and the Act are based upon 10 principles:

   (i)   accountability

   (ii) identifying purposes

   (iii) knowledge and consent

   (iv) limiting collection

   (v)   limiting use disclosure and retention

   (vi) accuracy

   (vii) safeguards

   (viii) openness

   (ix) individual access

   (x)   challenging compliance.

The Act places two key categories of obligations on entities: (i) obligations concerning the processing of personal information and (ii) various administrative obligations. In terms of the substantive obligations concerning the processing of personal information, entities will be required to identify and document the limited purposes for which the personal data they collect will be processed. They will also have to ensure that they have data subjects' consent for the processing of their data for that specific identified purpose.

On the administrative side, companies will be required to designate an individual who will be in charge of the personal data, adopt policies to give effect to the Act, maintain the accuracy of the personal information, retain personal information for only as long as is necessary for the purpose of its processing, adopt security safeguards to protect personal information, provide access and rectification procedures to data subjects, and adopt procedures to respond to inquiries and complaints concerning compliance with the Act.

The Act specifies exceptions to the requirement that an organization acquire consent before collection, use, or disclosure of personal information. It also provides for exceptions to the access requirements. The following exceptions are not exhaustive but reflect some of the situations where information may be collected, used, or disclosed without knowledge and consent and where access may be denied or limited. The Act stipulates that consent is not required when (i) collection of information clearly benefits the individual (which is not defined) and consent cannot be obtained in a timely way; (ii) it is reasonable to expect that the collection would compromise the availability or the accuracy of the information and the collection is reasonable for purposes related to investigating a breach of an agreement or a contravention of the laws of Canada or a province; (iii) the collection is solely for journalistic, artistic, or literary purposes; or (iv) the information is publicly available and is specified by the regulations.[7]

The Act also stipulates that knowledge and consent are not required when, in addition to foregoing exceptions, the information is used (i) because the organization reasonably believes the information would be useful, and is used, to investigate an ongoing, past, or proposed contravention of the laws of Canada, a province, or a foreign jurisdiction; (ii) for an emergency that threatens the life, health, or security of an individual; (iii) for statistical, scholarly, or research purposes that cannot be achieved without using the information; or (iv) in a manner that will ensure its confidentiality; or when it is impracticable to obtain consent and the organization informs the Commissioner of the anticipated use before the information is used.

The Act stipulates that knowledge and consent are not required when the information is disclosed for many reasons. Those reasons include disclosures (i) made for the purposes of collecting a debt owed by the individual to the organization or (ii) additional purposes that echo those set forth above and include disclosure made in the interest of national security and the conservation of historical records.

The Act sets forth various exceptions to the requirement that organizations provide access to an individual's personal information. Many of them concern access to information provided to a government institution concerning subpoena, law enforcement, investigations, or matters of national security. The Act also provides that access may be refused where (i) the information is protected by solicitor–client privilege or (ii) to do so would reveal confidential commercial information (and the confidential information is not severable from the requested information).

Under the Canadian Act, complaints of privacy violations can be initiated by anyone. In practice, this means that an organization's customers, suppliers, and competitors could all be in a position to initiate complaints. The Privacy Commissioner is empowered to investigate all complaints under the Act and to attempt to resolve them by many methods, including mediation or conciliation. The Privacy Commissioner has very broad investigative powers. Provided that the Commissioner is satisfied that there are reasonable grounds to proceed with the pursuit of a complaint, the Commissioner can direct his or her staff search and investigate entities' premises, administer oaths, and conduct interviews. Notwithstanding the powers of the Privacy Commissioner, individuals who contend that their rights under the Act have been violated still have recourse to the courts. Entities that violate the Act are subject to a range of penalties including public disclosure of the information practices, fines (for which company directors, officers, and employees may be personally liable), and court-ordered damages.

In Canada, the Office of the Privacy Commissioner is very active. To date, there have been more than 300 official cases for which the Privacy Commissioner has issued a formal finding.[8] This is in addition to the numerous cases that were settled[9] or otherwise reached an early resolution.[10] The Privacy Commissioner's office also publishes many advisory and educational documents.

Privacy Rights and Anti-Terror Measures after September 11

Anti-Terror Laws

Shortly after September 11, in December 2001, to be precise, Canada enacted an anti-terror law (hereinafter, Anti-Terror Act).[11] The act was a comprehensive "package" of legislative changes that, according to the government,

> creates measures to identify, prosecute, convict and punish terrorist groups; provides new investigative tools to law enforcement and national security agencies; and ensures that Canadian values of respect and fairness are preserved and the root causes of hatred are addressed through stronger laws against hate crimes and propaganda.[12]

The Anti-Terror Act also provided the government with additional investigative tools. First, the measure increased the government's ability to conduct electronic surveillance. Specifically, it extended the investigatory powers that were already in place in the Criminal Code and in Bill C-24 and that make it easier to use electronic surveillance against criminal organizations and terrorist groups. The law eliminated the need for authorities to demonstrate that electronic surveillance is a last resort in the investigation of terrorists. It also extends the period of validity of a wiretap authorization from 60 days to up to one year when police are investigating a terrorist group offence. To provide appropriate checks and balances, a Superior Court judge still must approve the use of electronic surveillance to ensure that these powers are used appropriately.

The Anti-Terror Act amended the Official Secrets Act (renamed as the Security of Information Act)[13] to address national security concerns, including threats of espionage by foreign powers and terrorist groups, and the intimidation or coercion of communities in Canada. The legislation also created new offences to cover counterintelligence-gathering activities by foreign powers and terrorist groups. Other new offences established by the legislation include:

- the unauthorized communication of special operational information by persons permanently bound to secrecy,

- engaging in harboring, threats, or violence for the purpose of increasing the capacity of a foreign power or of a terrorist group to harm Canadian interests.

With respect to foreign surveillance, the new law amended the National Defence Act[14] to allow for the interception of communications of foreign targets abroad and to permit the government to undertake security checks of government computer networks to protect them from terrorist activity. The Minister of National Defence's permission is required to authorize any interception of private communications to ensure that the privacy of individual Canadians is protected. The Act allows the Communications Security Establishment (CSE) to gather foreign intelligence concerning terrorist groups to protect Canadians and national security from terrorist activities as well as guard government communication networks from terrorists.

Amendments to the country's Criminal Code mandate that individuals with information relevant to an ongoing investigation of a terrorist crime can be required to appear before a judge to provide that information. This requires the consent of the Attorney General and increases the ability of law enforcement to effectively investigate and obtain evidence about terrorist organizations, subject to legal safeguards to protect the witness. The Criminal Code was also amended to create a "preventive arrest" power to arrest and impose conditions of release where appropriate on suspected terrorists. A warrant is required except where exigent circumstances exist, and the person has to be brought before a judge within 24 hours of an arrest. While the Anti-Terror Act does allow for preventative arrests without warrants and empowered authorities to conduct investigative hearings,[15] a report by the Solicitor General has observed that Canada has not exercised its detention powers[16] nor has it conducted any investigative hearings.[17]

The Anti-Terror Act also permitted Canada to ratify additional UN conventions regarding terrorism. At the time of the terrorist attacks against the United States, the Government of Canada had already signed all 12 U.N. conventions and protocols related to terrorism but had ratified only 10 of them. The legislation permitted the government to ratify the two remaining counterterrorism conventions: International Convention for the Suppression of the Financing of Terrorism and International Convention for the Suppression of Terrorist Bombings. Specifically, the Anti-Terror Act amended the Criminal Code[18] to allow for the implementation of the conventions.

According to the Canadian government, the changes to the government's system regarding terrorism, especially through the enactment and implementation of the Anti-Terror Act, are being carried out with proper checks and balances to protect the rights of Canadian citizens. Cited safeguards include the following:

- the requirement for a parliamentary review of the anti-terrorism legislation in three years from its passage;

- the utilization of clearly defined provisions so that (i) the requirements of the legislation are targeted at terrorists and terrorist groups and (ii) legitimate political activism and protests are protected;

- ensuring that the state has the burden of proof for establishing that there was intent on the part of the accused "for the purpose of facilitating or carrying out terrorist activity";

- ensuring that the process of adding a group to the list of terrorists incorporates many protections including provisions for removal, judicial review, and safeguards to address cases of mistaken identity;

- requiring the Attorney General's consent to prosecute the financing of terrorism offences;

- requiring the Minister of Defence's authorization for the Communications and Security Establishment to intercept foreign communications that may have a Canadian connection.

Surveillance

Like in the United States and many other countries around the world, after September 11, in Canada there was a dramatic increase in surveillance activities. The transit attacks in Madrid and London then provided the government with further impetus to conduct additional surveillance activity. After such attacks, there were wide reports of the government devoting resources to installing cameras and surveillance equipment in a wide range of areas, including, most notably, on the country's transit systems.[19] In the fall of 2005, following the attacks in London, the government announced a plan to spend $110 million on efforts to improve transit security in Vancouver, Calgary, Edmonton, Toronto, Ottawa, and Montréal.[20]

There has also been increased monitoring of certain Internet-related activities, and such efforts to increase surveillance appear to have been generating positive developments. In June 2006, the government achieved a major victory in using an online sting operation to detect and prevent a very detailed and large-scale terror plot from occurring.[21] In light of such a victory, it is quite likely that, at least for the immediate future, public support for surveillance efforts will grow and the government will continue to carry out a range of activities of this nature.

International Cooperation and Privacy Concerns

While Canada has been very active in developing and implementing terror measures at home as well as in lending significant support to the United States in its war on terror, there are many in Canada who are concerned about the effects that such cooperation and participation will have on the rights of the populace. Provincial authorities have been particularly active in bringing such attentions to light and attempting to mitigate the reach of foreign anti-terrorism laws. Authorities in the provinces of British Colombia, Alberta, and Nova Scotia have all taken steps to block private companies from transferring personal data regarding local citizens to countries such as the United States, for fear that once stored with a service provider in the United States such data could become subject to collection and review by U.S. governmental authorities.

Recently, Québec proposed modifying the province's own data protection legislation to "require public bodies and private companies to ensure the information they send outside the province is as secure as it is in Quebec."[22] Under the measure, which has not yet been enacted, companies would face fines for data breaches and would have to make public disclosures about such breaches. According to reports, the new measures are a specific response to concerns about the ability of U.S. authorities to access and use the data of Canadian residents for a range of purposes once such data are transferred across borders.[23] According to reports, there are concerns that such data will be used by the government not only for fighting terrorism but for other ancillary reasons and could result in an individual being placed upon a no-fly list, having trouble entering the country, or even being discriminated against in efforts to obtain health insurance.[24] The lack of full disclosure by the U.S. government of its plans and intentions for collecting and using data appears to be feeding into public concerns about potential abuse.

MEXICO

The Privacy Rights prior to September 11

Mexico does not have comprehensive federal privacy or data protection legislation; however, there are limited protections for privacy found in other legislation, and there is a fairly broad privacy law in place in the state of Colima. In addition, the country's constitution does provide limited protection for privacy rights, including the right to be free from unlawful searches.[25] In addition, with respect to privacy rights in the commercial sector, it is of interest to note that the country does have a rather thorough consumer protection law that, because of relatively recent amendments, has application to certain aspects of privacy online. In 2000, the Procuraduría Federal del Consumidor, Profeco (Office of the Federal Attorney for Consumer Protection) of Mexico reformed the Federal Law for Consumer Protection (FLCP)[26] to add a chapter related to consumer protection in the context of electronic commerce.

Privacy Rights and Anti-Terror Measures after September 11

Updates to Consumer Privacy Laws

Pursuant to a Decree of February 4, 2004, the FLCP was further revised to include additional provisions regarding data privacy, most of which concerned the transmission of unsolicited commercial email. Significant portions of such reforms as they relate to data privacy are as set forth below.

- *Article 16: Marketing and Advertising Information for Consumers.* Under this section, companies that use consumer information for marketing and advertising purposes are obliged to inform those consumers at no cost if they keep information about them. Companies are also required to make such information available to consumers upon their request.

- *Article 17: Information Disclosures and Opt-Out Clause.* This provision requires companies sending commercial emails to include their contact details as well as opt-out information.

- *Article 18: Information Purpose and Consumer's Public Registry for Personal Data.* This section prohibits companies dedicated to credit and marketing research from using data collected for purposes other than credit and marketing research. It also authorizes the Procuraduria to develop a consumers' public registry, which would list those not wishing their personal data to be used for marketing or advertising purposes.

State Privacy Developments

One of the most notable privacy developments to occur in Mexico arose in Colima. In June 2003, the Constitutional Congress of the State of Colima enacted Personal Data Protection Law (as contained in Decree No. 356).[27] In enacting this measure, Colima became the first Mexican state to enact privacy legislation. It will be interesting to see whether other states and/or the federal legislators will follow Colima's lead and do the same in the near future.

Freedom of Information

In June 2002, President Vicente Fox signed into law the Federal Transparency and Access to Public Government Information Law.[28] This measure was approved by Parliament in April 2002 and entered into force in May 2003. The law allows citizen access to information held by all government bodies. The measure also created a National Commission on Access to Public Information to supervise the implementation of the law. Exemptions are made for several categories of information.

Surveillance

Mexico, particularly in the areas near the border with the United States, has become subject to an increasing amount of surveillance after the September 11 attacks. Such surveillance has increased on both sides of the border. Reportedly, since September 11, the country has also had increased military checkpoints throughout the country.[29]

Anti-Terror Laws

After September 11, the government worked on enacting various measures designed to assist Mexico in making its contributions to the war on terror. During 2002, the country's Senate ratified three significant international conventions on counterterrorism: the UN International Convention for the Suppression of Terrorist Bombings, the UN International Convention for the Suppression of the Financing of Terrorism, and the Inter-American Counterterrorism Convention.

SUMMARY AND CONCLUSION

As close neighbors to the United States, both Canada and Mexico have been the subject of particular focus by the U.S. government and its law enforcement agencies. Notwithstanding previous as well as more recent efforts, the northern and southern borders to the United States remain porous and penetrable to entry by terrorists and/or materials to be used in a terrorist attack. Therefore, it is likely that these countries will continue to receive significant attention—and pressure—from the U.S. government to continue to undertake measures to prevent terrorism. While many of the measures taken domestically and/or in support of the U.S. initiatives are likely to continue to raise privacy concerns, as long as there is a perceived risk of terrorism and governments continue to achieve success in such battles—such as when the Canadian government thwarted a major attack—it is unlikely that such privacy concerns will be the focus of substantial remedial actions.

Six

South America

OVERVIEW

This chapter will focus upon South America. Privacy rights were somewhat slow in coming to the region. Even today, there are many countries in South America that have not enacted any privacy laws and do not provide any Constitutional protections to privacy rights. Nonetheless, in the late 1990s, certain South American countries began to consider and enact privacy laws. It is likely that such efforts were at least, in part, a response to the enactment of the European Data Protection Directive, which prohibits the export of personal data from the European Union (EU) to third countries that do not provide adequate protection to personal data. For the most part, efforts to enact new privacy laws and strengthen existing legislation were diminished by the war on terrorism. At the same time, throughout South America, many countries were influenced by September 11 and its aftereffects to renew efforts to enact new anti-terrorism legislation and/or get previously proposed, stalled bills passed.

PRIVACY RIGHTS PRIOR TO SEPTEMBER 11

Overview

Prior to September 11 and the subsequent terrorist attacks, many South American countries had already begun to follow the lead of countries in Europe and North America. These South American countries have started to enact and/or consider proposals for comprehensive privacy legislation. This action appeared to have been based at least in part upon the restrictions that European Data Protection Directive placed upon the transfer of personal data to countries outside the EU that are considered as failing to provide adequate protection to personal data.

Select National Issues

Argentina

Argentina enacted the Personal Data Protection Act.[1] This is a comprehensive law that addresses many different aspects of privacy rights. A review of this legislation suggests that it is intended to follow the European Data Protection Directive. The stated purpose of the law is to provide for "the full protection of personal information recorded in data files, registers, banks or other technical means of data-treatment, either public or private for purposes of providing reports, in order to guarantee the honor and intimacy of persons, as well as the access to the information that may be recorded about such persons, in accordance with the provisions of Section 43, Third Paragraph of the National Constitution."[2]

The law has very broad coverage. Under it, the definition of "personal data" extends to data concerning entities as well as individuals.[3] Aside from that, it closely follows the terms of Europe's Data Protection Directive in establishing conditions for the protection of data[4] and granting specified rights to data subjects.[5] Significantly, the measure also places restrictions on international transfers of data.[6] Argentina was the first South American country to have enacted a comprehensive data protection act and remains only one of a few countries worldwide to have been deemed by European data protection authorities as providing adequate protection to personal data.

Brazil

Brazil had modest privacy laws that predated the terrorist attacks. In Brazil, the 1990 Code of Consumer Protection and Defense[7] provides consumers with the right to access information concerning them that is stored in files, archives, and registries as well as the right to have incorrect data correct. This law also requires all consumer data files to be objective, clear, true, and written in a manner that is easily understood. Also significant in Brazil is the Informatics Law of 1984,[8] which provides certain protections to the confidentiality of stored, processed, and disclosed data. This law also provides individuals with the right to access and correct their personal information held in private or public databases.

Chile

While Argentina has gotten the most public attention for the enactment of its privacy legislation, the fact is that Chile's efforts in this area predate those of Argentina.

In 1999, Chile enacted the Law for the Protection of Private Life.[9] The legislation, which entered into force on October 28, 1999, covers the processing and use of personal data, whether through automated or manual means, in the public and private sector. In addition to setting forth guidelines pertaining to the collection, use, and disclosure of personal information, the Chilean act provides individuals with the right to access and correct their personal information and includes fines and damages for the unlawful denial of such access and correction rights.

Chile's law is divided into six sections: (i) general provisions about the use of personal data; (ii) rights of data subjects; (iii) use of personal data for economic, financial, banking, or commercial purposes; (iv) data processing by public authorities; (v) liability; (vi) transitional periods. The law includes some elements of Europe' Data Protection Directive, including, without limitation, the restrictions that are placed upon the processing of sensitive data. However, it is not as comprehensive as the European measure.

PRIVACY RIGHTS AND ANTI-TERROR MEASURES AFTER SEPTEMBER 11

Overview

Unfortunately, many South American countries have had a long history with terrorism. In addition to being a site for international terrorism,[10] South American countries have had to manage their own domestic terrorists for many years. Colombia and Peru, in particular, have been adversely affected by home-grown terrorism; however, such domestic terrorism has also been a significant force in many other countries in the region. In fact, it has been reported that more than 30,000 people in the region lost their lives to terrorist acts during the early 1990s alone.[11] There have also been many international terrorist acts in South America. Argentina, in particular, has been the site of at least two major international terrorist attacks: the 1992 bombing of the Israeli Embassy in Buenos Aires and the 1994 bombing of the Argentina–Israeli Community Center.

There has not been a consistent response to terrorism throughout the region. Even before the occurrence of the September 11 attacks, countries in the region were struggling to determine and implement the most effective legal mechanisms for halting terrorism within their jurisdiction. While some countries have considered tough anti-terrorism legislation, other nations have attempted to focus on greater transparency and openness.

While South American countries have been dealing with efforts to implement the most effective response to terrorism, the September 11 attacks and the resulting global war on terror also led to changes within the region. For those countries that had not yet developed anti-terrorism laws or that were finding it impossible to pass those laws, the September 11 attacks and subsequent U.S. governmental pressures gave local governments additional impetus to continue working toward the passage of their local measures. Shortly after September 11, there was a considerably strong response against terrorism within South America. Indeed, most South American countries voted for UN Resolution 1373 condemning terrorism,[12] and many countries got back to work on efforts to develop and implement new anti-terror measures.

Despite certain limited efforts, the ability of many countries in the region to make concrete progress against terrorism has been stymied by the lack of resources. As the U.S. Department of State has observed: "Overall, governments took modest steps to improve their counterterrorism (CT) capabilities and tighten border security, but corruption, weak government institutions, ineffective or lacking interagency cooperation, weak or non-existent legislation, and reluctance to allocate sufficient resources limited the progress of many."[13]

A more detailed description of the specific measures that were undertaken in certain South American countries follows below.

Select National Issues

Argentina

Argentina is no stranger to the threat of terrorism. The country was the site of two very significant acts of international terrorism. While the government has been supportive of the U.S. efforts in the war on terror, the country has not undertaken many significant steps toward the enactment of strict new anti-terrorism measures since the attacks on the United States. The country does, however, have certain laws in place regarding terrorism, many of which date way back and some of which were enacted after September 11. Some of the more significant anti-terror measures that have been enacted in Argentina are summarized below.

- *Law 25.241 (2000): Collaboration to Solve Terrorism Crimes.* Enacted in March 2000, this law defines acts of terrorism as those criminal acts committed by members of illegal associations or organization formed to cause alarm or fear in society and that used explosives or arms with high offensive power to threaten the life of undetermined number of people. The law allows for reducing prison term if the defendant collaborates with the criminal investigation before the final judgment.

- *Law No. 25.246 (2000): Regarding the Concealment and Laundering of Proceeds of Criminal Acts.* This legislation establishes the Financial Intelligence Unit and empowers it to monitor transactions in banks and other financial institutions in cases of money laundering.

- *Law 25.520 (2001): Regarding Intelligence Law.* This law, enacted after the September 11 terrorist attacks, represents a concerted effort to reorganize the intelligence system in Argentina, while also protecting constitutional guarantees of its citizens. The law forbids intelligence organizations from (i) doing enforcement and research, unless required by a judicial authority; (ii) obtaining and collecting personal data based on religion, race, private actions, or political opinions; (iii) exerting influence on the institutional, political, or cultural areas of the country or the political parties; and (iv) revealing or sharing personal data acquired related to any individual or legal entity, unless there is a judicial order (section 4). The law forbids interception and wiretapping of oral, written, or electronic communication of any kind, unless a judicial warrant is issued (section 5). The law regulates carefully how and when an intelligence agency may obtain a wiretap in Argentina. A judicial order is required and is only valid for 60 days. It can be renewed for another period. Upon completion of the period, the data must be destroyed if the government has not decided to initiate criminal proceedings (sections 18–22).

In addition to the laws specifically identified above, in the years immediately following the September 11 terrorist attacks, Argentina considered many additional legal measures against terrorism, including, most notably, Bill 2293[14] (the "Antiterrorism Project of Law"). This bill has been the subject of much criticism for its potential for running afoul of the country's privacy and data protection rules as well as individuals' constitutional rights. The objective of the bill is to "provide the government with exceptional measures to combat terrorism."[15] Of its main interesting provisions, section 5 of the bill authorizes the Secretariat of Intelligence to establish a national computer database to fight against terrorism and organized crime. The provision suggests that the objective of the establishment of such a database would be to ultimately share the information contained within the database with third parties. The bill does not include an express acknowledgement of sections 5 and 6 of the country's comprehensive data protection act, which requires the provision of notice to and the attainment of consent from data subjects prior to data collection and disclosure. The bill was subject to considerable criticism, and therefore, the Ministry of Justice announced plans to amend this bill at the Senate to result in a bill that would be more protective of privacy rights and constitutional guarantees.[16]

Brazil

In January 2002, former President Fernando Cardoso proposed a revision of Brazil's anti-terrorism laws. Under the amendments proposed by Cardoso, terrorism would have been defined more precisely. In addition, the revised legislation would have provided for more severe punishment for those involved in terrorist acts. The country has also been considering legislation that would allow wiretaps for court-approved investigations and would enable the country to become a party to the 1999 International Convention for the Suppression of the Financing of Terrorism. At the time of this writing, none of the aforementioned measures had been passed. Brazil did become a party to the International Convention for the Suppression of Terrorist Bombings in 2002. With this addition, Brazil then became a party to 9 of 12 international conventions and protocols relating to terrorism.[17]

Bolivia

Bolivia has been taking rapid and drastic action since the terrorist attacks of 9/11. Shortly after the September 11 attacks, Bolivia become a party to nine additional international conventions and protocols relating to terrorism, making it a party to all 12. Bolivia has also signed the Organization of American States (OAS) Inter-American Convention against Terrorism and the August 2003 Asuncion Declaration.

Ecuador

Ecuador has been publicly supportive of U.S. anti-terrorism efforts. However, in practice, its contributions have been limited. The country did recently sign the Inter-American Convention against Terrorism but has not yet ratified it. Ecuador is party to seven of the 12 international conventions and protocols relating to terrorism.

Uruguay

In recent years, Uruguay has not been a country in which terrorists have been particularly active. Nonetheless, subsequent to the 2001 attacks on America, the country's government has been supportive of the U.S.-initiated global war on terror. Uruguay is a party to eight of the 12 international conventions and protocols relating to terrorism.[18] The views of the U.S. government on the contributions made by Uruguay appear to be quite mixed. According to a 2005 Report issues by the U.S. Department of State, the Uruguay government cooperates with the United States on matters related to terrorism.[19] However, a 2006 report on counterterrorism also issued by the U.S. Department of State asserted that "[t]he Government of Uruguay allocates insufficient resources and lacks the political will to play a more significant role in the global war on terrorism."[20]

Venezuela

Venezuela undertook limited measures against terrorism subsequent to the September 11 attacks. For instance, in June 2002, it signed the OAS Inter-American Convention against Terrorism.[21] However, it has not yet ratified the convention. In sum, the country is a party to 4 of the 12 international conventions and protocols relating to terrorism. Still, the U.S. Department of State has remained critical of the response of the government, contending: "Venezuelan cooperation in the international campaign against terrorism remained negligible. President Hugo Chavez persisted in public criticism of U.S. counterterrorism efforts, publicly championed Iraqi terrorists, deepened Venezuelan collaboration with such state sponsors of terrorism as Cuba and Iran, and was unwilling to deny safe haven to members of Colombian terrorist groups, as called for in UN resolutions."[22]

In October 2003, the government introduced a bill[23] that proposes to criminalize the act of "anarchy," a crime that would be punishable with one to three years of prison.[24] The bill was approved once in a process of three rounds it requires to become law. Critics said that the bill is part of the U.S. pressure. Section 3 of the bill defines terrorism. Section 12 creates the crime of incitement against the government and punishes those who incite violence in the name of terrorism. Section 13 of the bill proposes to impose prison from 15 to 25 years to those who obtained and administer financial assets for terrorism. Under section 23, criminal proceedings can be suspended for those who collaborate in providing information. Also, under the proposed bill, the government is empowered to seize property related to terrorist organizations.[25] Under section 27, the government is authorized to wiretap any communication, provided that there is a presumption of terrorist acts and a judicial order.

SUMMARY AND CONCLUSION

Prior to the 2001 terrorist attacks against the United States, many initiatives to increase the protection for individual privacy rights were underway in South America. Leaders in this regard were Chile and Argentina, but proposals were also being considered in many other countries. After 2001, privacy rights appeared to have taken lesser of a priority in the region, with few countries considering and/or enacting privacy legislation.

For the most part, the countries of the region have undertaken various, relatively limited efforts to respond to the perception of an increased threat of terrorism. Immediately following the attacks of September 11, most countries of the region very quickly increased efforts of international cooperation against terrorism. Many countries also enacted new measures and/or began to increase the level of activity undertaken under the existing legal framework. Nonetheless, the efforts of many countries in this area have remained hampered by a lack of sufficient economic resources and internal problems of domestic terrorism and organized crime and in some countries corruption.

Seven

Australia, New Zealand, and Asia

INTRODUCTION

This chapter will focus on Australia, New Zealand, and Asia. It will examine the privacy trends that were under development throughout the region prior to September 2001 and will demonstrate how the war on terrorism has been negatively impacting the nascent privacy rights in many countries of the region.

Like in many other regions examined in this book, privacy rights were under development in this area of the world at the time of the 2001 terrorist attacks. But the development of these privacy laws took an about-face in the wake of the terrorist attacks and in response to increasing demands for information from the United States and other governments. The countries of the region have also been called upon to participate in the U.S.-launched war on terror, and many have responded in earnest.

ASIA

Privacy Rights prior to September 11

Overview

Prior to the September 11 terrorist attacks, many Asian countries had begun to undertake efforts to implement comprehensive data privacy laws. The countries of Asia have very disparate economies, cultures, and histories. Therefore, it is not too surprising that there are considerable differences in how—and whether—the countries of this region have elected to legislate these issues. The following sections will outline some of those efforts, on a country-by-country basis.

Select National Issues

China

Limited protections for privacy are found in the Constitution of China. Most notable is article 40, which provides as follows:

> The freedom and privacy of correspondence of citizens of the People's Republic of China are protected by law. No organization or individual may, on any ground, infringe upon the freedom and privacy of citizens' correspondence except in cases where, to meet the needs of state security or of investigation into criminal offences, public security or procuratorial organs are permitted to censor correspondence in accordance with procedures prescribed by law.

Of course, what is most notable here is the huge exception to the general principle of privacy protection. The exception would appear to allow most of the kinds of "infringements" into individual privacy rights that have been described in this publication.

Back at the time of the 2001 terrorist attacks, the country did not have, and continues to lack, any comprehensive legislation concerning privacy or data protection. However, as will be discussed in the section concerning privacy rights in China, post–9/11, there continues to be discussion regarding the possible enactment of new privacy legislation.

Hong Kong

Hong Kong has rather stringent data protection legislation. Hong Kong's main data protection law dates back to 1995, the same year that the European Data Protection Directive was passed. The personal data (Privacy) Ordinance[1] establishes six principles to regulate the collection, accuracy, use, and security of personal data. It also requires data users to inform data subjects about their data processing and grants data subjects the right to be provided a copy of their personal data and to demand corrections to such data. It imposes additional restrictions on certain uses of personal data, including data matching and cross-border transfers of personal data.

Also similar to the European Data Protection Directive, which requires EU member states to establish data protection supervisory authorities, the Ordinance establishes the Office of the Privacy Commissioner.[2] In Hong Kong, the mandate of the Privacy Commissioner is to promote and enforce compliance with the relevant statutory requirements. Similar to the situation in the United Kingdom, the Privacy Commissioner of Hong Kong has broad enforcement power and may initiate its own investigation of suspected violations of the statutory requirements.

India

India's 1950 Constitution does not provide express recognition of a right to privacy, but successive Supreme Court rulings have identified an implicit right under article 21 of the Constitution:[3] "No person shall be deprived of his life or personal liberty except according to procedure established by law." The Court also ruled that access to government information is an essential part of the fundamental right to freedom of speech and expression.

Despite much talk of doing so and many legislative proposals, at present, there is not any general national data protection or privacy laws in India. Instead, limited protection is provided on an uneven basis through sectoral enactments such as the 1993 Public Financial Institutions Act.[4]

Japan

Prior to the terrorist attacks of 2001, Japan did not have comprehensive national privacy and/or data protection legislation. However, as will be discussed in further detail in the section of this chapter addressing privacy rights post–9/11, in 2003, the country did enact a very comprehensive data protection regime.

The 1946 constitution enshrines "[f]reedom of assembly and association as well as speech, press and all other forms of the expression are guaranteed." In addition, the 1988 Act for the Protection of Computer Processed Personal Data Held by Administrative Organs and the 1990 Protection of Computer Processed Personal Data Act [based on the Organisation for Economic Co-operation and Development (OECD) guidelines] provide partial regulation of some national governmental agencies.

Malaysia

The country's constitution does not specifically recognize a right to privacy. Moreover, despite a few legislative proposals, the government has not accepted specific privacy and/or data protection laws.

Singapore

Prior to 2001, Singapore had not enacted a privacy and/or data protection law with general application in the private sector. With the exception of a small privacy division within the Ministry of Finance, Singapore has not charged any governmental authority with responsibility for privacy or data protection issues. Furthermore, the country's Constitution does not include any specific right to privacy.[5]

South Korea

South Korea's Constitution provides explicit protection of privacy. Article 17 declares: "The privacy of no citizen may be infringed." Article 16 states that "[a]ll citizens are free from intrusion into their place of residence," and article 18 provides that "[t]he privacy of correspondence of no citizen shall be infringed."

The country has also adopted the OECD guidelines and has enacted several pieces of privacy legislation, including (i) the 1994 Act on the Protection of Personal Information Managed by Public Agencies, (ii) the 1995 Act Relating to Use and Protection of Credit Information, and (iii) the 1996 Act on Disclosure of Information by Public Agencies. Furthermore, the 1999 Basic Act on Electronic Commerce provides:

> Electronic traders shall not use, nor provide to any third party, the personal information collected through electronic commerce, beyond the alleged purpose for collection thereof without prior consent of the person of such information or except as specifically provided in any other law.

In practice, however, implementation of the legislation has been uneven, with poor enforcement by government agencies and private sector bodies.

Thailand

Thailand's 1997 Constitution seeks to protect a "person's family rights, dignity, reputation or the right of privacy," indicating that "the assertion or circulation of a statement or picture in any manner whatsoever to the public, which violates or affect[s] a person's family rights, dignity, reputation or the right of privacy, shall not be made except for the case which is beneficial to the public" and that "[p]ersons have the freedom to communication with one another by lawful means." The 1997 Official Information Act establishes a code of governmental practice for personal information systems maintained by agencies.

Taiwan

There are limited protections for privacy rights in the country's constitution. The 1994 Constitution provides that people shall have a freedom of privacy of correspondence. Prior to the 2001 attacks, the country had also enacted limited privacy laws. Most notable in this regard is the 1995 Computer Processed Personal Data Protection Law.

This law addresses the collection and use of personally identifiable information by government agencies and some private sector bodies. The law requires that the "collection or utilization of personal data shall respect the rights and interest of the principal and such personal data shall be handled in accordance with the principles of honesty and credibility so as not to exceed the scope of the specific purpose." Significantly, under the measure, data flows to countries lacking privacy laws can be prohibited.

Privacy Rights and Anti-Terror Measures after September 11

Overview

Given the diversity of the jurisdictions under investigation in this chapter, it is not too surprising that there has not been a general, unified response to the terrorist threat. A number of countries in the region, including most notably, Australia, have put forth a very strong response to the attacks on the United States, and those that followed over the past few years. The horrific nightclub attacks in Bali appeared to have particularly influential in this regard. In other countries, however, whether due to a lack or resources or will, the response has been much more subdued.

There has also been a lack of uniformity on the privacy side. Although generally stymied by the effects of September 11 and the subsequent terrorist attacks that have occurred around the world, some Asian countries have continued to endeavor to make progress toward providing for enhanced privacy rights, including, in some jurisdictions, through the enactment of new privacy laws.

On a regional basis, one of the most notable developments occurred in November 2005, when ministers from the Asia-Pacific Economic Cooperation (APEC) endorsed a common privacy framework.[6] The APEC privacy framework is intended to "promote a flexible approach to information privacy protection for APEC Member Economies, while avoiding the creation of unnecessary barriers to information flows."[7] The APEC privacy framework is based upon the following nine principles:

(i) preventing harm

(ii) integrity of personal information

(iii) notice

(iv) security safeguards

(v) collection limitations

(vi) access and correction

(vii) uses of personal information

(viii) accountability

(ix) choice.

The APEC framework focuses on both domestic and international implementation of privacy standards for APEC member economies. It explores new ways of information sharing and cooperation across agencies and authorities to enable transfers of personal data across borders.

Select National Issues

China

Anti-Terror Efforts

According to reports, Chinese authorities—like many other governments—may have relied upon the events of September 11 and the general pubic outcry that followed to clamp down on certain groups within the country's territory.[8] Specifically, since 2001, there have been reports that the Chinese government has been blurring the distinction between terrorism and calls for independence by the ethnic Uighur community in the Xinjiang–Uighur Autonomous Region (XUAR).[9] "According to Amnesty International, Uighur exile sources estimated that at least 3,000 people were detained in the political crackdown from mid-September 2001 until the end of 2001. During the same period at least 20 people were tried on politically motivated charges and sentenced to death and executed. Many more were sentenced to prison terms."[10] China has also sought international assistance in its campaign against the separatists and has had some success in this regard.[11]

Human rights groups, on the other hand, have contended that the separatists in the XUAR region are very different from the terrorists who carried out the attacks on the United States. They allege that the authorities in China have been exploiting the newfound global concern about terrorism to launch a violent crackdown on the separatists.[12]

In addition to targeting the separatists, the Chinese government has also introduced new legislation in the wake of September 11. Specifically, on December 29, 2001, just a few months after the terrorist attacks, the Standing Committee of the National People's Congress (NPC, China's legislature) adopted amendments to the Criminal Law of the People's Republic of China. The stated purpose of the amendments, which entered into force the same day, was to "punish terrorist crimes, ensure national security and the safety of people's lives and property, and uphold social order."[13]

The changes entailed many amendments to existing law. First, two amendments were made to article 120 of the Criminal Law. The first amendment increases possible punishments for individuals who organize or lead a terrorist organization. Before the amendment, the punishment was a prison term of between 3 and 10 years. Under the amendment, it was increased to between 100 years of imprisonment and life imprisonment. The second amendment is the addition of a clause punishing those who "fund terrorist organizations or individuals engaging in terrorist activities." The new crime is punishable by penalties ranging from fines to a maximum of five years of imprisonment, except "when the circumstances of the case are serious, in which case five years' imprisonment is the minimum punishment."

Four of the amendments add new provisions in articles 114, 115, 125, and 127 of the Criminal Law to punish the dissemination; illegal manufacturing, trading, transporting, or storing; or the stealing, seizing or plundering of poisonous, radioactive substances or contagious-disease pathogens. The punishments provided in these articles remain unchanged. Articles 115, 125, and 127 all provide punishments ranging from varying terms of imprisonment to the death penalty.

Article 191 of the Criminal Law has also been amended. The article punishes illegal financial operations or gains related to a range of crimes, including narcotics and smuggling. One of the amendments has now added "terrorist crimes" to the list of offences. A second amendment provides that, when such crimes are committed by a "work unit," punishments will now range between 5 and 10 years' imprisonment if the "circumstances are serious" (i.e., a heavier punishment than previously provided).

The last amendment of the new legislation is a clause added to article 291 of the Criminal Law. The existing provisions in article 291 punish people who "disturb social order" by gathering in public places, blocking traffic, or obstructing agents of the state from carrying out their duties. The punishments for these offences, "if the circumstances are serious," range from "public surveillance" to a maximum five years' imprisonment.

The new clause added to article 291 provides that "whoever seriously disturbs social order by disseminating false explosive, poisonous or radioactive substances or contagious-disease pathogens, or by fabricating threats or information about an explosion or biological or radioactive threat, or by knowingly disseminating fabricated threats or messages" is to receive punishments ranging from "public surveillance" to five years' imprisonment or "if serious consequences have been caused" a sentence of minimum five years' imprisonment. No maximum sentence is specified.

In addition to specific legislative measures, in the wake of September 11, China has also increased its surveillance activities. Reportedly, Shanghai has 200,000 security cameras and has plans to double that amount within five years.[14] Increased surveillance activity is occurring in other cities as well, including Guangzhou and Beijing.[15]

Privacy-Related Developments

At the time of this writing, China still had not enacted any data protection and/or privacy laws. However, recently, there has been increasing talks of emerging privacy rights in the country[16] and it is not beyond the realms of possibility that the country will enact legislation that provides at least limited protections for privacy rights.

India

Anti-Terror Efforts

India has been struggling with the challenges of terrorism since long before the 2001 attacks on the United States. India's response to perceived threats of terrorism only intensified in the wake of an attack by militants on the national parliament in December 2001. On March 26, 2002, the long-debated Prevention of Terrorism Act (POTA) was enacted. Like its predecessor—the much-misused and now-lapsed Terrorists and Disruptive Activities (Prevention) Act (TADA) of 1985 (amended 1987)[17]—there have been claims that POTA is "draconian" as well as allegations that the government has used POTA to target certain groups, in particular Muslims, as well as political opponents.[18]

One of the most significant concerns about POTA was that it, like other national anti-terrorism laws, created an overly broad definition of terrorism. It also expanded the authorities' investigative and procedural powers. POTA allowed suspects to be detained for up to three months without charge and up to three months and more with the permission of a special judge. There were also great concerns that the measure had "required the accused to prove their innocence rather than the prosecution to prove guilt."[19]

For some, POTA's close resemblance to TADA foreshadowed a return to a widespread and systematic curtailment of civil liberties. Under TADA, tens of thousands of politically motivated detentions, acts of torture, and other human rights violations were committed against Muslims, Sikhs, Dalits (so-called untouchables), trade union activists, and political opponents in the late 1980s and early 1990s.[20] In the face of mounting opposition to the act, India's government acknowledged these abuses and consequently let TADA lapse in 1995.

Indian and international human rights groups, journalists, opposition parties, and minority rights groups have unequivocally condemned POTA. Numerous political parties have alleged the misuse of POTA against political opponents in states such as Uttar Pradesh, Jammu and Kashmir. Since it was first introduced, the government has added some safeguards to POTA to protect due process rights, but POTA's critics have stressed that the safeguards that were implemented did not go far enough and that existing laws were sufficient to deal with the threat of terrorism. In September 2004, just less than three years after the measure entered into force, the Indian cabinet agreed to repeal the controversial POTA.[21] The government's decision was well received by human rights groups, which also called upon the government to dismiss all pending cases that had been brought under POTA.[22] Others have contended that the repeal was largely a political, cosmetic change, as many of POTA's controversial provisions were set to expire in December 2004 in any event.[23]

Japan

Privacy Laws

Japan is one of the few jurisdictions to have had strengthened its privacy laws post–9/11. The country's Personal Information Protection Act (PIPA),[24] which provides very broad and comprehensive protection to personal information, within the private and public sectors, entered into force in 2003. The PIPA establishes the basic ideals and principles that will serve for future legislation on the protection of privacy in both the public and the private sectors. Cabinet ministers are charged with its implementation and are authorized to issue recommendations or orders to businesses dealing with personal information. Many of the obligations it imposes on organizations processing personal information are similar to those contained in the European Data Protection Directive. For example, under Japan's PIPA, among other requirements, businesses must specify a "Purpose of Use" to process personal information.[25] Businesses are also obliged to maintain personal data as accurately and up to date as necessary to achieve the stated purpose of using the same.[26] In addition, businesses must take steps to prevent the unauthorized disclosure, loss, or destruction of personal information and must protect information security.[27]

Singapore

Privacy Laws

Recently, reports have suggested that Singapore is in the process of developing new data protection legislation. According to such published reports, the upcoming data protection law will include provisions designed to clamp down on the ability of private companies to collect and disseminate personal data from individuals.[28] It is not expected that the new law will be enacted before early 2008. But it remains to be seen whether this will really occur at all. There have, after all, been reports that comprehensive privacy legislation was "under review" in the country for well over 10 years.

At present, Singapore's data privacy laws only regulate how public bodies, such as the Inland Revenue Authority of Singapore, collect and use personally identifiable data. If the reports are correct and new privacy legislation is in the works, such legislation will represent the first efforts to impose limitations on the ability of private companies to collect, use, and transfer personal data.

Anti-Terror Measures

Singapore has actively and aggressively used surveillance since well before the September 11 terrorist attacks. Under national law, the government has extensive powers to review and monitor anything, including private communications, that can be considered a threat to national security. The extent of monitoring and surveillance in Singapore was noted by the U.S. Department of State in a 2002 Report:

> Law enforcement agencies, including the Internal Security Department and the Corrupt Practices Investigation Board, had extensive networks for gathering information and conducting surveillance, and highly sophisticated capabilities to monitor telephone and other private conversations. No court warrants were required for such operations. It was believed that the authorities routinely monitored telephone conversations and the use of the Internet; however, there were no confirmed reports of such practices during the year.[29]

While authorities in Singapore have long enjoyed very broad rights of surveillance and investigation, certain rights were strengthened even further after the terrorist attacks on the United States. Shortly after the attacks, in November 2001, the country's Ministry of Law announced that it adopted regulations that would criminalize the funding of terrorism and the spreading of hoax threats.[30] In addition, in July 2002, the country passed the Terrorism (Suppression of Financing) Act, which penalizes those found sheltering or dealing with the property of terrorists and withholding financial information of terrorist acts.[31]

Indonesia

Not too surprisingly, given the attacks in Bali, there has been a fair amount of anti-terror activity in Southeast Asia. Following the attacks in Bali on October 12, 2002, the government of Indonesia bestowed upon law enforcement agencies the power to detain individuals without evidence.[32] This power evolved into law in March 2003. The law also allows intelligence to be used as evidence and increases the ability of authorities to intercept private communications. The U.S. Department of State has voiced public concerns regarding the application of state powers, particularly in the conviction of a political activist in June 2003.[33]

The Philippines

The Philippines has also been actively confronting terrorism and devising new policies. A proposed law provides for longer periods of detention without a warrant, and the Anti-Terrorism Action Council (including eight cabinet members and the governor of the Central Bank) may authorize the interception of communications and freeze bank accounts.[34] Recently, in July 2006, Philippine President Gloria Macapagal-Arroyo asserted that the enactment of a new anti-terrorism law was urgent.[35]

AUSTRALIA

Privacy Rights prior to September 11

In late 1998, the Government announced its intention to legislate to support and strengthen privacy protection in the private sector. After widespread consultation, the Privacy Amendment (Private Sector) Act 2000 was passed in December 2000, with a commencement date of December 21, 2001. It aimed to establish a single comprehensive national scheme governing the collection, holding, use, correction, disclosure, and transfer of personal information by private sector organizations. It did so by the National Privacy Principles (NPP) and provisions allowing organizations to adopt approved privacy codes.

Privacy Rights and Anti-Terror Measures after September 11

Anti-Terror Measures

Overview

Australia has been very active in proposing and adopting anti-terror measures in cooperation with the United States in its war on terror. It would far exceed the intended scope of this book to examine all such measures in detail. Instead, the following section shall endeavor to examine some of the most notable developments to have arisen in the country since the 2001 attacks on the United States.

At least one commentator has specifically observed that Australia may have been under influence from third-party countries including, most notably, the United States and the United Kingdom to develop and implement new, tough anti-terrorism legislation. In a research paper regarding laws in Australia, Nathan Hancock of the Law and Bills Digest Group commented:

> Australia is under pressure from two sides to take measures to address terrorism both locally and globally. On one side is an open-ended requirement from the United Nations Security Council requiring States to take comprehensive measures to combat terrorism. On the other side are strong precedents set by the United Kingdom and United States which far exceed these requirements, particularly in the context of law enforcement powers.[36]

Detention Measures

Most notably, the country has enacted tough detention measures. One of the most controversial initiatives has been the Australian Security Intelligence Organisation (ASIO) Legislation Amendment (Terrorism) Bill 2002 (the law, as modified by the bill). The measure was subject to intense debate and scrutiny in Australia. In fact, an early version of the bill gave rise to a 27-hour debate that had to be shut down by the prime minister.[37] The measure was reintroduced in late 2002, debated intensely again in 2003, and eventually passed in 2003. Some of the most controversial provisions are contained in division 3, part III of the ASIO Act, which gives a number of powers to the federal, State, and Territory police. These powers include:

- the power to conduct an ordinary search or a strip search of a person detained under a warrant;

- the right to use necessary and reasonable force when taking a person into custody under a warrant, preventing their escape and detaining such a person;

- the right to enter premises to take a person into custody under a warrant;

- the ability to make arrangements for a person taken into custody under a warrant to be immediately brought before a prescribed authority for questioning.

The revisions to the ASIO allow for warrants to detain citizens 18 years of age and older for seven days if it is believed that the citizen has information that may be useful to combat terrorism, while citizens aged 16 and older may be detained if they are suspected of terrorist activity. Interrogation may occur for three eight-hour periods. Warrants may be applied successively, with no limit. The particularly controversial provisions of the legislation have a three-year sunset provision and were scheduled to expire on July 23, 2006. However, the government proposed and passed an amendment (the ASIO Legislation Amendment 2006[38]) that extended these controversial provisions for another ten years.[39]

Surveillance Measures

In the wake of the 2001 attacks against the United States and the subsequent attacks in Bali and in Europe, Australia has increased its surveillance efforts as a means of countering the threat of terrorism. Recently, it was reported that Australia authorities were "tightening security on public transport and cracking down on bookshops in Sydney and Melbourne that sell Islamic literature which preaches jihad against the West."[40]

The government has also been working on legislation that would enhance its ability to conduct surveillance. On December 8, 2004, the Australian parliament adopted two very significant laws regarding surveillance: the Surveillance Devices Bill[41] and the Telecommunications (Interception) Amendment (Stored Communications) Bill 2004 (the "Interception Bill").[42]

The Surveillance Devices Bill 2004 has attracted many critics. In formal comments submitted regarding the bill, Electronic Frontiers Australia, Inc., for example, expressed concern that the Surveillance Devices Bill would (i) remove the need for law enforcement agencies to obtain a telecommunication interception (TI) warrant to covertly record electronic communications consisting of written information; (ii) enable law enforcement agencies to record covertly electronic communications and other written information in circumstances where a TI warrant was not allowed; and (iii) allow the intercepted information to be given to foreign countries (whereas the information could not be provided to a foreign country if it had been obtained under a TI warrant).[43]

The Surveillance Devices Bill does employ certain safeguards, with respect to both warrant[44] and emergency authorizations,[45] noting:

> Nothing in this section authorizes the doing of anything for which a warrant would be required under the Telecommunications (Interception) Act 1979. A data surveillance device warrant ("data SD warrant") could be used to covertly install software or hardware (e.g. a keystroke logger) in a computer. Such a device could record all information entered into the computer before it passes over a telecommunications system, thereby obviating the need for a TI warrant because the information is not passing over the telecommunications system at the time it is being recorded.

Electronic Frontiers Australia has observed that such assurances are inadequate for electronic communications because the Telecommunications (Interception) Act 1979 is not clear with regard to where a telecommunication system begins and ends or when a TI warrant is required to intercept electronic communications.[46]

Also notable within the context of Australia are the amendments to the country's Interception Bill. Once Schedule 1 of the Telecommunications (Interception) Amendment Act 2006 becomes operative, which is expected to be on or before June 14, 2006, the Protection of the Telecommunications (Interception and Access) Act 1979 will apply to "stored communications" such as email, short message service (SMS), and voice mail messages. The bill will allow for easy access to email, SMS, and voice mail by police. Under existing law, an interception warrant is required to access the contents of email, SMS and voice mail messages that are temporarily delayed and stored during passage over the telecommunication system. The bill will eliminate the protection from interception of email, SMS, and voice mail messages that have not been delivered to the intended recipient, thereby allowing government agencies (not only police), private investigation agencies, telephone companies, and Internet service providers (ISPs) and other businesses to access such communications, without a warrant of any type.

NEW ZEALAND

Privacy Rights before September 11

New Zealand had comprehensive privacy legislation that applies to both the public and the private sectors, well before the terrorist attacks on the United States. The country's key legislation is the Privacy Act of 1993, entered into force on July 1, 1993, and was amended several times thereafter, including many times after September 11.[47] The Privacy Act of 1993 applies broadly to the collection, use, and dissemination of personal information (defined as any information about an identifiable individual, whether automatically or manually processed).[48]

At the root of the legislation are 12 Information Privacy Principles that are generally based on the 1980 OECD guidelines. Significantly, however, such general Information Privacy Principles can be replaced by enforceable codes of practice for particular sectors or classes of information. This has been done in certain sectors, namely, the health and telecommunication sectors, through the Health Information Privacy Code 1994[49] and the Telecommunications Information Privacy Code 2003.[50]

In New Zealand, there is an Office of the Privacy Commissioner, an independent oversight authority that was established pursuant to the 1991 Privacy Commissioner Act. Today, the Office of the Privacy Commissioner oversees compliance with the Privacy Act 1993. Unlike the data protection supervisory authorities in Europe, New Zealand's Office of the Privacy Commissioner does not function as a central data registration or notification authority.

Privacy Rights and Anti-Terror Measures after September 11

Legislative Developments of Note

Overview

New Zealand has responded swiftly to the 2001 terrorist attacks against the United States. Since 2001, it has proposed and enacted a wide range of measures regarding issues related to terrorism. The country has also undertaken efforts to increase the level of its cooperation in the international field. Before September 11, 2001, New Zealand was a party to only 8 of the 12 United Nations conventions regarding terrorism. Presently, it is a party to all 12.[51] The next sections shall examine some of the most important legislative developments related to counterterrorism efforts that arose in the country after September 11.

Counter-Terrorism Act

There have been several interesting developments in New Zealand since the 2001 terrorist attacks against the United States. One of the most interesting developments has been the passage of a new comprehensive counterterrorism measure. The government introduced the Counter-Terrorism Bill on December 17, 2002. The country's parliament voted to approve the bill at its third and final reading in October 2003. It aims to implement obligations arising from many international conventions related to terrorism.

One of the most significant aspects of the new measure has been its role in creating new criminal offences regarding terrorism. Given the importance of agriculture to the country and concerns that the country's farming industry could fall victim to acts of bioterrorism, a fair number of the new criminal offenses concern acts intended to poison or otherwise harm the country's food supply. Specific new offenses include (i) infecting animals with, for example, foot and mouth diseases; (ii) contaminating food crops or water; and (iii) unauthorized possession of radioactive materials. Some of the offenses in this area are punishable by up to 10 years' imprisonment.

The legislation criminalizes a wide range of additional activities, as well. For instance, threatening or "communicating information" about harm to persons or property, including making hoax calls, now carries a maximum jail sentence of seven years. It also proposes new penalties for harboring terrorists, and anyone found harboring or concealing terrorists can be imprisoned for seven years. The law also amended the Crimes Act[52] to provide prison terms of up to seven years for any person found guilty of carrying out an act with the intention of causing "significant disruption to commercial interests or government interests."

The measure has been sharply criticized for the powers it provides authorities to intrude on the lives of citizens engaged in ordinary activities. Under the measure, individuals can be forced to disclose their passwords, even in non-terrorism–related investigations, or face three months in jail or a fine of NZ$2,000.[53] Significantly, in addition to the actual computer owners, any person with "a sufficient connection" to a computer system can be required by the police to help access data. Moreover, the new powers apply not only to terrorism investigations, but to any case where agencies are able to obtain a search warrant.

The law also gives law enforcement agencies greater rights to search and seize computer databases and seize and detain goods at border checks.

Terrorism Suppression Act 2002

The latest legislation, the Terrorism Suppression Act 2002,[54] builds upon the Terrorism Suppression Act 2001 which was enacted after going through Parliament just six weeks after the attack on the World Trade Center.

At that time, an existing new piece of legislation—the Terrorism (Bombings and Financing) Bill—had just been presented to parliament and largely agreed to by the multi-party Foreign Affairs, Defence and Trade Select Committee. In the immediate wake of September 11, the Labour government rapidly replaced this bill and pushed through the far more draconian Terrorism Suppression laws, with minimal opportunity for public comment. [55]

Legislation Regarding Surveillance

The country has also enacted new legislation regarding surveillance powers. The Crimes Amendment Bill, which was passed by Parliament in July 2003 and became effective on October 1, 2003, grants broader powers to police and security agencies to intercept electronic communications.[56] The measure provides intelligence agencies additional powers to intercept communications, with the approval of the High Court.[57] The controversial anti-hacking legislation also gives police explicit authority to intercept electronic communications.

The new law makes it illegal to intercept, access, use, or damage data stored on computers without proper authorization. It also makes the sale, distribution, or possession of hacking programs illegal. The act prohibits the unauthorized interception of electronic communications and makes hacking and denial-of-service attacks illegal but grants exemptions to the police, the Government Communications Security Bureau (GCSB), and the Security Intelligence Service (SIS). Those agencies are allowed to secretly hack into individuals' computers and intercept email, text messages, and faxes. Police are required to specify a person, place, and specific electronic address, telephone number, or similar facility when applying for an interception warrant.

Another very significant development was the enactment of the Telecommunications (Interception Capabilities), which was introduced into Parliament on November 12, 2002, and enacted as the Telecommunications (Interception Capability) Act 2004.[58] This controversial legislation requires all ISPs and telephone companies to upgrade their systems so that they are able to assist the police and intelligence agencies (including the GCSB and SIS) in intercepting communications. The law also requires telecommunication companies and ISPs to intercept telephone calls and emails at the behest of the police and security service. Significantly, it also requires a telecommunication operator to decrypt the communications of a customer if that operator had provided encryption facility. It does not, however, require individuals to hand over encryption keys.

SUMMARY AND CONCLUSION

The response to the 2001 attacks taken by the diverse group of countries discussed in this chapter has not been entirely uniform. There have, however, been some common trends. For the most part, the jurisdictions under investigation in this chapter enacted new legislation and/or strengthened their existing laws to provide their law enforcement authorities with greater power to conduct surveillance, detain subjects, and engage in related activities, all in effort to prevent terrorism and apprehend terrorists. For the most part, such measures have had a negative effect on the further development of privacy rights and individual liberties.

The next chapter will show why the erosion of privacy rights on a worldwide basis is detrimental to society. It will present recommendations for improving the protection of privacy rights on a worldwide basis. While it is clear that efforts to prevent terrorism are essential, it is the thesis of this publication that such efforts can be carried out with greater respect for individual privacy rights. The next chapter will present and analyze specific suggestions in this regard.

Conclusion

OVERVIEW

The previous chapters have documented some of the ways that the 9/11 attacks, together with the ensuing U.S.-led war on terror, have impacted privacy rights on a global level. The consequences of these events and the changes they have caused in the day-to-day lives of people all around have been profound. The efforts to prevent future terrorist attacks continue to infringe on individual privacy rights and civil liberties in more frequent and increasingly significant ways, as they intrude on the most routine activities—commuting to work, talking on the phone, using the Internet. Even still, it may actually be several more years before we have a full understanding of the effects that the events of September 11 have had on privacy and civil liberties worldwide.

The fact that this current debate is necessary is not too surprising. Promptly after the attacks, many began to ruminate and speculate over the repercussions that the attacks have upon all aspects of society. Scholars and commentators have been warning about our descent down this slippery slope for some time now. Consider, for example, the comments of former Justice Sandra Day O'Connor, just shortly after the terrorist attacks in 2001: "We're likely to experience more restrictions on our personal freedom than has ever been the case in our country . . . . It will cause us to re-examine some of our laws pertaining to criminal surveillance, wiretapping, immigration and so on."[1] Justice O'Connor's premonitions were right on target, and it is now due time to commence in earnest the reexamination that she mentioned.

SPECIFIC CONCERNS

General Observations

The quest to prevent terrorism is a significant and crucial mission. It is in fact the duty of governments to protect their citizens from harm, including the harm posed by the threat of terrorism. It is, however, also the duty of governments to uphold the rule of law, and arguably, it is detrimental (instead of beneficial) to society for governments to trample over fundamental human rights and liberties in an effort to protect citizens from the threat of terrorism.

Feelings of loss and horror about previous attacks, coupled with fear and anxiety about the prospect of future attacks, can cause some to accept the premise that anything that can be done to possibly prevent terrorism should indeed be done. Even today, as there continue to be shocking revelations about the numerous and incredibly profound violations of privacy rights that have occurred under the guise of terrorism prevention, there are many who still assert that they would trade privacy for security. Those who speak so freely of forfeiting privacy for security more often than not mean that they are happy to barter someone else's privacy rights for their own— or for the perceived collective security of society. Sure, they say it is perfectly acceptable to install governmental surveillance cameras in mosques and to subject young people wishing to study at U.S. universities to much greater scrutiny. But inform these same people that their telephone calls will be monitored or that their children's library habits will be tracked and you are likely to elicit a much different response.

The current debate cannot be viewed within a vacuum. It is not any of the individual cases of privacy infringements and rights violations that matter; rather it is the collective and cumulative impact of a general deterioration of the very freedoms and values on which our society was based.

While it is clear that the privacy as legal right is still developing and that people's conceptions—and significance—of privacy continue to evolve, one need only to look at the etymology of the word "privacy" to get a sense of its role and proper place in our lives. The word "private" derives from the Middle English "privat," which, in turn, comes from the Latin term "privates," which significantly means "not belonging to the state" or "not in public life." Such a distinction between that which is public and that which is private is a fundamental cornerstone of Western traditions and culture.

Some opponents of the recent initiatives have cautioned that when considered cumulatively, these measures are resulting in fundamental societal changes. Of particular concern has been the role that the military and various agencies traditionally involved in activities occurring solely outside one's local border have begun to play within one's own country. Consider, in this regard, the comments of Michael Ratner, president of the Center for Constitutional Rights, as quoted in a recent news story:

> We are seeing the increasing militarisation of our American streets. Shame on the Senate for permitting the military to prowl our streets, spy on us,

entrap unknowing people and terrify America. Are we living in (Francisco) Franco's Spain? The military is not trained in constitutional rights; they belong on the battlefield and not in our homes.[2]

Diminishing Privacy and Human Rights Worldwide

As a world leader, the United States has an incredibly important position to fill as a role model to the world. It is simply not possible to separate the actions that the United States is taking against its "terrorists" from the actions that other governments worldwide are taking against the individuals and groups they have elected to label as terrorist—whether because it is an accurate term or a political convenience. The United States has long been a voice of reason and moral authority in the world. If we are to trample on privacy rights, individual liberties, and other fundamental human rights in our quest to detect and apprehend the enemy, how can we speak out against other governments when they commit similar violations? The answer is simple, we can't.

Stuck in the Middle

While the impacts on individual liberties and human rights have clearly been among the most vexing problems, the war on terror has also led to serious and significant changes in the ways in which companies are being asked to conduct their businesses. Companies are now placed in the unenviable position of having to attempt to decipher the meaning of divergent legislative imperatives. Companies have to comply with a slew of privacy legislation passed near the turn of the century by President Bill Clinton's administration; on the other hand, these game companies are being required to comply with legislation and "requests" put forth by a post–September 11 Republican administration that places a high value on increasing the government's ability to collect, use, and analyze an extraordinarily large and diverse collection of personal data. Not only are such legislative imperatives competing, they are in many ways completely contradictory.

So what is a company to do? Increasingly, private enterprises are being asked to decide whether to (A) comply with established privacy laws, its own stated privacy policies, and the terms of agreements it has entered into with various third parties or (B) comply with governmental demands for information. In the present environment, it is truly a lose–lose scenario. Select option B, and face private class-action lawsuits, fines for violating privacy laws, breach-of-contract lawsuits, and a slew of negative publicity. Choose option A and face serious repercussions, including fines, criminal sanctions, and worse.

Significantly, this phenomenon is not limited to the United States. As we have seen in a previous chapter, unless an appropriate solution is soon negotiated, European airlines will soon have to make the impossible choice of complying with U.S. law and providing passenger name records to U.S. authorities or complying with European data protection rules.

OBSERVATIONS AND CONCLUSIONS

Terrorism has been said to achieve three effects: (i) the immediate effect of killing and/or injuring in the intended acts of terrorism; (ii) the intermediate effects of intimidating the population at large; and (iii) the aggregate effect of undermining public order generally.[3] If we continue to change our entire system, our most basic beliefs, and fundamental freedoms—and guide the rest of the world to do the same—are we not allowing our entire system of public order to be undermined?

As Charles Krouthammer prophetically noted in *Time* magazine back in March 2001, several months before the terrorist attacks, "America is no mere international citizen. It is the dominant power in the world, more dominant than any since Rome. America can reshape norms, alter expectations and create new realities."[4] It is due time to ask ourselves: Is this truly the direction we wish to be showing the rest of the world to take? More importantly: Is this the direction we wish to take ourselves?

Appendix 1

PRIVACY IN INTERNATIONAL INSTRUMENTS

Privacy is well established in a wide range of international instruments. Some of these clauses are summarized below.

International Instrument	Clause
Declaration of Principles on Freedom of Expression in Africa, April 14, 2002. Adopted by the African Commission on Human and Peoples' Rights, 32nd Session, October 17–23, 2002, Banjul, The Gambia	Article IV Freedom of Information 1. Public bodies hold information not for themselves but as custodians of the public good and everyone has a right to access this information, subject only to clearly defined rules established by law. 2. The right to information shall be guaranteed by law in accordance with the following principles: – everyone has the right to access information held by public bodies; – everyone has the right to access information held by private bodies which is necessary for the exercise or protection of any right; – any refusal to disclose information shall be subject to appeal to an independent body and/or the courts; – public bodies shall be required, even in the absence of a request, actively to publish important information of significant public interest; – no one shall be subject to any sanction for releasing in good faith information on wrongdoing, or that which would disclose a serious threat to health, safety or the environment save where the imposition

of sanctions serves a legitimate interest and is necessary in a democratic society; and

– secrecy laws shall be amended as necessary to comply with freedom of information principles.

3. Everyone has the right to access and update or otherwise correct their personal information, whether it is held by public or by private bodies.

African [Banjul] Charter on Human and Peoples' Rights, April 14, 2002. Adopted June 27, 1981, OAU Doc. CAB/LEG/67/3 rev. 5, 21 I.

I.L.M. 58 (1982), entered into force October 21, 1986

Article 9

1. Every individual shall have the right to receive information.

2. Every individual shall have the right to express and disseminate his opinions within the law.

International Covenant on Civil and Political Rights. Adopted and opened for signature, ratification, and accession by General Assembly resolution 2200A (XXI) of December 16, 1966; entry into force March 23, 1976, in accordance with article 49

Article 17

1. No one shall be subjected to arbitrary or unlawful interference with his privacy, family, home or correspondence, nor to unlawful attacks on his honor and reputation.

2. Everyone has the right to the protection of the law against such interference or attacks.

Universal Declaration of Human Rights. Adopted by the United Nations General Assembly, December 10, 1948

Article 12

No one shall be subjected to arbitrary interference with privacy, family, home or correspondence, nor to attacks upon his honor and reputation. Everyone has the right to the protection of the law against such interference or attacks.

(*Continued*)

International Instrument	Clause
Convention on the Rights of the Child. Adopted and opened for signature, ratification, and accession by General Assembly resolution 44/25 of November 20, 1989; entry into force September 2, 1990, in accordance with article 49	Article 16 1. No child shall be subjected to arbitrary or unlawful interference with his or her privacy, family, home or correspondence, nor to unlawful attacks on his or her honor and reputation. 2. The child has the right to the protection of the law against such interference or attacks.
Convention for the Protection of Human Rights and Fundamental Freedoms. Rome, 4.XI.1950: the text of the convention had been amended according to the provisions of Protocol No. 3 (ETS No. 45), which entered into force on September 21, 1970; of Protocol No. 5 (ETS No. 55), which entered into force on December 20, 1971; and of Protocol No. 8 (ETS No. 118), which entered into force on January 1, 1990, and comprised also the text of Protocol No. 2 (ETS No. 44) which, in accordance with article 5, paragraph 3 thereof, had been an integral part of the Convention since its entry into force on September 21, 1970. All provisions which had been amended or added by these protocols are replaced by Protocol No. 11 (ETS No. 155), as from the date of its entry into force on November 1, 1998. As from that date, Protocol No. 9 (ETS No. 140), which entered into force on October 1, 1994, is repealed and Protocol No. 10 (ETS No. 146) has lost its purpose	Article 8 "Everybody has the right of esteem to his private and family life, inviolability of home, and secrecy of correspondence." According to clause 2 of the same article, governmental intrusion of privacy is permitted only in certain cases determined by law "for the sake of national security, public order or economic welfare of the country, maintenance of order and prevention of criminality, in order to prevent disorders or crimes, health protection or defense of morality or protection of rights and freedoms of other persons."

Appendix 2

**SURVEY OF PRIVACY LAWS PASSED AND/OR ENACTED
AT THE CLOSE OF THE PAST CENTURY**

MAJOR FEDERAL PRIVACY LEGISLATION

Number	Legislation	Key dates	Type of data covered	Main functions
Public Law 90-351	The Federal Wiretap Act (expanded in 1986)	1968	Electronic data and voice data	Sets procedures for court authorization of real-time surveillance of all kinds of electronic communications, including voice mail, email, fax, and Internet in criminal investigations
Public Law 91-508	Fair Credit Reporting Act (FCRA)	October 1970	Consumer data	Designed to promote accuracy and ensure the privacy of the information used in consumer reports. Recent amendments to the act expand consumer rights and place additional requirements on Credit Reporting Agencies
Public Law 93-579	The Privacy Act of 1974	1974	Personal data	Covers government documents charting individuals and regulates government control of documents that concern citizens. It gives one "(1) the right to see records about [one]self, subject to the Privacy Act's exemptions, (2) the right to amend that record if it is inaccurate, irrelevant, untimely, or incomplete, and (3) the right to sue the government for violations of the statute including permitting others to see [one's] records unless specifically permitted by the Act." In conjunction with the Freedom of Information Act (FOIA), the Privacy Act is used to further the rights of an individual to gain access to information held by the government

Public Law 95-511	Foreign Intelligence Surveillance Act	October 1978	Electronic surveillance and physical search	Prescribes procedures for requesting judicial authorization for electronic surveillance and physical search of persons engaged in espionage or international terrorism against the United States on behalf of a foreign power. Requests are adjudicated by a special 11-member court called the Foreign Intelligence Surveillance Court (amended by USA PATRIOT Act)
Public Law 99-508	Electronic Communications Privacy Act of 1986	October 1986	Electronic data	Extends government restrictions on wiretaps from telephone calls to include transmissions of electronic data by computer. Also creates privacy protection for stored electronic communications
Public Law 102-243	Telephone Consumer Protection Act of 1991 (TCPA)	1991 (entered into force one year after the date of enactment of the act)	Advertisements via voice	Updates the Communications Act of 1934. It is the primary law governing the conduct of telephone solicitation (telemarketing). The TCPA restricts the use of automatic dialing systems, artificial or prerecorded voice messages, and fax machines to send unsolicited advertisements
Public Law 104-104	Telecommunications Act of 1996	January 1996	Electronic data and voice data	Governs (i) radio and television broadcasting, (ii) cable television, (iii) telephone services, (iv) Internet and online computer services, and (v) telecommunication equipment manufacturing
Public Law 104-191	Health Insurance Portability and Accountability Act	1996 (privacy rule entered into force as of April 2003)	Personal health information	Addresses the security and privacy of health data. Requires the establishment of national standards for electronic health care transactions and national

(Continued)

MAJOR FEDERAL PRIVACY LEGISLATION (*Continued*)

Number	Legislation	Key dates	Type of data covered	Main functions
				identifiers for providers, health insurance plans, and employers. The standards encourage the widespread use of electronic data interchange
Public Law 104-208	Consumer Credit Reporting Reform Act of 1996	September 1996 (entered into force one year after the date of enactment of the act)	Personal data	Contained amendments and improvements to the FCRA. The act narrowed the broad "legitimate need" purpose for which credit reports could be disseminated. Under the act, consumer credit reports could be furnished for employment purposes only if the employer certifies that the employee has consented in writing. Consumers are able to have access to the nature and substance of the material collected, excluding medical information; the source of the information; the recipients of the information and the "date, original papers, and amounts of any checks" that form the basis for adverse decisions regarding that consumer's creditworthiness
Public Law 104-231	FOIA (and amendments)	July 1966 (amendments enacted in 1974 and 1986; entered into force 180 days after date of	Government records	The U.S. FOIA is a law ensuring public access to U.S. government records. FOIA carries a presumption of disclosure; the burden is on the government—not the public—to substantiate why information

| Public Law 105-272 | Intelligence Authorization Act for Fiscal Year 1999 | October 1998 | International terrorism data | Authorizes the Attorney General (AG) or a designated Federal attorney to apply for an order authorizing or approving the use of a trace device for any investigation to gather foreign intelligence or international terrorism information which is being conducted by the FBI under guidelines approved by executive order. Authorizes the AG to allow the use of such a device to obtain such information without a court order for a period not exceeding 15 days following a declaration of war by the Congress. Requires notification to the person involved that information so obtained is to be used or disclosed. Act allows the person to move to suppress such evidence |

enactment; sections 7 and 8 take effect one year after enactment of the act) — may not be may not be released. upon writing request, agencies of the U.S. government are required to disclose those records, unless they can be lawfully withheld from disclosure under one of nine specific exemptions in the FOIA. This right of access is ultimately enforceable in federal court

| Public Law 105-277 | Children's Online Privacy Protection Act | April 2000 | Minor's personal data on the Internet | Online collection of personal information by persons or entities under from children under U.S. jurisdiction 13 years of age. The act details what a Web site operator |

(Continued)

MAJOR FEDERAL PRIVACY LEGISLATION (*Continued*)

Number	Legislation	Key dates	Type of data covered	Main functions
				must include in a privacy policy, when and how to seek verifiable consent from a parent or guardian, and what responsibilities an operator has to protect children's privacy and safety online including restrictions on the marketing to those under 13
Public Law 105-277	Communications Decency Act of 1996 (§230)	October 1998	Electronic data	Added protection for online service providers and users from action against them for the actions of others, stating in part that "[n]o provider or user of an interactive computer service shall be treated as the publisher or speaker of any information provided by another information content provider." Effectively, this section immunizes Internet service providers (ISPs) and other service providers from torts committed by users over their systems
Public Law 106-102	Gramm–Leach–Bliley Act	November 1999	Consumer financial data	Declares it is the policy of Congress that each financial institution has an affirmative, continuing obligation to respect the privacy and to protect the confidentiality of customer nonpublic personal information. Instructs specified regulatory agencies to establish standards for financial institution safeguards that

Public Law	Title	Date	Topic	Description
				(i) ensure security and confidentiality of customer records and information and (ii) protect against hazards or unauthorized access to such information. Stipulates disclosure of customer nonpublic personal information to a nonaffiliated third party must comply with consumer notification requirements: (i) clear, conspicuous disclosures that such information may be disseminated to third parties and (ii) consumer opportunity to prevent such dissemination. Prohibits a financial institution from disclosing a consumer's information to a nonaffiliated third party for use in telemarketing, direct mail marketing, or other marketing through email to the consumer. Exempt are (i) law enforcement agencies, (ii) financial institutions and insurance institutions which are engaged in specified activities, (iii) customer information of financial institutions available as a public record under Federal securities laws, and (iv) State-licensed private investigators acting under court authorization to collect child support from a person adjudged delinquent
Public Law 106-229	Electronic Signatures in Global and National Commerce Act	June 2000	Commerce	Enforces the legal effect of certain transactions in interstate or foreign commerce on the ground that (i) the signature, contract, or record of such transaction is in electronic form and (2) with respect to a contract, an electronic signature or electronic record was used in its formation
Public Law 106-81	Wireless Communications and	October 1999	Emergency voice communications	Amends the Communications Act of 1934 to direct the Federal Communications Commission (FCC)

(Continued)

MAJOR FEDERAL PRIVACY LEGISLATION *(Continued)*

Number	Legislation	Key dates	Type of data covered	Main functions
	Public Safety Act of 1999			and any delegated authority to designate 911 as the universal emergency telephone number within the United States for reporting an emergency to appropriate authorities and requesting assistance. Applies such designation to both wire and wireless telephone service. Provides immunity for public safety answering points (emergency dispatchers) and users of wireless or non-wireless 911 services. Authorizes telecommunication carriers to provide call location information to (i) emergency dispatchers and emergency service personnel to respond to the user's call, (2) the user's legal guardian or family member in an emergency situation that involves the risk of death or serious physical harm, or (3) providers of information or database management services solely for assisting in the delivery of emergency services. Requires a customer's express prior authorization for disclosure to any other person. Requires telephone exchange service providers to provide both listed and unlisted subscriber information to providers of emergency and emergency support services

Public Law 107-204	Sarbanes–Oxley Act of 2002	2002	Accounting data	Establishes public company accounting oversight board, auditor independence, corporate responsibility, and enhanced financial disclosure
Public Law 107-296	Stored Communications Act (amended)	November 2002 (amended 60 days after date of enactment)	Electronic data	Regulates when an electronic communication service provider may release the contents of, or other information about, a customer's emails and other electronic communications to private parties. Refers to electronic communications that are in electronic storage with an ISP
Public Law 107-305	Cyber Security Research and Development Act	November 2002	Computer and network security	Authorizes appropriations to the National Science Foundation and to the Secretary of Commerce for the National Institute of Standards and Technology to establish new programs and to increase funding for certain current programs, for computer and network security (CNS) research and development and CNS research fellowships
Public Law 107-347	E-Government Act of 2002	December 2002	Electronic government services	Establish Internet-based information technology to enhance citizen access to government information and services. Directs that data or information acquired by an agency under a pledge of confidentiality and for exclusively statistical purposes be used exclusively for statistical purposes. Bars the data from being disclosed in identifiable form for use other than an exclusively statistical purpose, except with the respondent's informed consent

(*Continued*)

MAJOR FEDERAL PRIVACY LEGISLATION (*Continued*)

Number	Legislation	Key dates	Type of data covered	Main functions
Public Law 108-10	Do-Not-Call Implementation Act of 2003	March 2003	Voice data	Establishes the FCC's National Do Not Call Registry to facilitate compliance with the Telephone Consumer Protection Act of 1991
Public Law 108-159	Fair and Accurate Credit Transactions Act of 2003 (FACTA)	December 2003	Consumer credit data	Amends the FCRA to prevent identity theft, improve resolution of consumer disputes, improve the accuracy of consumer records, and make improvements in the use of, and consumer access to, credit information. Includes free annual consumer credit reports
Public Law 108-187	CAN-SPAM Act of 2003	December 2003	Electronic data	Sets national standards for the sending of commercial email and requires the Federal Trade Commission to enforce the provisions. Also requires the Federal Trade Commission to promulgate rules to shield consumers from unwanted mobile service commercial messages
Public Law 108-281	E-Government Act of 2002 with respect to rulemaking authority of the Judicial Conference	August 2004	Redacted court filings	Amends the E-Government Act of 2002 to provide for court rules allowing parties in a Federal court proceeding to file under seal a reference list that would include both a complete and a partially redacted version of protected information, e.g., social security numbers and credit card account numbers, contained in pleadings

Public Law 108-82	Do-Not-Call-Registry	September 2003	Voice marketing data	Authorized the Federal Trade Commission, under the Telemarketing and Consumer Fraud and Abuse Prevention Act, to implement and enforce a national Do-Not-Call registry. Also ratifies the Do-Not-Call registry provision of the Telemarketing Sales Rule of March 2003
Public Law 109-13	REAL ID Act of 2005	May 2005	Terrorism data	Implements regulations for state driver's license and identification document security standards, to prevent terrorists from abusing the asylum laws of the United States. Unifies terrorism-related grounds for inadmissibility and removal, and ensures expeditious construction of the San Diego border fence
Public Law 109-21	Junk Fax Prevention Act of 2005	July 2005	Advertisements via fax machine	Prohibits using any telephone facsimile machine, computer, or other device to send an unsolicited advertisement to a person who has requested that such sender not send advertisements unless (i) the sender has an established business relationship with the person, (ii) the sender obtained the fax number through voluntary communication from the recipient or from an Internet directory or site to which the recipient voluntarily made the fax number available for public distribution, and (iii) the advertisement contains a conspicuous notice on its first page that the recipient may request not to be sent any further unsolicited advertisements, and includes a domestic telephone and fax number (neither of which can be a pay-per-call number) for sending such a request

(Continued)

MAJOR FEDERAL PRIVACY LEGISLATION (*Continued*)

Number	Legislation	Key dates	Type of data covered	Main functions
Public Law 109-8	Bankruptcy Abuse Prevention and Consumer Protection Act of 2005	February 2005	Public data	All public record data held in electronic form by bankruptcy clerks should be released in electronic form in bulk to the public, subject to appropriate privacy concerns and safeguards as Congress and the Judicial Conference may determine; and a bankruptcy data system should be established that employs a single set of data definitions to collect data nationwide and that aggregates in the same electronic record all data for any particular bankruptcy case
Public Law 109-9	Family Entertainment and Copyright Act of 2005	April 2005	Intellectual property rights	Protects intellectual property rights by authorizing up to three years' imprisonment for illegally recording a motion picture in a theater. Prohibits unauthorized use of a video camera or similar device to transmit or make a copy of a motion picture or other copyrighted audiovisual work from a performance of such work in a movie theater
H. R. 4127 (pending)	Data Accountability and Trust Act		Personal data	To protect consumers by requiring reasonable security policies and procedures to protect computerized data containing personal information and to provide for nationwide notice in the event of a security breach

Appendix 3

SAFE HARBOR PRINCIPLES

NOTICE   An organization must inform individuals about the purposes for which it collects and uses information about them, how to contact the organization with any inquiries or complaints, the types of third parties to which it discloses the information, and the choices and means the organization offers individuals for limiting its use and disclosure. This notice must be provided in clear and conspicuous language when individuals are first asked to provide personal information to the organization or as soon thereafter as is practicable, but in any event before the organization uses such information for a purpose other than that for which it was originally collected or processed by the transferring organization or discloses it for the first time to a third party

CHOICE   An organization must offer individuals the opportunity to choose (opt out) whether their personal information is (i) to be disclosed to a third party or (ii) to be used for a purpose that is incompatible with the purpose(s) for which it was originally collected or subsequently authorized by the individual. Individuals must be provided with clear and conspicuous, readily available, and affordable mechanisms to exercise choice

For sensitive information (i.e., personal information specifying medical or health conditions, racial or ethnic origin, political opinions, religious or philosophical beliefs, trade union membership, or information specifying the sex life of the individual), they must be given affirmative or explicit (opt in) choice if the information is to be disclosed to a third party or used for a purpose other than those for which it was originally collected or subsequently authorized by the individual through the exercise of opt-in choice. In any case, an organization should treat as sensitive any information received from a third party where the third party treats and identifies it as sensitive

ONWARD TRANSFER   To disclose information to a third party, organizations must apply the Notice and Choice Principles. Where an organization wishes to transfer information to a third party that is acting as an agent, it may do so if it first either ascertains that the third party subscribes to the Principles or is subject to the Directive or another adequacy finding or enters into a written agreement with such third party requiring that the third party provide at least the same level of privacy protection as is required by the relevant principles. If the organization complies with these requirements, it shall not be held responsible (unless the organization agrees otherwise) when a third party to which it transfers such information processes it in a way contrary to any restrictions or representations, unless the organization knew or should have known the third party would process it in such a contrary way and the organization has not taken reasonable steps to prevent or stop such processing

SECURITY   Organizations creating, maintaining, using, or disseminating personal information must take reasonable precautions to protect it from loss, misuse, and unauthorized access, disclosure, alteration, and destruction

DATA INTEGRITY   Consistent with the Principles, personal information must be relevant for the purposes for which it is to be used. An organization may not process personal information in a way that is incompatible with the purposes for which it has been collected or subsequently authorized by the individual. To the extent necessary for those purposes, an organization should take reasonable steps to ensure that data are reliable for their intended use, accurate, complete, and current

ACCESS   Individuals must have access to personal information about them that an organization holds and be able to correct, amend, or delete that information where it is inaccurate, except where the burden or expense of providing access would be disproportionate to the risks to the individual's privacy in the case in question, or where the rights of persons other than the individual would be violated

ENFORCEMENT   Effective privacy protection must include mechanisms for assuring compliance with the Principles, recourse for individuals to whom the data relate affected by noncompliance with the Principles, and consequences for the organization when the Principles are not followed. At a minimum, such mechanisms must include (i) readily available and affordable independent recourse mechanisms by which each individual's complaints and disputes are investigated and resolved by reference to the Principles and damages awarded where the applicable law or private sector initiatives so provide, (b) follow-up procedures for verifying that the attestations and assertions businesses make about their privacy practices are true and that privacy practices have been implemented as presented, and (c) obligations to remedy problems arising out of failure to comply with the Principles by organizations announcing their adherence to them and consequences for such organizations. Sanctions must be sufficiently rigorous to ensure compliance by organizations

Notes

Preface

1. Quoted in "Terrorism in Historical Perspective," *Digital History: Using New Technologies to Enhance Teaching and Research*, available at <http://www.digitalhistory.uh.edu/historyonline/terrorism.cfm> (last visited June 1, 2003).

Introduction

1. See Council Directive No. 95/46/EC of October 24, 1995, on the protection of individuals with regard to the processing of personal data and on the free movement of such data, O.J. L 281/31 (1995).

2. See *Appendix 2* for further details regarding the main federal privacy laws in the United States, including those that were enacted during this time period.

3. During this time period, in the United States, for example, the Federal Trade Commission launched many enforcement actions against companies for allegedly having failed to have honored their own stated privacy policies. See, generally, <http://www.ftc.gov/privacy/privacyinitiatives/promises_enf.html> (last visited March 25, 2006).

4. See "World Leaders Express Outrage," *The Guardian* (London), September 11, 2001, available at <http://www.guardian.co.uk/september11/story/0,11209,600809,00.html> (last visited June 1, 2006).

5. See, for example, "National Briefing | Washington: F.B.I. Discloses Subpoenas," *The New York Times*, April 29, 2006.

6. S.C. Res. 1368, UN SCOR, 56th Sess., 4370th mtg., UN Doc. S/Res/1368 (2001), available at <http://daccessdds.un.org/doc/UNDOC/GEN/N01/533/82/PDF/N0153382.pdf?OpenElement> (last visited July 31, 2006).

7. S.C. Res. 1373, UN SCOR, 56th Sess., 4385th mtg., UN Doc. S/Res/1373 (2001), available at <http://daccessdds.un.org/doc/UNDOC/GEN/N01/ 557/43/ PDF/N0155743.pdf?OpenElement> (last visited July 31, 2006).

8. Charter of the United Nations, at article 42, available at <http://www.un.org/ aboutun/charter/> (last visited July 31, 2006).

9. Ibid., at article 39.

10. See UN Counter-Terrorism Committee, Reports of Member States, available at <http://www.un.org/Docs/sc/committees/1373/submitted_reports.html> (last visited May 13, 2004).

11. Council of Europe Committee of Ministers, Declaration of the Committee of Ministers on the fight against international terrorism, adopted by the Committee of Ministers at the 763rd meeting of the Ministers' Deputies, September 12, 2001.

12. Council of Europe Parliamentary Assembly, Recommendation 1534 (2001), Democracies Facing Terrorism, September 26, 2001 (28th Sitting), available at <http://assembly.coe.int/main.asp?Link=/documents/workingdocs/doc01/edoc9282. htm> (last visited July 31, 2006).

13. See RFE/RL, "Moldovan Parliament Approves Presidential Bill on Fighting Extremism," *Newsline* Vol.7, No.35, Part II, February 24, 2003, for Moldova's bill; see also Georgia's bill providing for the restriction on suspending the activities of organizations that receive foreign funding and whose activities "threaten Georgia's national interests," but failing to define those interests.

14. Mike Branom, "Judge Cites Terrorism Concerns for Ruling on Muslim Woman's Veil," *The Associated Press*, June 7, 2003.

15. Giles Wilson, "Terrorism Fear Derails Train-Spotters," *BBC NewsOnline*, May 28, 2003, available at <http://212.58.226.30/1/hi/uk/2943304.stm> (last visited July 31, 2006).

16. Michael Isikoff, "Intelligence: The Pentagon—Spying in America?" *Newsweek*, June 21, 2004, available at <http://www.msnbc.msn.com/id/5197014/site/ newsweek> (last visited July 31, 2006).

17. Human Rights News, "Human Rights Watch World Report 2006, US Policy of Abuse Undermines Rights Worldwide," available at <http://www.hrw.org/wr2k6/> (last visited July 31, 2006).

18. See Jeffrey Tayler, "Putin's Policy of Realpolitik," *The Atlantic Monthly*, December 2001, available at <http://www.theatlantic.com/doc/prem/200112/tayler> (last visited July 31, 2006); see also Peter Baker, "Old Enemies Enlist in US Terror War: Former Soviet Republics Become Allies," *The Washington Post*, January 1, 2004, at A18.

19. See Lale Sariibrahimoglu, "News Analysis: Allies Help to Corner Turkish Extremists Abroad to Take Away Turkish Card," *Turkish Daily News*, December 15, 2001, noting: "A Turkish security official . . . describes the latest moves by Germany to close down almost 19 associations of the Union of Islamic Communities and Societies known as 'Supporters of Kaplan', seizing its assets as a serious indication of a mental change within German government since the September 11, terror."

20. Quoted in Robin Kirk, "Colombia and the 'War' on Terror: Rhetoric and Reality," *The World Today*, a publication of the Royal Institute of International Affairs, March 2004, and on *Human Rights Watch*, available at <http://hrw.org/english/docs/2004/03/04/colomb7932.htm> (last visited July 31, 2006).

21. See "Press Freedom being Tested by Bush Administration's Anti-Terrorist Policy," *Reporters Without Borders*, May 23, 2002, available at <http://www.rsf.org/article.php3?id_article=2277> (last visited July 31, 2006).

22. "National Briefing | Washington: F.B.I. Discloses Subpoenas," *The New York Times*, April 29, 2006.

23. See International Telecommunication Union, "Promoting Global Cybersecurity: Cybersecurity Awareness Survey," available at <http://www.itu.int/newsroom/wtd/2006/survey/charts/index.asph> (last visited June 1, 2006).

24. See Cyber Security Industry Alliance, "Internet Security Voter Survey," June 2005, available at <https://www.csialliance.org/publications/surveys_and_polls/CSIA_Internet_Security_Survey_June_2005.pdf> (last visited July 31, 2006).

25. "'Chaos' Warning over Airport Security Plan," *BBC News Online*, July 6, 2002, available at <http://news.bbc.co.uk/2/hi/uk_news/2104280.stm> (last visited July 31, 2006).

26. See, generally, Ryan Cormier, "Spies on the Friendly Skies," *Capital News Online*, October 18, 2002, available at <http://temagami.carleton.ca/jmc/cnews/18102002/n4.shtml> (last visited July 31, 2006).

27. See Robert O'Harrow, Jr., "Financial Database To Screen Accounts: Joint Effort Targets Suspicious Activities," *The Washington Post*, May 30, 2002, at E01; see also Financial Action Task Force on Money Laundering, "Nine Special Recommendations on Terrorist Financing," available at <http://www.fatf-gafi.org/document/9/0,2340,en_32250379_32236920_34032073_1_1_1_1,00.html> (last visited July 31, 2006); Glenn R. Simpson and Jathon Sapsford, "New Rules for Money-Laundering," *The Wall Street Journal*, April 23, 2002.

28. See NPR/Kaiser/Kennedy School Poll on Security and Civil Liberties, Results and Follow-up, available at <http://www.npr.org/news/specials/civillibertiespoll/011130.poll.html> (last visited on May 20, 2006).

29. Gary Langer (Analysis), "Broader Concern on Privacy Rights But Terrorism Threat Still Trumps," ABCNews.com, January 10, 2006, available at <http://abcnews.go.com/images/Politics/1003a3WiretapsandPrivacy.pdf> (last visited July 31, 2006).

30. Ibid.

Chapter 1

1. Public Law 104–191.
2. 45 C.F.R. 164.501 (Definitions).
3. 45 C.F.R. 164.512(k)(2).
4. 50 U.S.C. 401.
5. Executive Order 12333.

6. 50 U.S.C. 1861.

7. Statute (Public Law 106-102, 15 U.S.C. §6801, et seq.) (hereinafter GLB Act).

8. Any institution the business of which is engaging in financial activities as described in section 4(k) of the Bank Holding Company Act (12 U.S.C. §1843(k)).

9. GLB Act, supra note 7, at §§313.14 and 313.15.

10. Ibid., at §313.14(b).

11. FTC, Standards for Safeguarding Customer Information, Final Rule, 16 C.F.R. 314 (2002).

12. Children's Online Privacy Protection Act of 1998, 15 U.S.C. 6501 (1999). On October 20, 1999, the FTC issued the final rule implementing COPPA. FTC, Children's Online Privacy Protection Rule; Final Rule 16 CFR Part 312 (1999). Such final rule, along with the act, is referred to herein as "COPPA."

13. 144 Cong. Rec. S12741 (October 7, 1998) (Statement of Senator Bryan).

14. Under the terms of COPPA, the term "verifiable personal consent" means "any reasonable effort (taking into consideration available technology), including a request for authorization for future collection, use, and disclosure described in the notice, to ensure that a parent of a child receives notice of the operator's personal information collection, use, and disclosure practices, and authorizes the collection, use, and disclosure practices, and authorizes the collection, use, and disclosure, as applicable, of personal information and the subsequent use of that information before that information is collected from that child." COPPA, supra note 12, at §1302(9).

15. COPPA defines "disclosure" in a rather broad manner. Under the act, disclosure, with respect to personal information, is said to constitute: "(A) the release of personal information collected from a child in identifiable form by an operator for any purpose, except where such information is provided to a person other than the operators who provides support for the internal operations of the website and does not disclose or use that information for any other purpose; and (B) making personal information collected from a child by a website or online service directed to children or with actual knowledge that such information was collected from a child, publicly available in an identifiable form, by any means including by a public posting, through the Internet, or through (i) a home page of a web site; (ii) a pen pal service; (iii) an electronic mail service; (iv) a message board; or (v) a chat room." Ibid., at §1302(4).

16. Ibid., at §1303(b)(1).

17. A copy of the complaint is available at <http://www.ftc.gov/os/1999/02/9823015cmp.htm> (last visited August 1, 2006).

18. See "FTC Announces Settlements with Web Sites That Collected Children's Personal Data Without Parental Permission," FTC Release, April 19, 2001, available at <http://www.ftc.gov/opa/2001/04/girlslife.htm> (last visited August 1, 2006). Copies of the complaints and consent orders are available from the FTC's Web site at <http://www.ftc.gov>.

19. See *United States of America (for the Federal Trade Commission) v. Hershey Foods Corporation (Middle District of Pennsylvania)*, Consent Decree and Order for Civil Penalties, Injunctive, and Other Relief.

20. See *United States of America (for the Federal Trade Commission) v. Mrs. Fields Famous Brands, Inc., Mrs. Fields Holding Company, Inc. and Mrs. Fields Original Cookies, Inc. (District of Utah, Central Division)*, Consent Decree and Order for Civil Penalties, Injunctive, and Other Relief.

21. See "FTC Protecting Children's Privacy Online," FTC Release, April 22, 2002, available at <http://www.ftc.gov/opa/2002/04/coppaanniv.htm> (last visited July 31, 2006).

22. Electronic Communications Privacy Act, Pub. L. No. 99-508, 100 Stat. 1848 (1986) (codified at 18 U.S.C. 2510–2521, 2701–2710, 3117, 3121–3126 (1986)) (hereinafter ECPA).

23. ECPA defines "electronic communication" as "any transfer of signs, signals, writing, images, sounds, data, or intelligence of any nature transmitted in whole or in part by a wire, radio, electromagnetic, photoelectronic or photooptical system that affects interstate or foreign commerce but does not include—

(A) the radio portion of a cordless telephone communication that is transmitted between the cordless telephone handset and the base unit;

(B) any wire or oral communication;

(C) any communication made through a tone-only paging device; or

(D) any communication from a tracking device."
   Ibid., at §2510(12).

24. Omnibus Crime Control and Safe Streets Act of 1968, 42 U.S.C. §3789d.

25. 18 U.S.C. §§2510–2521.

26. 18 U.S.C. §2501(1).

27. Codified at 18 U.S.C. §§2701–2710.

28. Ibid., at §2702.

29. Ibid.

30. Codified at 18 U.S.C. §§3117–3126.

31. Ibid., at §2707(b)(1).

32. Ibid., at §2707(c).

33. Ibid., at §2707(b)(3).

34. 18 U.S.C. §2710.

35. Under the act, the term "video service provider" is defined as "any person, engaged in the business, in or affecting interstate or foreign commerce of rental, sale or delivery of prerecorded video cassette tapes or similar audio visual materials." 18 U.S.C. §2710(a)(4).

36. Under the act, "personally identifiable information" includes information which identifies a person as having requested or obtained specific video materials from a video tape service provider. Ibid., at (a)(4).

37. 18 U.S.C. §2710(b).

38. 18 U.S.C. §2710(c).

39. See, for example, Ark. Code Ann. §14-14-110(b) (Michie 1998); Haw. Rev. Stat. Ann. §92F-14 (Michie 1996); Kan. Stat. Ann. §72-6214 (1992); Mont. Code Ann. §20-25 (1997); N.Y. Penal Law §250.05 (McKinney 1989); W. Va. Code §46A-2-126 (1998).

40. California Business and Professions Code §§350–352.

41. Ibid., at §350(a); see the Web site of California's Office of Privacy Protection available at <http://www.privacy.ca.gov/> (last visited August 3, 2006).

42. "FTC Announces Settlement With Bankrupt Web site, Toysmart.com, Regarding Alleged Privacy Policy Violations," FTC Release, July 21, 2000, available at <www.ftc.gov/opa/2000/07/toysmart2.htm> (last visited August 1, 2006).

43. *FTC v. Toysmart.com, LLC and Toysmart.com, Inc.*, Civil Action No. 00=11341-RGS, Stipulated Consent Agreement and Final Order, available at <http://www.ftc.gov/os/2000/07/toysmartconsent.htm> (last visited August 1, 2006).

44. See *In the Matter of Eli Lilly & Co.*, No. 012 3214, available at <http://www.ftc.gov/os/2002/01/lillycmp.pdf> (last visited August 1, 2006).

45. See "Eli Lilly Settles FTC Charges Concerning Security Breach," FTC Release, January 18, 2002, available at <http://www.ftc.gov/opa/2002/01/elililly.htm> (last visited August 1, 2006).

46. See *In the Matter of Eli Lilly & Co.*, No. 012 3214, Agreement Containing Consent Order, available at <http://www.ftc.gov/os/2002/01/lillycmp.pdf> (last visited August 1, 2006).

47. See *In the Matter of Guess? Inc. and Guess.com, Inc.*, File No. 022 3260, available at <http://www.ftc.gov/opa/2003/06/guess.htm> (last visited August 1, 2006).

48. CAN-SPAM Act of 2003 (Pub. L. 108-187, S. 877).

49. See, for example, "LexisNexis Concludes Review of Data Search Activity, Identifying Additional Instances of Illegal Data Access," April 12, 2005, available at <http://www.lexisnexis.com/about/releases/0789.asp> (last visited July 15, 2005); Robert Lemos, "Bank of America Loses a Million Customer Records," CNET News.com, February 25, 2005, available at <http://news.com.com /Bank+of+America+loses+a+million+customer+records/2100-1029_3-5590989.html> (last visited August 1, 2006); see also the Web pages of the Electronic Privacy Information Center on the Choicepoint security breach, available at <http://www.epic.org/privacy/choicepoint/> (last visited July 17, 2005).

50. (Pub. L. 108–159).

51. 15 U.S.C. §§1681, 1681a–1681t.

52. Consumer reporting agencies are entities that regularly engage in assembling or evaluating consumer credit information for the purpose of furnishing consumer reports to third parties (15 U.S.C. §1681 a(f) (1988)).

53. Security Breach Notice—Civil Code §§1798.29 and 1798.82–1798.84, available at <http://www.leginfo.ca.gov/cgi-bin/displaycode?section=civ&group=01001-

02000&file=1798.25-1798.29> and <http://www.leginfo.ca.gov/cgi-bin/ displaycode? section=civ&group=01001-02000&file=1798.80-1798.84> (last visited August 1, 2006).

54. Ibid., at §1798.29(e).

55. Ibid., at §1798.29(a).

56. Ibid., at §1798.29(a).

57. See also National Conference of State Legislatures, 2005 Breach of Information Security Legislation, available at <http://www.ncsl.org/programs/lis/ CIP/priv/breach.htm> (last visited December 18, 2005).

58. Online Privacy Protection Act of 2003—Business and Professions Code Section 22575–22579, available at <http://www.leginfo.ca.gov/cgi-bin/displaycode? section=bpc&group=22001-23000&file=22575-22579> (last visited December 10, 2005).

59. Ibid., at 22575(a).

60. Ibid., at 22577(a).

61. See California Business and Professions Code §17200.

62. The Online Privacy Protection Act is merely one example of the various measures that have been enacted in California in recent years. Additional information about other measures that have been proposed and/or enacted is available through the Web site of California's Office of Privacy Protection. See <http://www.privacy.ca.gov/ lawenforcement/laws.htm#six> (last visited December 10, 2005).

63. See "Petco Settles FTC Charges. Security Flaws Allowed Hackers to Access Consumers' Credit Card Information," File No. 032 3221, November 17, 2004, available at <http://www.ftc.gov/opa/2004/11/petco.htm> (last visited August 1, 2006).

64. See "Gateway Learning Settles FTC Privacy Charges: Company Rented Customer Information it Pledged to Keep Private," *In the Matter of Gateway Learning Corp.*, File No. 042 3047, July 7, 2004, available at <http://www.ftc.gov/opa/ 2004/07/gateway.htm> (last visited August 1, 2006).

65. See "BJ'S Wholesale Club Settles FTC Charges: Agency Says Lax Security Compromised Thousands of Credit and Debit Cards," File No. 042 3160, June 16, 2005, available at <http://www.ftc.gov/opa/2005/06/bjswholesale.htm> (last visited August 1, 2006).

Chapter 2

1. Office of Management and Budget, Stimulating Smarter Regulation: 2002 Report to Congress on the Costs and Benefits of Regulations and Unfunded Mandates on State, Local, and Tribal Entities, published in March 2003.

2. H.R. 3162, incorporating elements from several earlier anti-terrorism bills; passed by the House of Representatives on October 24, 2001 and the Senate on October 25, 2001, becoming Public Law 107-56 upon the signature of President Bush on October 26, 2001 (hereinafter "Patriot Act").

3. See, for example, Geoffrey Stone and Richard Posner debate, "What's Wrong With the Patriot Act?" October 3, 2005, available at <http://www.legalaffairs.org/webexclusive/debateclub_patact1005.msp> (last visited August 2, 2006), noting: "The act was hastily drafted by the Department of Justice and presented to Congress and the nation by Attorney General John Ashcroft as vital to the nation's safety. The administration voiced barely veiled threats that anyone who questioned the legislation would be deemed unpatriotic and accused of aiding the terrorists."

4. Patriot Act, supra note 2, at sections 201 and 202.

5. Ibid., at section 217.

6. With a roving wiretap order, it would not be necessary to specify the identity of the surveillance target or the location or nature of the communication system that is being tapped.

7. Patriot Act, supra note 2, at section 206.

8. Ibid., at section 219.

9. Ibid., at 220 and 216(c).

10. Ibid., at section 213, providing:

> (b). DELAY—With respect to the issuance of any warrant or court order under this section, or any other rule of law, to search for and seize any property or material that constitutes evidence of a criminal offense in violation of the laws of the United States, any notice required, or that may be required, to be given may be delayed if—
>
> > (1). the court finds reasonable cause to believe that providing immediate notification of the execution of the warrant may have an adverse result (as defined in section 2705);
> >
> > (2). the warrant prohibits the seizure of any tangible property, any wire or electronic communication (as defined in section 2510), or, except as expressly provided in chapter 121, any stored wire or electronic information, except where the court finds reasonable necessity for the seizure; and
> >
> > (3). the warrant provides for the giving of such notice within a reasonable period of its execution, which period may thereafter be extended by the court for good cause shown . . .

11. Ibid., at section 209.

12. Ibid., at section 203(b).

13. Ibid., at section 203(d).

14. Frost & Sullivan, "World Video Surveillance Software Markets," MarketResearch.com, June 29, 2005, available for purchase at <http:// www.marketresearch.com> (last visited June 1, 2006).

15. See James Risen and Eric Lichtblau, "Bush Lets U.S. Spy on Callers Without Courts," *The New York Times*, December 16, 2005, available at <http://www.nytimes.com/2005/12/16/politics/16program.html?ex=1292389200&en=e320 72d786623ac1&ei=5090&partner=rssuserland&emc=rss>; (last visited August 2,

2006); see also Dan Eggen and Charles Lane, "On Hill, Anger and Calls for Hearings Greet News of Stateside Surveillance," *The Washington Post*, December 17, 2005, at A01, available at <http://www.washingtonpost.com/wp-dyn/content/article/2005/12/16/AR2005121601825.html> (last visited August 1, 2006).

16. See "Camera-Shy America Weighs Merits of Video Surveillance," *Agence France Presse*, July 24, 2005.

17. Ibid.

18. Greg Lucas, "Local Transit Agencies Debate Use of Cameras: U.S. Has Invested Little in Type of Device that Helped British Identify 4 Bombing Suspects," *The San Francisco Chronicle*, July 18, 2005, at A1.

19. See, for example, "Washington Subway System Considering Bag Searches: Officials," *Agence France Presse*, July 18, 2005.

20. See, for example, Leslie Cauley, "NSA has Massive Database of Americans' Phone Calls," *USA Today*, May 11, 2006, available at <http://www.usatoday.com/news/washington/2006-05-10-nsa_x.htm> (last visited August 2, 2006).

21. Ibid.

22. Ibid.

23. It should be noted that the "international program" raised great concerns as well, and in January of 2006, privacy advocacy group Electronic Privacy Information Center (EPIC) filed a class-action suit against AT&T for its role.

24. John O'Neil and Eric Lichtblau, "Qwest's Refusal of NSA Query's Explained," *The New York Times*, May 12, 2006.

25. Communications Act of 1934, as amended by the Telecommunications Act of 1996, 47 U.S.C. 151, available at <http://www.fcc.gov/Reports/1934new.pdf> (last visited August 2, 2006).

26. "USA TODAY/Gallup poll, Government Phone Records Reaction," available at <http://www.usatoday.com/news/polls/tables/live/2006-05-14-nsa-poll.htm> (survey conducted May 12, 2006; last visited May 26, 2006).

27. David Jefferson, "Newsweek Poll: Americans Wary of NSA Spying. Bush's Approval Ratings Hit New Lows as Controversy Rages," MSNBC.com, May 14, 2006, available at <http://www.msnbc.msn.com/id/12771821/site/newsweek> (last visited August 2, 2006).

28. *Riordon v. Verizon Communications Inc.*, Cal. Super. Ct., No. CGC-06-45268, complaint filed May 26, 2006; *Campbell v. AT&T Communications of California*, Cal. Super. Ct., No. CGC-06-45626, complaint filed May 26, 2006; *Terkel v. AT&T Inc.*, N.D. Ill., No. 06 cv 2837, complaint filed May 22, 2006 (100 PRA, May 24, 2006); *Mayer v. Verizon Commc'ns Inc.*, S.D.N.Y., No. 1:06-cv-03650-LBS/AJP, complaint filed May 12, 2006 (94 PRA, May 16, 2006); *Driscoll v. Verizon Commc'ns Inc.*, D.D.C., No. 1:06-cv-00916-RBW, complaint filed May 15, 2006 (95 PRA, May 17, 2006); *Ludman v. AT&T Inc.*, D.D.C., No. 1:06-cv-00917-RBW, complaint filed May 15, 2006 (95 PRA, May 17, 2006); *Phillips v. BellSouth Corp.*, D.D.C., No. 1:06-cv-00918-RBW, complaint filed May 15, 2006.

29. A copy of the letter sent by EPIC to the FCC is available on the Web site of EPIC at <http://www.epic.org/privacy/phone/fcc-letter5-06.html> (last visited May 26, 2006).

30. *Terkel v. AT&T Inc.*, N.D. Ill., No. 06 CV 2837, complaint filed May 22, 2006.

31. As quoted in Michael Bologna, "Studs Terkel, Civic Leaders, ACLU File Class Action over Phone Records," *Privacy Law Watch*, May 24, 2006.

32. *Riordon v. Verizon Communications Inc.*, Cal. Super. Ct., No. CGC-06-45268, complaint filed May 26, 2006; *Campbell v. AT&T Communications of California*, Cal. Super. Ct., No. CGC-06-45626, complaint filed May 26, 2006.

33. See <http://att.sbc.com/gen/privacy-policy?pid=2506> (last visited August 1, 2006).

34. Sara Kehaulani Goo, "Concerns Raised Over AT&T Privacy Policy," *The Washington Post*, June 23, 2006, at DO5.

35. *In the Matter of JetBlue Airways and Acxiom Corporation* (complaint filed with the FTC).

36. 18 U.S.C. §2701.

37. *In the Matter of Northwest Airlines*, Docket No. 16939 (complaint filed with the DOT).

38. Eric Lichtblau and James Risen, "Bank Data Is Sifted by U.S. in Secret to Block Terror," *The New York Times*, June 23, 2006, available at <http://www.nytimes.com/2006/06/23/washington/23intel.html?ei=5088&en=168d69d26685c26c&ex=1308715200&partner=rssnyt&emc=rss&pagewanted=print> (last visited August 4, 2006).

39. See, generally, the Web site of SWIFT, available at <http://www.swift.com> (last visited August 2, 2006).

40. See Sheryl Gay Stolberg and Eric Lichtblau, "Cheney Assails Press on Report on Bank Data," *The New York Times*, June 24, 2006, available at <http://www.nytimes.com/2006/06/24/washington/24swift.html?ex=1308801600&en=7ab995f0b77a7226&ei=5090&partner=rssuserland&emc=rss> (last visited August 4, 2006).

41. SWIFT statement on compliance policy, June 23, 2006, available at <http://www.swift.com/index.cfm?item_id=59897> (last visited August 4, 2006).

42. Ben Worthen, "What to do When Uncle Sam Wants Your Data: How to Serve Your Company and Your Country," *CIO Magazine*, April 15, 2003, available at <http://www.cio.com/archive/041503/data.html> (last visited May 23, 2006).

43. Bob Sullivan, "Are Private Firms Helping Big Brother Too Much?" *MSBNC*, August 20, 2004, available at <http://www.msnbc.msn.com/id/5737239> (last visited September 8, 2006).

44. See Eunice Moscoso, "Demand for Data by Feds on Rise. Patriot Act: Businesses Feel Burden of Subpoenas, Court Orders about Patrons," Atlanta Journal—Constitution, August 17, 2003, E1.

45. See Patrick Healy, "Colleges Giving Probers Data on Foreign Students' Finances," *Boston Globe*, October 3, 2001.

46. Stephanie Stoughton, "Poll: Firms Relaxed Privacy Rules," *Boston Globe*, October 8, 2001.

47. GAO Report, "Data Mining: Federal Efforts Cover a Wide Range of Uses," May 2004, available at <http://www.epic.org/privacy/profiling/gao_dm_rpt.pdf> (last visited August 2, 2006).

48. See, for example, "The Federal Bureau of Investigation's Efforts to Improve the Sharing of Intelligence and Other Information," Office of the Inspector General, U.S. Department of Justice, December 2003, available at <http:// www.usdoj.gov/ oig/reports/FBI/a0410/index.htm> (last visited August 8, 2006); see also White House Press Release, "Executive Order: Further Strengthening the Sharing of Terrorism Information to Protect Americans," October 25, 2005, available at <http://www.whitehouse.gov/news/releases/2005/10/20051025-5.html> (last visited August 8, 2006).

49. A copy of the court order is available at the Web site of the Electronic Privacy Information Center, at <http://www.epic.org/privacy/carnivore/cd_cal_order.html> (last visited August 2, 2006).

50. Verne Kopytoff, "FBI's Controversial Cyber-Snooping System Plays Key Part in Terrorism Probe," *The San Francisco Chronicle*, October 15, 2001, at G1.

51. See, generally, the Web pages of the Electronic Privacy Information Center, devoted to Carnivore at <http://www.epic.org/privacy/carnivore /review_comments.html> (last visited August 2, 2006).

52. Wendy Hart and Diana Johnson, "Taking a Bite out of Internet Privacy," Georgia State University College of Law, Summer 2003, available at <http://gsulaw. gsu.edu/lawand/papers/su03/hart_johnson/> (last visited August 2, 2006).

53. "Report to Congress regarding the Terrorism Information Awareness Program," May 20, 2003, available at <http://wyden.senate.gov/leg_issues/reports /darpa_tia_summary.pdf> (last visited August 2, 2006).

54. See, generally, EPIC's Total Terrorism Information Awareness Web page at <http://www.epic.org/privacy/profiling/tia> (last visited August 8, 2006).

55. See Carl Hulse, "Poindexter's Office Closed: Department Tried Terrorism Futures," *San Francisco Chronicle*, September 26, 2003, available at <http:// www.sfgate. com/cgi-bin/article.cgi?file=/chronicle/archive/2003/09/26/ MN301359.DTL> (last visited August 8, 2006).

56. Fred Bayles, "Air-Traveler Screening, Privacy Concerns Collide," *USA Today*, October 3, 2003.

57. Eric Wieffering, "Stricter Air Passenger Screening On Track," *Star Tribune* (Minneapolis, MN), January 25, 2004.

58. Ibid.

59. Ibid.

60. Ibid.

61. See, for example, Mimi Hall and Alan Levin, "Revised Flier-Screening Plan in Works," *USA Today*, July 16, 2004.

62. Jane Black, *At Justice, NSEERS Spells Data Chaos*, Business Week Online, May 2, 2003.

63. Department of Homeland Security Press Release, "Fact Sheet: Changes to National Security Entry/Exit Registration System (NSEERS)," December 1, 2003, available at <http://www.dhs.gov/dhspublic/display?content=3020> (last visited August 2, 2006).

64. Rachel L. Swarns, "More than 13,000 May Face Deportation," *The New York Times*, June 7, 2003.

65. The Web site of the PBS displays many interesting documents regarding the program. See, for example, Unclassified Information Paper, DoD Talon, available at <http://www.pbs.org/now/politics/TALON.pdf> (last visited May 20, 2006).

66. Quoted in William Fisher, "Watchdogs Protest Pentagon's 'Mission Creep,'" *Inter Press Services News Agency*, December 15, 2005, available at <http://www.ipsnews.net/news.asp?idnews=31437> (last visited August 2, 2006).

67. See "Pentagon Caught Spying on U.S. Anti-War and Anti-Nuclear Activists," December 15, 2005, available at <http://www.democracynow.org/ article.pl?sid= 05/12/15/155219> (last visited August 2, 2006).

68. See Michael Isikoff, "Intelligence: The Pentagon—Spying in America?" *Newsweek*, June 21, 2004, available at <http://www.msnbc.msn.com/id/5197014/site/newsweek> (last visited August 8, 2006).

69. Nancy Kranich, "MATRIX and the New Surveillance States: The Multistate Anti-Terrorism Information Exchange," October 16, 2003, available at <http://www.fepproject.org/commentaries/matrix.html> (last visited August 8, 2006).

70. See Robert O'Harrow, Jr., "U.S. Backs Florida's New Counterterrorism Database: 'Matrix' Offers Law Agencies Faster Access to Americans' Personal Records," *The Washington Post*, August 6, 2003, at A01, available at <http:// www.washingtonpost.com/ac2/wp-dyn/A21872-2003Aug5> (last visited August 2, 2006).

71. Ibid.

72. Ibid.

73. Madeleine Baran, "Welcome to the Matrix: Inside the Government's Secret, Corporate-Run Mega-Database," *The NewStandard*, July 9, 2004, available at <http://newstandardnews.net/content/?action=show_item&itemid=662> (last visited August 2, 2006).

74. Ibid.

75. FACTS Success Stories, January 26, 2004, pamphlet obtained from the Florida Department of Law Enforcement, available on the Web site of the ACLU at <http://www.aclu.org>.

76. Robert O'Harrow, Jr., "U.S. Backs Florida's New Counterterrorism Database: 'Matrix' Offers Law Agencies Faster Access to Americans' Personal Records," *The Washington Post*, August 6, 2003, at A01, available at <http:// www.washingtonpost.com/ac2/wp-dyn/A21872-2003Aug5> (last visited August 8, 2006).

77. Institute for Intergovernmental Research, MATRIX Web site, section on Program Objectives: Data Security, available at <http://www.iir.com/matrix/objectives_1.htm> (last visited March 20, 2003). Note that the public Web site has since been taken down.

78. Allen Pusey, "Experts Wary of Personal Data Use," *The Mercury News*, May 28, 2006, available at <http://www.mercurynews.com/mld/mercurynews/news/politics/14689011.htm> (last visited August 8, 2006).

79. Ibid.

80. See Ann Davis, "Why a No Fly List Aimed At Terrorists Delays Others," *Wall Street Journal*, April 22, 2003.

81. See Tamara Lytle and Jim Leusner, "The Price of Protection: Push for Safety Clouds Individual Rights," *Orlando Sentinel*, August, 29, 2002, at A1.

82. Privacy Act of 1974, 5 U.S.C. §552a (2000).

83. See Testimony of Maureen Cooney, Acting Chief Privacy Officer, U.S. Department of Homeland Security, Protection of Privacy, Statement to the Committee on House Homeland Security Subcommittee on Intelligence, Information Sharing and Terrorism Risk Assessment, April 6, 2006.

84. Ibid.

85. See Paul M. Sniderman, Joseph F. Fletcher, Peter H. Russell, and Philip E. Tetlock, *The Clash of Rights: Liberty, Equality, and Legitimacy in Pluralist Democracy* (New Haven: Yale University Press, 1996).

86. See, for example, James L. Gibson and Amanda Gouws, "Social Identities and Political Intolerance: Linkages Within the South African Mass Public," *American Journal of Political Science* 44 (2000): 278–292.

Chapter 3

1. Fadwa El Guindi, *Veil: Modesty, Privacy and Resistance* (Oxford, UK: Berg Publishers, 1999) 81–82.

2. Margaret K. Nydell, *Understanding Arabs* (Boston, MA: Intercultural Press, 2002) 33.

3. See "The Internet Under Surveillance: Reporters Without Borders: 2003 Report," available at <http://www.rsf.org/IMG/pdf/doc-2236.pdf> (last visited May 20, 2006).

4. See, for example, Constitution of the Kingdom of Bahrain, at article 26, available at <http://www.oefre.unibe.ch/law/icl/ba00000_.html> (last visited August 3, 2006), providing:

The freedom of postal, telegraphic, telephonic and electronic communication is safeguarded and its confidentiality is guaranteed. Communications shall not be censored or their confidentiality breached except in exigencies specified by law and in accordance with procedures and under guarantees prescribed by law.

5. This observation has been noted in many U.S. Department of State reports. For a recent observation, see US Department of State, Bahrain, Country Reports on Human Rights Practices – 2005, March 8, 2006, available at <http://www.state.gov/g/drl/rls/hrrpt/2005/61686.htm> (last visited August 3, 2006), observing:

The constitution provides for freedom from arbitrary interference with privacy, home, and correspondence except under the provisions of the law and under judicial supervision; however, the government continued to infringe on citizens' right to privacy. The government carried out some illegal searches. Telephone calls and personal correspondence remained subject to monitoring . . .

6. The Constitution of Egypt, available at <http://www.egypt.gov.eg/english/laws/constitution/index.asp> (last visited June 1, 2006).

7. See "Egypt: Troops Smother Protests, Detain Activists," *Human Rights Watch*, May 5, 2006.

8. U.S. Department of State, "Egypt: Country Reports on Human Rights Practices—2003," February 25, 2004, available at <http:// www.state.gov/g/drl/rls/hrrpt/2003/27926.htm> (last visited August 3, 2006).

9. Supra note 6, article 44, providing: "Homes shall have their sanctity and they may not be entered or inspected except by a causal judicial warrant as prescribed by the law."

10. Basic Law: Human Dignity and Liberty (5752 – 1992) (Israel), Passed by the Knesset on the 21st Adar, 5754, March 9, 1994, available at <http://www.mfa.gov.il/mfa/go.asp?MFAH00hi0> (last visited June 1, 2006).

11. The Protection of Privacy Law 5741 – 1981, 1011 Laws of the State of Israel 128. Amended by the Protection of Privacy Law (Amendment) 5745 – 1985.

12. Ahmad Al Akhal, "The Virtual Law Firm—Privacy Issue. World Wide Activates: Middle East—Jordan," available at <http://vlf.juridicum.su.se/master99/staff/akhal/privacy.html> (last visited April 10, 2006).

13. The Constitution of the Hashemite Kingdom of Jordan, adopted January 1, 1952, available at <http://www.kinghussein.gov.jo/constitution_jo.html> (last visited August 3, 2006).

14. Ibid.

15. Constitution of Tunisia (1959), at article 9, available at <http://www.oefre.unibe.ch/law/icl/ts00000_.html> (last visited June 1, 2006).

16. Constitution of the United Arab Emirates (1971).

17. See, for example, supra note 8.

18. Quoted in Steve Negus, "Egyptian Justice, US-Style," *The Nation*, January 3, 2002, available at <http://www.thenation.com/doc/20020107/negus20020103> (last visited August 3, 2006).

19. Ibid.

20. U.S. Department of State, "Jordan: Country Reports on Human Rights Practices—2005," released by the Bureau of Democracy, Human Rights, and Labor, March 8, 2006, available at <http://www.state.gov/g/drl/rls/hrrpt/2005/61691.htm> (last visited August 3, 2006).

21. Electronic Transactions Law No. (85) of 2001 (Jordan), December 31, 2001, section 37. An English translation is available at <http://www.bakernet.com/ecommerce/e-transactions%20law.doc> (last visited August 3, 2006).

22. Ibid., at section 38.

23. A French translation is available at <http://www.kalimatunisie.com/>.

24. U.S. Department of State, "United Arab Emirates: Country Reports on Human Rights Practices—2005," released by the Bureau of Democracy, Human Rights, and Labor, March 8, 2006, available at <http://www.state.gov/g/drl/rls/hrrpt/2005/61701.htm> (last visited August 8, 2006).

25. Electronic Transactions and Commerce Law No. 2/2002 (Dubai), available at <http://www.tecom.ae/law/law_2.htm> (last visited August 3, 2006).

26. 1999 Constitution of the Federal Republic of Nigeria, available at <http://www.nigeria-law.org/ConstitutionOfTheFederalRepublicOfNigeria.htm> (last visited August 3, 2006).

27. The Constitution of the Republic of South Africa, Act 108 of 1996, available at <http://www.info.gov.za/documents/constitution/index.htm> (last visited August 3, 2006).

28. Ibid.

29. See Uganda Human Rights Commission, Annual Report January 2001—September 2002, 2003.

30. Ibid.

31. The Suppression of Terrorism Bill, 2003 (Kenya), Kenya gazette Supplement No. 38, publication date April 30, 2003, available at <http://www.ealawsociety.org/statutes/Kenya%20Suppression%20of%20Terrorism%20Bill%202003.pdf> (last visited August 3, 2006).

32. See Amnesty International, Amnesty International Press Release, "Kenya: Draft Anti-Terrorism Legislation may Undermine Kenyan Constitution and International Law," September 9, 2004, available at <http://news.amnesty.org/index/ENGAFR320042004> (last visited August 3, 2006).

33. Ahmed Issack Hassan, "Pitfalls of the Anti-Terrorism Bill: Draft Reverses Major Gains Made in Human Rights Crusade," InfoShop.com, June 27, 2003, available at <http://www.infoshop.org/inews/article.php?story=03/06/27/4176099> (last visited August 3, 2006).

34. Michelle Kagari, "Anti-Terror Bill an Affront to Human Rights," Comment, *Daily Nation*, November 18, 2003, available at <http://www.nationaudio.com/News/DailyNation/18112003/Comment/Comment181120036.html> (last visited August 3, 2006).

35. Interception and Monitoring [Prohibition] Act of 1992, (South Africa) [1992 (Act No. 127 of 1992)] 2001.

36. Regulation of Interception of Communications and Provision of Communication-related Information Act 70 of 2002 (hereinafter, SA Interception Act).

37. Telecommunications Act (South Africa), Act No. 103 of 1996, as amended.

38. A Interception Act, supra note 36, at section 13(5).

39. Ibid., at section 8.

40. See "Newspaper Uncovers 'Unlawful' Tapping by Intelligence Units," *The Star*, February 21, 1996.

41. See "South Africa Admits to Spying on German Embassy," *Reuters*, February 6, 2000.

42. Electronic Communications and Transactions Act (South Africa), Act No. 25 of 2002.

43. Ibid., at chapter III.

44. Ibid., at chapter VIII.

45. Ibid., at chapter XI.

46. Regulation of Interception of Communications and Provision of Communication-Related Information Amendment Bill [B9-2006] (South Africa), available at <http://www.doj.gov.za/2004dojsite/legislation/notices/n2006/Bill_final.pdf> (last visited August 2, 2006).

47. Barbara Slaughter, "South Africa: ANC Government Pushes through Draconian Anti-Terrorism Legislation," World Socialist Web Site, November 9, 2001, available at <http://www.wsws.org/articles/2001/nov2001/sa-n09.shtml> (last visited August 3, 2006).

48. Issue Paper 24 (Project 124), Privacy and Data Protection, available at <http://www.doj.gov.za/salrc/media/2005-prj_124_media.pdf> (last visited August 3, 2006).

49. Discussion Paper 109 (Project 124), Privacy and Data Protection (South Africa), available at <http://www.doj.gov.za/salrc/dpapers.htm> (last visited August 8, 2006).

50. Ant-Terrorism Act, 2002, No. 14/2002 (Uganda), available at <http://www.kituochakatiba.co.ug/anti.htm>, at section 7.

51. Ibid., at section 9(2).

52. Ibid., at section 11(3).

53. Ibid., at section 19(1).

54. David Ouma Balikowa, "The Anti-Terrorism Act 2002: The Media and Free Speech," *The Defender*, Volume 8, Issue 1, 2003.

55. Supra note 34.

Chapter 4

1. Council Directive No. 95/46/EC of 24 October 1995 on the Protection of Individuals with Regard to the Processing of Personal Data and on the Free Movement of Such Data, O.J. L 281/31 (1995) (hereinafter, Directive).

2. Ibid., at article 2(a).

3. Ibid., at article 4, which provides:

1. Each Member State shall apply national provisions it adopts pursuant to this Directive to the processing of personal data where:

(a) the processing is carried out in the context of the activities of an establishment of the controller on the territory of the Member State; when the same controller is established on the territory of several Member States, he must take the necessary measures to ensure that each of these establishments complies with the obligations laid down by national law applicable;

(b) the controller is not established on the Member State's territory, but in a place where is national law applies by virtue of international public law;

(c) the controller is not established on Community territory and, for purposes of processing personal data, makes use of equipment, automated or otherwise, situated in the territory of the said Member States, unless such equipment is used only for purpose of transit through the territory of the Community.

4. Directive, supra note 1, at article 7(a).

5. Ibid., at article 7(b).

6. Ibid., at article 7(c).

7. Ibid., at article 7(d).

8. Ibid., at article 7(e).

9. Ibid., at article 7(f).

10. Ibid., at article 8(1).

11. Ibid., at article 8(2)(a).

12. Ibid., at article 8(2)(b).

13. Ibid., at article 8(2)(c).

14. Ibid., at article 8(2)(d).

15. Ibid., at article 8(2)(e).

16. Ibid., at article 8(2)(f).

17. Ibid., at article 8(2)(g).

18. Ibid., at article 18, requiring each member state to "provide that one or more public authorities are responsible for the application within its territory of the provisions adopted by the Member States . . . "

19. Directive, supra note 1, at article (1).

20. Ibid., at article 12(a).

21. Ibid.

22. Ibid., at article 17(1).

23. Ibid., at article 17(2).

24. The country's main data protection law contains security requirements that are quite similar to those of the Directive. See Organic Law 15/1999 of 13 December on the Protection of Personal Data; an unofficial translation is available at <http://ec.europa.eu/ justice_home/fsj/privacy/docs/organic-law-99.pdf> (last visited August 4, 2006), at article 9(1), providing: "[t]he controller or, where applicable, the processor shall adopt the technical and organisational measures necessary to ensure the security of the personal data and prevent their alteration, loss, unauthorised processing or access, having regard to the state of the art, the nature of the data stored and the risks to which they are exposed by virtue of human action or the physical or natural environment." For more specific data security requirements, see Royal Decree 994/1999, de 11 de junio of 11 June, which approves the Regulation on Mandatory Security Measures for the Computer Files which contain Personal Data, available at <https://212.170.242.148/upload/ reglamento_ingles_pdf.pdf> (last visited August 4, 2006).

25. Directive, supra note 1, at article 17(2).

26. Ibid.

27. Further information about this program is available on the Web site of the U.S. Department of Commerce, at <http://www.export.gov/safeharbor> (last visited June 1, 2006). Information about the countries approved as "adequate" is available on the Web site of the European Commission, at <http://ec.europa.eu/ justice_home/ fsj/privacy/thridcountries/index_en.htm> (last visited August 4, 2006).

28. Commission Staff Working Document—The implementation of Commission Decision 520/2000/EC on the adequate protection of personal data provided by the Safe Harbour privacy Principles and related Frequently Asked Questions issued by the US Department of Commerce, available at <http://europa.eu.int/comm/ internal_market/privacy/docs/adequacy/sec-2004-1323_en.pdf> (last visited July 18, 2006).

29. The study, entitled Safe Harbour Decision Implementation Study, was conducted by Professors Y. Poullet, J. Dhont, and M.V. Perez Asinary from the Centre de Researched Informatique et Droit (University of Namur, Belgium), Dr Bygrave (University of Oslo, Norway), and Dr Reidenberg (Fordham University School of Law, New York), available at <http://ec.europa.eu/justice_home/fsj/privacy/docs/studies/safe-harbour-2004_en.pdf> (last visited August 4, 2006).

30. Directive, supra note 1, at article 26(2)(b).

31. Ibid., at article 26(2)(d).

32. Ibid.

33. Ibid., at article 26(2)(f).

34. Ibid., at article 26(3).

35. See International Bar Association, Task Force on International Terrorism, International Terrorism: Legal Challenges and Responses 32–38, at 34 n. 30 (2004).

36. See, generally, Human Rights Watch, "Setting an Example? Counter-Terrorism Measures in Spain," January, 2005, volume 17, no. 1(D).

37. Organic Law 4/2000 of January 11 on the rights and freedoms of foreigners in Spain and their social integration, as amended.

38. Terrorism Act 2000 (UK), chapter 11, available at <http://www.opsi.gov.uk/acts/acts2000/20000011.htm#aofs> (last visited August 1, 2006).

39. Regulation of Investigatory Powers Act, 2000 (UK), at chapter 23, available at <http://www.opsi.gov.uk/acts/en2000/2000en23.htm> (last visited August 1, 2006).

40. European Union, "Structure of the European Union: The 'Three Pillars,'" available at <http://europa.eu.int/eur-lex/en/about/abc/abc_12.html> (last updated April 27, 2004; last visited June 1, 2006).

41. Conclusions Adopted by the Council (Justice and Home Affairs), September 20, 2001. Doc. SN 3926/6/01 REV 6.

42. Council of the European Union, "Note from the Presidency," available at <http://register.consilium.eu.int/pdf/en/01/st12/12800-r1en1.pdf> (last visited June 1, 2006).

43. Proposal for a Council Framework Decision on Combating Terrorism, Brussels, September 19, 2001—COM(2001) 0521 final, available at <http://europa.eu/eur-lex/en/com/pdf/2001/en_501PC0521.pdf> (last visited August 4, 2006).

44. Commission of the European Communities, Brussels, Report From The Commission, Overview of European Union action in response to the events of the 11 September and assessment of their likely economic impact, October 17, 2001, COM(2001) 611 final.

45. Letter from President George W. Bush to Mr Romano Prodi, President, Commission of the European Communities, Brussels, October 16, 2001, forwarded by the Deputy Chief of Mission, United States Mission to the European Union, available at <http://www.statewatch.org/news/2001/nov/06Ausalet.htm> (last visited August 1, 2006).

46. Prepared statement of the United States of America, presented at European Union Forum on Cybercrime, Brussels, November 27, 2001, a copy of which is available at <http://cryptome.sabotage.org/eu-dataspy.htm> (last visited August 1, 2006).

47. See "Recommendations for Tracing Networked Communications Across National Borders in Terrorist and Criminal Investigations," available at <http://www.justice.gc.ca/en/news/g8/doc2.html> (last visited August 3, 2006); see also, generally, Chairperson's Summary, G8 Justice and Interior Ministers' Meeting, Mont-Tremblant, May 13–14, 2002, available at <http://www.g8.utoronto.ca/adhoc/justice2002chair.htm> (last visited August 1, 2006).

48. Public Law 107-071.

49. Ibid., at section 115(c)(1) and (2), now codified at 49 U.S.C. 44909.

50. Article 29 Data Protection Working Party, Opinion 4/2003 on the Level of Protection ensured in the US for the Transfer of Passengers' Data, 11070/03/EN, adopted on June 13, 2003.

51. *European Parliament v. Council of the European Union and European Parliament v. Commission of the European Communities* (C-317/04 and C-318/04), available at <http://curia.eu.int/jurisp/cgi-bin/gettext.pl?where=&lang=en&num=79939469C1904 0317&doc=T&ouvert=T&seance=ARRET> (last visited August 1, 2006).

52. See News Release, No. 50/06, EU Commission Adopts Initiatives To Open New Talks With The Us On Passenger Name Records, June 19, 2006, available at <http://www.eurunion.org/News/press/2006/20060050.htm> (last visited August 1, 2006).

53. Quoted in "Passenger Data Judgment Attacked by Privacy Chief," *Out-Law News*, May 30, 2005, available at <http://www.out-law.com/page-6960> (last visited August 1, 2006).

54. See Peter J. Hustinx, European Data Protection Supervisor, "A Framework in Development: Third Pillar and Data Protection," available at <http://www.edps.europa.eu/publications/speeches/06-05-12_article_Warsaw_third_pillar_EN.pdf> (last visited June 1, 2006), for a general discussion on the efforts to progress with such a framework.

55. Council of Europe Convention on Cybercrime, Budapest, 23.X1.2001, available at <http://conventions.coe.int/Treaty/EN/Treaties/Html/185.htm> (last visited August 1, 2006).

56. Ibid., at Preamble.

57. Ibid., at chapter II, section 1.

58. Ibid., at chapter II, section 1, title 1.

59. Ibid., at chapter II, section 1, title 2.

60. Ibid., at chapter II, section 1, title 3.

61. Ibid., at chapter II, section 1, title 4.

62. Ibid., at chapter II, section 2.

63. Ibid., at chapter III.

64. Ibid., at chapter II, section 3.

65. See Opinion 4/2001 On the Council of Europe's Draft Convention on Cybercrime, adopted March 22, 2001, available at <http://www.statewatch.org/news/2001/mar/data01.pdf> (last visited August 1, 2006).

66. Ibid.

67. See "How the World Clamped Down on the Threat of More Violence," *The Observer*, July 24, 2005.

68. Some analysts have contended that many factors, including the London bombings, the recent youth riots, and the informational campaign put forth by Interior Minister Nicolas Sarkozy, contributed to the passage of the legislation. Consider the comments of Jim Bittermann on CNN regarding the legislation:

I don't think the results would have been quite the same as they were this afternoon. But nonetheless, I think probably it would have passed anyway because Nicolas Sarkozy has done a very good job of softening the ground for this legislation. As much as six weeks ago he began saying that France was a very real target for terrorists. He said the ingredients and the threat really do exist. So he laid the groundwork very well in a way that a lot of people were concerned about the possibility of an outside threat. There's kind of been sort of a laissez-faire, a blasé attitude about terrorism here because there's always been the feeling that France has this special relationship with the Middle East and is viewed differently than the rest of the world, perhaps.

But I think that's changed the last few months. There's a lot of notice for the police. They've put out warnings that in fact they've heard of threats to France—French targets. And a number of round-ups have taken place that have led to suspects being arrested who had in fact plans in their possession for attacks on French targets. So I think the threat has become more real over the last few months.

Michael Holmes, Rosemary Church, Jim Bittermann, Christiane Amanpour, Tony Harris, Dana Bash, Robin Oakley, and Guy Raz, "French Lawmakers Advance New Anti Terror Measures; Interview with French Prime Minister Dominque de Villepin; Bush Takes Border Campaign to El Paso," *CNN: Your World Today*, November 29, 2005, Transcript 112901CN.V10.

69. Joshua Pantesco, "French Senate Gives Final Approval to Anti-Terror Bill," December 22, 2005, available at <http://jurist.law.pitt.edu/ paperchase/2005/12/french-senate-gives-final-approval-to.php> (last visited August 1, 2006).

70. For a copy of the measure in French, please see <http://www.senat.fr/dossierleg/pjl05-109.html> (last visited August 1, 2006). In addition, the Commission Nationale de l'Informatique et des Libertes (CNIL) analysis of the proposed legislation is available, in French, at <http://www.cnil.fr/index.php?id=1884&news[uid] =286&cHash=dad76fea63> (last visited August 1, 2006).

71. Projet de loi relatif à la lutte contre le terrorisme et portant dispositions diverses relatives à la sécurité et aux contrôles frontaliers, available at <http://www.senat.fr/dossierleg/pjl05-109.html> (last visited December 23, 2005).

72. Human Rights Watch, "France: More Safeguards Needed in Anti-Terrorism Bill. Letter to French Senators," December 9, 2005, available at <http://hrw.org/english/docs/2005/12/09/france12182.htm> (last visited August 1, 2006).

73. Decree-Law n. 374, Emergency Measures to Fight against International Terrorism (18 October 2001), available at <http://www.legislationline.org/legislation.php?tid=46&lid=1397> (last visited August 1, 2006).

74. The detention provisions of the legislation have already been criticized by many human rights groups. See, for example, Amnesty International, Public Statement, Italy: New "counter-terrorist" legislation jeopardizes exercise of human rights, AI Index: EUR 30/011/2005 (Public), News Service No: 210, August 4, 2005.

75. Conversione in legge, con modificazioni, del decreto-legge 27 luglio 2005, n. 144, recante misure urgenti per il contrasto del terrorismo internazionale, LEGGE 31 luglio 2005, n.155, Gazzetta Ufficiale N. 177 dell' 1 Agosto 2005, available at <http://www.gazzette.comune.jesi.an.it/2005/177/3.htm> (last visited August 1, 2006).

76. Sofia Celeste, "Want to Check Your E-mail in Italy? Bring Your Passport," *The Christian Science Monitor*, October 4, 2005, available at <http://www.csmonitor.com/2005/1004/p07s01-woeu.html> (last visited August 1, 2006).

77. Ibid.

78. See "How the World Clamped Down on the Threat of More Violence," *The Observer*, July 24, 2005, at 5.

79. Betsy Powell, "Heavy Security Measures a Way of Life in London," *Toronto Star*, October 10, 2001, at A14.

80. Terrorism Act 2006, C. 11 (United Kingdom), available at <http://www.opsi.gov.uk/acts/acts2006/20060011.htm> (last visited August 1, 2006).

81. Thomas, Kim, "Cilip Says Security Services can Demand Records: Spooks Have Powers to Access Information on Books Borrowed and Websites Accessed," *News Reports: Information World Review*, November 16, 2005, at 1.

82. Anti-terrorism, Crime and Security Act 2001 (United Kingdom), available at <http://www.hmso.gov.uk/acts/acts2001/20010024.htm> (last visited August 1, 2006).

83. The Retention of Communications Data (Code of Practice) Order 2003, SI 2003 No. 3175, (United Kingdom), December 4, 2003. Retention of Communications

Data under Part 11: Anti-Terrorism, Crime & Security Act 2001 – Voluntary Code of Practice, available at <http://www.legislation.hmso.gov.uk/si/ si2003/draft/5b.pdf> (last visited August 1, 2006).

84. Opinion of Ben Emmerson QC and Helen Mountfield, Matrix Chambers, July 2002, available at <http://www.privacyinternational.org/countries/uk/surveillance/ ic-terror-opinion.htm> (last visited August 1, 2006).

85. "U.K.: New Anti-Terror Law Rolls Back Rights," Human Rights Watch, December 14, 2001, available at <http://hrw.org/english/docs/2001/12/14/uk3427 .htm> (last visited August 1, 2006).

86. Prevention of Terrorism Act 2005, C. 12, (United Kingdom), available at <http://www.opsi.gov.uk/acts/acts2005/20050002.htm> (last visited August 1, 2006).

87. Ibid., at section 1(3).

88. Ibid., at section 1(4).

89. Regulation of Investigatory Powers Act 2000 (c. 23) (United Kingdom), available at <http://www.legislation.hmso.gov.uk/acts/acts2000/20000023.htm> (last visited August 1, 2006), replacing Interception of Communications Act 1985 (c. 56) (United Kingdom), available at <http://www.archive.official-documents.co.uk/ document/cm47/4778/4778.htm> (last visited August 8, 2006).

90. See "Nowhere to Hide as Britain Tops CCTV League," *Sunday Times*, April 18, 2004.

91. See "Security Role for Traffic Cameras," *The Observer*, February 9, 2003.

92. Greg Lucas, "Local Transit Agencies Debate Use of Cameras: U.S. Has Invested Little in Type of Device that Helped British Identify 4 Bombing Suspects," *The San Francisco Chronicle*, July 18, 2005, at A1.

93. See Justin Davenport, "Hi-Tech Scanners Will Detect Explosives on Tube, Rail Passengers," *The Evening Standard*, November 14, 2005.

94. See, for example, David Leppard, "Police Snipers Track Al-Qaeda Suspects," *Sunday Times*, July 17, 2005, at 2.

95. Quoted in Nigel Morris, "Hundreds of Terror Suspects Under Surveillance," *The Independent*, September 14, 2005.

96. See Mark Rice-Oxley, "How Should Britain Tackle Terror?" *The Christian Science Monitor*, November 15, 2005, at 7.

97. For a very good but somewhat dated summary of privacy in Russia, see "Privacy in the Russian Internet," available at <http://www.hro.org/docs/reps/privacy/2002/ eng/index.htm> (last visited August 1, 2006).

98. The Constitution of Russian Federation, available at <http://www.russianembassy. org/RUSSIA/CONSTIT> (last visited August 1, 2006).

99. Russian Federation, Law of the Russian Federation on Information, Informatisation and Information Protection, January 25, 1995; extracts available at <http://www.datenschutz-berlin.de/gesetze/internat/fen.htm> (last visited August 1, 2006).

100. Ibid., at article 11, providing:

> (1) Lists of personal data included in Federal information resources, joint-management information resources, information resources of Russian Federation subjects, and information resources of organs of local self-government, and also data obtained and collected by nonstate organizations must be established on the Federal-law level. Personal data shall be referred to the category of confidential information.
>
> Collection, storage, use and dissemination of information on the private life, and of information disclosing personal secret, family secret, secret of correspondence, telephone conversations, postal, telegraph and other communications of natural person without his or her consent, except under court decision, shall not be allowed.
>
> (2) Personal data may not be used for the purpose of inflicting property or moral harm on citizens or hampering the exercise of Russian Federation citizens' rights and freedoms. Restriction of Russian Federation citizens' rights through the use of information on their social origins, racial, national, language, religious or party affiliation shall be prohibited and shall be punishable in conformity with legislation.
>
> (3) Legal and natural persons in possession, in accordance with their powers, of information on citizens, and obtaining and making use thereof shall bear liability in conformity with the effective legislation of the Russian Federation for breach of the regime of protection, processing, and rules of use of this information.
>
> (4) The activity of nonstate organizations and private persons involved in the processing and provision of personal data to users shall be subject to mandatory licensing. The rules of licensing shall be determined by the effective legislation of the Russian Federation.
>
> (5) Unlawful activity by the organs of state power and organizations in the collection of personal data may be established in judicial proceedings on the appeal of persons acting under Articles 14 and 15 of the present Federal Act and legislation on personal data.

101. Ibid., at articles 11 and 21. The relevant provision of article 11 is quoted in the previous note. The relevant provision of article 21 provides in part:

> The information-protection regime shall be established:
>
> with respect to facts and figures classified as state secret by authorized agencies, on the basis of the Russian Federation State Secrets Act;
>
> with respect to confidential documented information by the owner of information resources or by duly authorized person, on the basis of the present Federal Act;
>
> with respect to personal data—by the Federal Act.

102. The Criminal Code of The Russian Federation, Adopted by the State Duma on May 24, 1996, Adopted by the Federation Council on June 5, 1996, Federal Law No. 64-FZ of June 13, 1996 on the Enforcement of the Criminal Code of the Russian Federation, available at <http://www.russian-criminal-code.com> (hereinafter, Russian Criminal Code) (last visited August 1, 2006).

103. Ibid., at article 138.

104. Ibid., at article 139.

105. Ibid., at article 372.

106. Ibid., at article 272.

107. Ibid.

108. Civil Code, article 150, part 2.

109. Ibid., at article 151.

110. United Nations Human Rights Committee, Comments on Russian Federation, U.N. Doc. CCPR/C/79/Add.54 (1995), available at <http://sim.law.uu.nl/SIM/CaseLaw/uncom.nsf/0/9172bc5146972b6dc125663c00343b49?OpenDocument> (last visited August 1, 2006).

111. The Federal Law on Operational Investigative Activity, No. 144-FZ of August 12, 1995 (Russian Federation).

112. Ibid., at article 5.

113. Susan B. Glasser and Peter Baker, "Putin, Bush Weigh New Unity against a 'Common Foe,'" *The Washington Post*, September 13, 2001, at A25.

114. Signed 28 February 1996, ratified 5 May 1998, entered into force 5 May 1998; information available at <http://conventions.coe.int/>.

115. Signed November 8, 2001; further information available at <http://conventions.coe.int>.

116. Federal Law No. 114-FZ of July 25, 2002 on the Counteraction of Extremist Activity. Under the measure, extremist activity is defined very broadly as:

> (1) the activity of public and religious associations or any other organisations, or of mass media, or natural persons to plan, organise, prepare and perform the acts aimed at:
> – the forcible change of the foundations of the constitutional system and the violation of the integrity of the Russian Federation;
> – the subversion of the security of the Russian Federation;
> – the seizure or acquisition of peremptory powers;
> – the creation of illegal military formations;
> – the exercise of terrorist activity;
> – the excitation of racial, national or religious strife, and also social hatred associated with violence or calls for violence;
> – the abasement of national dignity;
> – the making of mass disturbances, ruffian-like acts, and acts of vandalism for the reasons of ideological, political, racial, national or religious hatred or hostility toward any social group;

> – the propaganda of the exclusiveness, superiority or deficiency of individuals on the basis of their attitude to religion, social, racial, national, religious or linguistic identity;
>
> (2) the propaganda and public show of nazi attributes or symbolics or the attributes or symbolism similar to nazi attributes or symbolics to the extent of blending;
>
> (3) public calls for the said activity or for the performance of the said acts;
>
> (4) the financing of the said activity or any other encouragement of its exercise or the performance of the said acts, including by the extension of financial resources for the exercise of the said activity, the supply of real estate, educational facilities, printing and publishing facilities and the material and technical base, telephone, fax and other communications, information services and other material and technical facilities.

117. Ibid. See also Declan McCullagh, "Russia Poised to Restrict Net Activities," CNET, June 24, 2002, available at <http://news.com.com/2100-1023-938810.html> (last visited August 9, 2006).

118. Law of the Russian Federation "On Mass Media," No. 2124-1 of December 27, 1991 (Russian Federation), as of December 8, 2003 (as amended on January 13, 1995; June 6, 1995; July 19, 1995; December 27, 1995; March 2, 1998; June 20, 2000; August 5, 2000; August 4, 2001; March 21, 2002; July 25, 2002; July 4, 2003; and December 8, 2003), available at <http://www.medialaw.ru/e_pages/laws/russian/massmedia_eng/massmedia_eng.html> (last visited August 8, 2006) (hereinafter, Law on Mass Media).

119. Russian Federal Law on Communications, No. 15-FZ (1995) (Russia), available at <http://www2.internews.ru/law/comm_eng/index.html> (last visited August 1, 2006).

120. Ibid.

121. Available in Russian at <http://www.legislationline.org/legislation.php?tid=46&lid=6007> (last visited August 1, 2006).

122. Russian Criminal Code, supra note 102.

123. Criminal-Procedural Code of the Russian Federation, No. 174-FZ of December 18, 2001 (with the Amendments and Additions of May 29, July 24, 25, October 31, 2002, June 30, July 4, 7, December 8, 2003, April 22, June 29, December 2, 28, 2004, June 1, 2005), available at <http://legislationline.org/upload/legislations/9a/eb/3a4a5e98a67c25d4fe5eb5170513.htm> (last visited August 1, 2006).

124. Law on Mass Media, supra note 118.

125. Privacy International, Media Release, "What is Wrong with Europe? PI Report Criticises EU Anti-Terror Policies," December 14, 2005, available at <http://www.privacyinternational.org/article.shtml?cmd%5B347%5D=x-347-494877> (last visited August 1, 2006). For the full study, see Gus Hosein, "Threatening the Open Society: Comparing Anti-Terror Policies and Strategies in the U.S. and Europe," Privacy International, December 15, 2005.

126. Ibid.

Chapter 5

1. The Personal Information Protection and Electronic Documents Act, introduced as Bill C-6, assented to April 13, 2000 (Canada), available at <http://www.privcom.gc.ca/legislation/02_06_01_e.asp> (last visited July 19, 2006).

2. Ibid., at part 1, §3.

3. Ibid., at part 1, §2(1).

4. Personal Information Protection and Electronic Documents Act, supra note 1, at part 1, §2(1).

5. Ibid., at part 1.

6. Model Code for the Protection of Personal Information, CAN/CSA Q830 96, Prepared by Canadian Standards Association, Approved by Standards Council of Canada, available at <http://www.privacyexchange.org/buscodes/standard/canadianstandards. html> (last visited August 5, 2006).

7. Personal Information Protection and Electronic Documents Act, supra note 1, at part 1, division 1 (Protection of Personal Information), subdivision 7(1)(a)–(d).

8. See "Summaries of Findings under the Personal Information Protection and Electronic Documents Act," available at <http://www.privcom.gc.ca/cf-dc/2005/index2-5_e.asp> (last visited March 1, 2005).

9. See "Summaries of Cases Settled during the Course of the Investigation under the Personal Information Protection and Electronic Documents Act," available at <http://www.privcom.gc.ca/ser/index_01_e.asp> (last visited March 1, 2005).

10. See "Summary of an Early Resolution Case under the Personal Information Protection and Electronic Documents Act," available at <http://www.privcom.gc.ca/ser/index_02_e.asp> (last visited March 10, 2005).

11. Bill C-36 (as assented to December 18, 2001, proclaimed in force December 24, 2001): An Act to amend the Criminal Code, the Official Secrets Act, the Canada Evidence Act, the Proceeds of Crime (Money Laundering) Act and other Acts, and to enact measures respecting the registration of charities in order to combat terrorism, available at <http://www.parl.gc.ca/LEGISINFO/index.asp?Lang=E&Chamber=N&StartList=A&EndList=Z&Session=9&Type=0&Scope=I&query=2981&List=toc-1> (last visited August 4, 2006).

12. Canadian Department of Justice, "Backgrounder: Highlights of Anti-Terrorism Act," available at <http://canada.justice.gc.ca/en/news/nr/2001/doc_27787 .html> (last visited June 1, 2006).

13. Security of Information Act (R.S., 1985, c. O-5) (Canada), available at <http://laws.justice.gc.ca/en/O-5/text.html> (last visited August 5, 2006).

14. National Defence Act (R.S., 1985, c. N-5) (Canada), available at <http://laws.justice.gc.ca/en/N-5/text.html> (last visited August 4, 2006).

15. Ibid., at section 83.28.

> (2) Subject to subsection (3), a peace officer may, for the purposes of an investigation of a terrorism offence, apply ex parte to a judge for an order for the gathering of information.

(3) A peace officer may make an application under subsection (2) only if the prior consent of the Attorney General was obtained.

(4) A judge to whom an application is made under subsection (2) may make an order for the gathering of information if the judge is satisfied that the consent of the Attorney General was obtained as required by subsection (3) and

(a) that there are reasonable grounds to believe that

(i) a terrorism offence has been committed, and

(ii) information concerning the offence, or information that may reveal the whereabouts of a person suspected by the peace officer of having committed the offence, is likely to be obtained as a result of the order; or

(b) that

(i) there are reasonable grounds to believe that a terrorism offence will be committed,

(ii) there are reasonable grounds to believe that a person has direct and material information that relates to a terrorism offence referred to in subparagraph (i), or that may reveal the whereabouts of an individual who the peace officer suspects may commit a terrorism offence referred to in that subparagraph, and

(iii) reasonable attempts have been made to obtain the information referred to in subparagraph (ii) from the person referred to in that subparagraph.

16. Department of the Solicitor General of Canada, Annual Report on the Use of Arrest Without Warrant Pursuant to the Antiterrorism Act 2002, May 2003.

17. Attorney General of Canada, Annual Report Concerning Investigative Hearings and Recognizance With Conditions for Period of December 24, 2001–December 23 2002, May 2003.

18. Criminal Code. R.S., c. C-34, s. 1. (Canada), available at <http://laws.justice. gc.ca/en/c-46/text.html> (last visited August 4, 2006).

19. See Darah Hansen, "$18-million in Transit Cameras part of Federal Security Drive: SkyTrain, West Coast Express Cars and Possibly Buses to be Monitored," *The Vancouver Sun*, November 24, 2005, at A3.

20. Ibid.

21. See Beth Duff-Brown and Rob Gillies, "Links Sought in Canada Bomb Plot: More Arrests Expected; Authorities Investigating Possible Foreign Connections," *The Mercury News*, June 6, 2006, available at <http://www.mercurynews.com/mld/ mercurynews/news/world/14750816.htm> (last visited August 4, 2006).

22. Ross Marowits, "Quebec to Amend Law to Protect Transfer of Personal Information to U.S.," *Canadian Press*, June 5, 2006, available at <http://www.canada. com/topics/news/national/story.html?id=87998cec-106f-4623-8f9b-36cbe 74949d8&k=47450> (last visited August 8, 2006).

23. Ibid.

24. Ibid.

25. See Constitution of Mexico (1917), an English translation of which is available at <http://www.ilstu.edu/class/hist263/docs/1917const.html#TitleIChapterI> (last visited August 4, 2006), at article 16, providing:

> No one shall be molested in his person, family, domicile, papers, or posses-sions except by virtue of a written order of the competent authority stating the legal grounds and justification for the action taken. No order of arrest or detention shall be issued against any person other than by the competent judi-cial authority, and unless same is preceded by a charge, accusation, or com-plaint for a credible party or by other evidence indicating the probable guilt of the accused; in cases of flagrante delicto, any person may arrest the offender and his accomplices, turning them over without delay to the nearest authori-ties. Only in urgent cases instituted by the public attorney without previous complaint or indictment and when there is no judicial authority available, may the administrative authorities, on their strictest accountability, order the detention of an accused person, turning him over immediately to the judicial authorities. Every search warrant, which can be issued only by judicial author-ity and which must be in writing, shall specify the place to be searched, the person or persons to be arrested, and the objects sought, the proceedings to be limited thereto; at the conclusion of which a detailed statement shall be drawn up in the presence of two witnesses proposed by the occupant of the place searched, or by the official making the search in his absence or should he refuse to do so.
>
> Administrative officials may enter private homes for the sole purpose of ascertaining whether the sanitary and police regulations have been complied with; and may demand to be shown the books and documents required to prove compliance with fiscal rulings, in which latter cases they must abide by the provisions of the respective laws and be subject to the formalities pre-scribed for cases of search.

26. The Decree of May 29, 2000, amended three federal statutes, including the Federal Consumer Protection Law, available at <http://www.firmadigital.gob.mx/marcolegal/29-05-2000.doc> (last visited August 4, 2006).

27. Decreto No. 356.—Se Aprueba La Ley De Proteccion De Datos Personales Del Estado De Colima, Ley publicada en el Suplemento No. 1 del Periódico Oficial "El Estado de Colima" No. 27, el sábado 21 de junio del 2003, available at <http://www.congresocol.gob.mx/leyes/ley-de-proteccion-datos.zip> (last visited August 5, 2006).

28. An unofficial English translation of the measure is available at <http://www.gwu.edu/~nsarchiv/NSAEBB/NSAEBB68/laweng.pdf> (last visited August 4, 2006).

29. See <http://www.state.gov/g/drl/rls/hrrpt/2002/18338.htm> (last visited August 5, 2006).

Chapter 6

1. Personal Data Protection Act, Law No. 25,326 (Argentina), available in English at <http://www.privacyinternational.org/countries/argentina/argentine-dpa.html> (last visited August 4, 2006).

2. Ibid., at section 1.

3. Ibid., at section 2, in which personal data is defined as: "Information of any kind referred to certain or ascertainable physical persons or legal entities."

4. Ibid., at chapter II.

5. Ibid., at chapter III.

6. Ibid., at section 12, providing: "The transfer of any type of personal information to countries or international or supranational entities which do not provide adequate levels of protection, is prohibited." Such general prohibition is, however, subject to the following exceptions:

  (a) international judicial cooperation;

  (b) exchange of medical information, when so required for the treatment of the party affected, or in case of an epidemiological survey, provided that it is conducted in pursuance of the terms of Paragraph e) of the foregoing Section;

  (c) stock exchange or banking transfers, to the extent thereof, and in pursuance of the applicable laws;

  (d) when the transfer is arranged within the framework of international treaties which the Argentine Republic is a signatory to;

  (e) when the transfer is made for international cooperation purposes between intelligence agencies in the fight against organized crime, terrorism and drug-trafficking.

7. Law No. 8078, September 11, 1990 (Brazil).

8. Law No. 7.232, October 29, 1984 (Brazil).

9. Law No. 19628, August 30, 1999 (Chile).

10. See Stephen Johnson, "U.S. Coalition against Terrorism should include Latin America," The Heritage Foundation, October 9, 2001, available at <http://www.heritage.org/Research/NationalSecurity/BG1489.cfm> (last visited May 20, 2006) (arguing that from 30 terrorist organizations operating worldwide, at least 10 of them, including one linked to Bin Laden, were operating in Latin America).

11. See Noah Leavitt, "Peru as Our Crystal Ball? One Possible Future for America's War on Terrorism, and the Lessons that can Help us Avoid It," FindLaw, June 5, 2003, available at <http://writ.findlaw.com/commentary/20030605_leavitt.html> (last visited April 10, 2006).

12. S.C. Res. 1373, U.N. SCOR, 56th Session, 4385th mtg., U.N. Doc. S/Res/1373 (2001), available at <http://daccessdds.un.org/doc/UNDOC/GEN/N01/557/43/PDF/N0155743.pdf?OpenElement> (last visited August 2, 2006); see also the reports about UN Res. 1373 and anti-terrorism implementation measures in the

countries of Argentina, Belize, Bolivia, Brazil, Chile, Colombia, Costa Rica, Ecuador, El Salvador, Honduras, Mexico, Nicaragua, Panama, Paraguay, Peru, Uruguay, and Venezuela, available at <http://www.un.org/Docs/sc/committees/1373/ submitted_ reports. html> (last visited August 3, 2006).

13. U.S. Department of State, Country Reports on Terrorism: Released by the Office of the Coordinator for Counterterrorism, April 28, 2006, Chapter 5—Country Reports: Western Hemisphere Overview, available at <http://www.state.gov/s/ct/rls/crt/2005/ 64346.htm> (last visited August 6, 2006) (hereinafter, "Western Hemisphere Report").

14. See Bill 2293/02, Sen. Pichetto, Proyecto de Ley Antiterrorista, available at <http://www.senado.gov.ar>.

15. Ibid., at section 1.

16. See Daniel Santoro, "El Gobierno enviará en breve una ley antiterrorista al Congreso," *Diario Clarin,* November 3, 2003, available at <http://old.clarin.com/diario/ 2003/11/03/p-00801.htm> (last visited August 6, 2006).

17. See "Patterns of Global Terrorism. Brazil: 2003 overview," available at <http:// www.tkb.org/MorePatterns.jsp?countryCd=BR&year=2003> (last visited August 5, 2006); see also additional yearly reports, also in the same site.

18. "Patterns of Global Terrorism. Uruguay: 2002 Overview," available at <http:// www.tkb.org/MorePatterns.jsp?countryCd=UY&year=2002> (last visited August 6, 2006).

19. U.S. Department of State, Bureau of Western Hemisphere Affairs, Background Note: Uruguay, March 2006, available at <http://www.state.gov/ r/pa/ei/bgn/2091.htm> (last visited August 6, 2006).

20. Western Hemisphere Report, supra note 13.

21. The Inter-American Convention against Terrorism, available at <http://www. cicte.oas.org/Docs/Treaty%20as%20approved.doc> (last visited August 6, 2006).

22. Western Hemisphere Report, supra note 13.

23. The bill is available at <http://www.asambleanacional.gov.ve> (last visited August 6, 2006); see also <http://brasil.indymedia.org/pt/blue/2003/10/265132.shtml> (last visited August 6, 2006) and <http://ecuador.indymedia.org/es/2003/10/3686.shtml> (last visited August 6, 2006).

24. Ibid., at section 11.

25. Ibid., at section 24.

Chapter 7

1. Chapter of Laws (Cap) 383: 288, available at <http://www.justice.gov.hk>.

2. The home page of the Office of the Privacy Commissioner in Hong Kong is <http://www.pco.org.hk>.

3. The Constitution of India, available at <http://www.oefre.unibe.ch/law/icl/ in00000_.html> (last visited August 6, 2006).

4. The Public Financial Institutions (Obligation As to Fidelity and Secrecy) Act, 1983 (Act No. 48 of 1983).

5. Constitution of the Republic of Singapore, September 1963, available at <http:// statutes.agc.gov.sg/non_version/cgi-bin/cgi_retrieve.pl?&actno=Reved-CONST&date= latest&method=part> (last visited August 6, 2006).

6. See "Ministers Approve APEC Privacy Framework to Strengthen E-commerce and the Protection of Personal Information," a press release issued by the APEC Electronic Commerce Steering Group, November 16, 2005, available at <http://www.apec.org/apec/news___media/2005_media_releases/161105_kor_minsapproveapecpriva cyframewrk.html> (last visited July 10, 2006); see also "APEC Ministers Approve Privacy Framework," ZDNet Asia, November 17, 2005, available at <http://www.zdnetasia.com/news/security/0,39044215,39291594,00.htm> (last visited July 10, 2006).

7. Ibid.

8. Chien-peng Chung, "China's 'War on Terror': September 11 and Uighur Separatism," *Foreign Affairs*, July/August 2002, available at <http://www.foreignaffairs.org/20020701facomment8515/chien-peng-chung/china-s-war-on-terror-september-11-and-uighur-separatism.html> (last visited August 5, 2006); Bay Fang, "Troubles in the Neighborhood: Cracking Down on its Muslim Separatists, China has Reasons for Backing U.S. Actions," *U.S. News & World Report*, October 17, 2001, available at <http://www.usnews.com/usnews/news/terror/articles/china011017.htm> (last visited August 7, 2006).

9. Angela Pagano and James Conachy, "Bush's Pay-Off to China over Iraq: Uighur Group Declared 'Terrorist,'" World Socialist Website, September 20, 2002, available at <http://www.wsws.org/articles/2002/sep2002/uigh-s20.shtml> (last visited July 10, 2006).

10. As quoted in John Chan, "China's 'War on Terrorism'—Brutal Repression of Ethnic Unrest in Xinjiang," World Socialist Website, August 8, 2002, available at <http://www.wsws.org/articles/2002/aug2002/chin-a08.shtml> (last visited July 10, 2006).

11. See "Bush's Pay-Off to China over Iraq," supra note 9.

12. Amnesty International, "People's Republic of China: China's Anti-Terrorism Legislation and Repression in the Xinjiang Uighur Autonomous Region," March 22, 2002, available at <http://web.amnesty.org/library/index/engasa170102002> (last visited August 6, 2006).

13. See "Amendment to the Criminal Law of the PRC," Xinhua News Agency (Beijing), December 29, 2001, AS1; and United Nations, Security Council, S/2001/1270/Add.1, January 10, 2002. In early January 2002, the Chinese government transmitted the text of the amendments to the UN Security Council Counter-Terrorism Committee, as an addendum to a report it had submitted to the Committee in December 2001 on its implementation of Security Council resolution 1373 (2001).

14. "The Long March to Privacy," *The Economist*, January 12, 2006, available at <http://www.economist.com/world/asia/displaystory.cfm?story_id=5389362> (last visited August 7, 2006).

15. Ibid.

16. Ibid.

17. See Human Rights Watch, "India Human Rights Press Backgrounder. Anti-Terrorism Legislation," *Human Rights Watch*, November 20, 2001, available at <http://www.hrw.org/backgrounder/asia/india-bck1121.htm> (last visited August 6, 2006) (hereinafter, "Backgrounder").

18. Amnesty International, "India: Abuse of the law in Gujarat: Muslims detained illegally in Ahmedabad," Amnesty International, November 6, 2003, available at <http://web.amnesty.org/library/Index/ENGASA200292003> (last visited September 9, 2006).

19. "India Withdraws Anti-Terror Law," *BBC News,* September, 17, 2004, available at <http://news.bbc.co.uk/2/hi/south_asia/3665098.stm> (last visited August 6, 2006).

20. See Backgrounder, supra note 17.

21. "India Withdraws Anti-Terror Law," *BBC News*, September, 17, 2004, available at <http://news.bbc.co.uk/2/hi/south_asia/3665098.stm> (last visited August 6, 2006).

22. Human Rights Watch, "India: POTA Repeal a Step Forward for Human Rights: Government Should Dismiss All POTA Cases," *Human Rights Watch*, September 22, 2004, available at <http://hrw.org/english/docs/2004/09/22/india9370.htm> (last visited August 6, 2006).

23. See Kranti Kumara, "Repeal of India's Draconian Anti-Terrorism Law: Largely a Cosmetic Change," World Socialist Web Site, November 27, 2004, available at <http://www.wsws.org/articles/2004/nov2004/ind-n27.shtml> (last visited August 6, 2006).

24. Personal Information Protection Act (2003, Law No. 57), available at <http://www.privacyexchange.org/japan/PIPA-offtrans.pdf> (last visited August 7, 2006).

25. Ibid., at chapter 4, article 15(1)(2).

26. Ibid., at chapter 4, article 19.

27. Ibid., at chapter 4, article 20.

28. See May Wong, "New Data Protection Law Likely to Reduce Junk Mails, Marketing Ploys," *Channel NewsAsia*, May 21, 2006, available at <http://www.channelnewsasia.com/stories/singaporelocalnews/view/209498/1/.html> (last visited July 10, 2006).

29. U.S. Department of State, "Singapore: Country Reports on Human Rights Practices – 2002," March 31, 2003, available at <http://www.state.gov/g/drl/rls/hrrpt/2002/18263.htm> (last visited July 10, 2006).

30. "Singapore Tightens Anti-Terrorism Laws," *BBC News*, November 13, 2001, available at <http://news.bbc.co.uk/1/hi/world/asia-pacific/1653797.stm> (last visited July 10, 2006).

31. Terrorism (Suppression of Financing) Act (No. 16 of 2002), available at <http://statutes.agc.gov.sg> (last visited July 10, 2006).

32. "Jakarta Debates Terror Decree," *BBC News Online*, October 15, 2002.

33. Richard Boucher, Spokesman for Department of State, Press Statement: Conviction of Muhammad Nazar by Indonesian Court, July 2, 2003.

34. An Act Defining Terrorism, Establishing Institutional Mechanisms to Prevent and Suppress Its Commission, Providing Penalties Therefor and For Other Purposes, draft as of September 28, 2005, available at <http://pcij.org/blog/wp-docs/house-anti-terror-bill-sept28.pdf> (last visited August 6, 2006).

35. "PGMA Certifies Enactment of Anti-Terrorism Law as Urgent," Gov.Ph News, July 3, 2006, available at <http://www.gov.ph/news/default.asp?i=15559> (last visited August 6, 2006).

36. Nathan Hancock, Law and Bills Digest Group, Research Paper No. 12 2001–2002, "Terrorism and the Law in Australia: Legislation, Commentary and Constraints," March 2002, available at <http://www.aph.gov.au/library/pubs/rp/2001-02/02rp12.htm> (last visited August 1, 2006).

37. Cosima Marriner and Mark Riley, "ASIO Gets Sweeping Powers of Arrest," *Sydney Morning Herald*, June 12, 2003.

38. ASIO Legislation Amendment 2006, May 5, 2006, no. 114, 2005–2006, available at <http://202.14.81.34/library/pubs/bd/2005-06/06bd114.pdf> (last visited August 6, 2006).

39. Mike Head, "Australian Government Retains Detention Powers," World Socialist Web Site, June 22, 2006, available at <http://wsws.org/articles/2006/jun2006/terr-j22.shtml> (last visited August 6, 2006).

40. "How the World Clamped Down on the Threat of More Violence," *The Observer*, July 24, 2005.

41. Surveillance Devices Bill (No. 2) 2004 (Australia).

42. Telecommunications (Interception) Amendment (Stored Communications) Bill 2004 on 8 December 2004 (Australia).

43. Electronic Frontiers Australia, Inc., Comments on the Surveillance Devices Bill 2004, Submission, May 18, 2004, available at <http://www.efa.org.au/Publish/efasubm-slclc-sdbill2004.html> (last visited July 10, 2006).

44. Surveillance Devices Bill, supra note 41, at s18(9).

45. Ibid., at s32(4).

46. See Electronic Frontiers Australia, Inc., Comments on the Surveillance Devices Bill 2004, supra note 43.

47. Privacy Act 1993, available at <http://www.knowledge-basket.co.nz/privacy/legislation/1993028/toc.html> (last visited August 6, 2006); all subsequent amendments are available at <http://www.legislation.govt.nz/browse_vw.asp?content-set=pal_statutes> (last visited August 7, 2006).

48. Interestingly, recent case law has found that the definition of personal information in the Privacy Act includes "mentally processed" information. See Re Application by L – Information stored in person's memory (1997) 3 HRNZ 716 (Complaints Review Tribunal).

49. Health Information Privacy Code 1994, available at <http://www.privacy.org.nz/privacy-act/health-information-privacy-code-1994> (last visited August 6, 2006).

50. Telecommunications Information Privacy Code 2003, available at <http://www.privacy.org.nz/privacy-act/telecommunications-information-privacy-code> (last visited August 6, 2006).

51. See Hon Phil Goff, "NZ Now Party to All 12 UN Terrorism Conventions," December 23, 2003, available at <http://www.beehive.govt.nz/ViewDocument.cfm?DocumentID=18735> (last visited August 7, 2006).

52. Crimes Act of 1961, as amended (New Zealand), available at <http://www.legislation.govt.nz/browse_vw.asp?content-set=pal_statutes> (last visited August 7, 2006).

53. Scott MacLeod, "Search Bill Breaks Password Barriers," *The New Zealand Herald*, June 20, 2003.

54. Terrorism Suppression Act 2002 034 (New Zealand), Commenced: 18 October 2002, available at <http://rangi.knowledge-basket.co.nz/gpacts/public/text/2002/an/034.html> (last visited August 7, 2006).

55. John Braddock, "New Zealand Anti-Terror Legislation Gives Police Sweeping New Powers," World Socialist Web Site, November 27, 2003, available at <http://www.wsws.org/articles/2003/nov2003/newz-n27.shtml> (last visited August 7, 2006).

56. For a general discussion of the measure, see Francis Till, "Police Win Intercept Rights," *The National Business Review*, July 11, 2003, at 31.

57. See, generally, Associated Press, "NZ Police Get Tech Crime Powers," AustralianIT, July 4, 2003.

58. Telecommunications (Interception Capability) Act 2004 (New Zealand) 019, available at <http://rangi.knowledge-basket.co.nz/gpacts/public/text/2004/an/019.html> (last visited August 6, 2006).

Conclusion

1. Justice Sandra Day O'Connor, *New York Times*, September 29, 2001, quoted in Darren W. Davis and Brian D. Silver, "Civil Liberties vs. Security: Public Opinion in the Context of the Terrorist Attacks on America," *American Journal of Political Science* 48 (2004): 28.

2. Quoted in William Fisher, "Watchdogs Protest Pentagon's 'Mission Creep,'" *Inter Press Services News Agency*, December 15, 2005, available at <http://www.infoshop.org/inews/article.php?story=20051219111219174> (last visited August 8, 2006).

3. W. Michael Reisman, "International Legal Reponses to Terrorism," *Houston Journal of International Law*, 22 (1999): 3.

4. Charles Krauthammer, "The Bush Doctrine. In American Foreign Policy, A New Motto: Don't Ask. Tell," *Time*, March 5, 2001, at 42, also available at <http://www.time.com/time/archive/preview/0,10987,999353,00.html>.

Selected References

Articles and News Stories

Al Akhal, Ahmad, "The Virtual Law Firm—Privacy Issue, World Wide Activates: Middle East—Jordan," available at <http://vlf.juridicum.su.se/master99/staff/akhal/privacy.html>.

Amnesty International, "Italy: New 'Counter-Terrorist' Legislation Jeopardizes Exercise of Human Rights," AI Index: EUR 30/011/2005 (Public), News Service No: 210, August 4, 2005, available at <http://web.amnesty.org/library/Index/ENGEUR300112005?open&of=ENG2EU>.

Amnesty International, "Kenya: Draft Anti-Terrorism Legislation May Undermine Kenyan Constitution and International Law," September 9, 2004, available at <http://news.amnesty.org/index/ENGAFR320042004>.

Amnesty International, "People's Republic of China: China's Anti-Terrorism Legislation and Repression in the Xinjiang Uighur Autonomous Region," March 22, 2002, available at <http://web.amnesty.org/library/index/engasa170102002>.

Baker, Peter, "Old Enemies Enlist in US Terror War: Former Soviet Republics Become Allies," *The Washington Post*, January 1, 2004, at A18.

Baran, Madeleine, "Welcome to the Matrix: Inside the Government's Secret, Corporate-Run Mega-Database," *The NewStandard*, July 9, 2004, available at <http://newstandardnews.net/content/?action=show_item&itemid=662>.

Bayles, Fred, "Air-Traveler Screening, Privacy Concerns Collide," *USA Today*, October 3, 2003.

"Camera-Shy America Weighs Merits of Video Surveillance," *Agence France Presse*, July 24, 2005.

Cauley, Leslie, "NSA has Massive Database of Americans' Phone Calls," *USA Today*, May 11, 2006, available at <http://www.usatoday.com/news/washington/2006-05-10-nsa_x.htm>.

Celeste, Sofia, "Want to Check Your E-mail in Italy? Bring Your Passport," *The Christian Science Monitor*, October 4, 2005, available at <http://www .csmonitor.com/2005/1004/p07s01woeu.html>.

Davenport, Justin, "Hi-Tech Scanners Will Detect Explosives on Tube, Rail Passengers," *The Evening Standard*, November 14, 2005.

Duff-Brown, Beth, and Rob Gillies, "Links Sought in Canada Bomb Plot: More Arrests Expected; Authorities Investigating Possible Foreign Connections," *The Mercury News*, June 6, 2006, available at <http://www.mercurynews.com/ mld/mercurynews/news/world/14750816.htm>.

Eggen, Dan, and Charles Lane, "On Hill, Anger and Calls for Hearings Greet News of Stateside Surveillance," *The Washington Post*, December 17, 2005, at A01, available at <http://www.washingtonpost.com/wpdyn/content/article/2005/ 12/16/AR2005121601825.html>.

El Guindi, Fadwa, *Veil: Modesty, Privacy and Resistance* (Oxford, UK: Berg Publishers, 1999) 81–82.

Fisher, William, "Watchdogs Protest Pentagon's 'Mission Creep,'" *Inter Press Services News Agency*, December 15, 2005, available at <http://www.ipsnews.net/ news.asp?idnews=31437>.

Gibson, James L., and Amanda Gouws, "Social Identities and Political Intolerance: Linkages Within the South African Mass Public," *American Journal of Political Science* 44 (2000): 278–292.

Glasser, Susan B., and Peter Baker, "Putin, Bush Weigh New Unity against a 'Common Foe,'" *The Washington Post*, September 13, 2001, at A25.

Hall, Mimi, and Alan Levin, "Revised Flier-Screening Plan in Works," *USA Today*, July 16, 2004.

Hansen, Darah, "$18-million in Transit Cameras part of Federal Security Drive: SkyTrain, West Coast Express Cars and Possibly Buses to be Monitored," *The Vancouver Sun*, November 24, 2005, at A3.

Hart, Wendy, and Diana Johnson, "Taking a Bite out of Internet Privacy," Georgia State University College of Law, Summer 2003, available at <http://gsulaw.gsu.edu/lawand/papers/su03/hart_johnson/>.

Hassan, Ahmed Issack, "Pitfalls of the Anti-Terrorism Bill: Draft Reverses Major Gains Made in Human Rights Crusade," InfoShop.com, June 27, 2003, available at <http://www.infoshop.org/inews/article.php?story=03/06/27/ 4176099>.

Hosein, Gus, "Threatening the Open Society: Comparing Anti-Terror Policies and Strategies in the U.S. and Europe," Privacy International, December 15, 2005.

"How the World Clamped Down on the Threat of More Violence," *The Observer*, July 24, 2005.

Hulse, Carl, "Poindexter's Office Closed: Department Tried Terrorism Futures," *San Francisco Chronicle*, September 26, 2003, available at <http://www.sfgate.com/ cgi-bin/article.cgi? file=/chronicle/archive/2003/09/ 26/MN301359.DTL>.

Human Rights News, "Human Rights Watch World Report 2006, US Policy of Abuse Undermines Rights Worldwide," available at <http://www.hrw.org/wr2k6/>.

Human Rights Watch, "France: More Safeguards Needed in Anti-Terrorism Bill. Letter to French Senators," December 9, 2005, available at <http://hrw.org/english/docs/2005/12/09/france12182.htm>.

Human Rights Watch, "Setting an Example? Counter-Terrorism Measures in Spain," January, 2005, volume 17, no. 1(D).

Human Rights Watch, "U.K.: New Anti-Terror Law Rolls Back Rights," December 14, 2001, available at <http://hrw.org/english/docs/2001/12/14/ uk3427.htm>.

Isikoff, Michael, "Intelligence: The Pentagon—Spying in America?" *Newsweek*, June 21, 2004, available at <http://www.msnbc.msn.com/id/5197014/site/ newsweek>.

Jefferson, David, "Newsweek Poll: Americans Wary of NSA Spying. Bush's Approval Ratings Hit New Lows as Controversy Rages," MSNBC.com, May 14, 2006, available at <http://www.msnbc.msn.com/id/12771821/site/newsweek>.

Kirk, Robin, "Colombia and the 'War' on Terror: Rhetoric and Reality," *The World Today*, available at <http://hrw.org/english/docs/2004/03/04 /colomb7932.htm>.

Kopytoff, Verne, "FBI's Controversial Cyber-Snooping System Plays Key Part in Terrorism Probe," *The San Francisco Chronicle*, October 15, 2001, at G1.

Lucas, Greg, "Local Transit Agencies Debate Use of Cameras: U.S. Has Invested Little in Type of Device that Helped British Identify 4 Bombing Suspects," *The San Francisco Chronicle*, July 18, 2005, at A1.

Lytle, Tamara, and Jim Leusner, "The Price of Protection: Push for Safety Clouds Individual Rights," *Orlando Sentinel*, August, 29, 2002, at A1.

MacLeod, Scott, "Search Bill Breaks Password Barriers," *The New Zealand Herald*, June 20, 2003.

Marriner, Cosima, and Mark Riley, "ASIO Gets Sweeping Powers of Arrest," *Sydney Morning Herald*, June 12, 2003.

McCullagh, Declan, "Russia Poised to Restrict Net Activities," CNET, June 24, 2002, available at <http://news.com.com/2100-1023-938810.html>.

Morris, Nigel, "Hundreds of Terror Suspects Under Surveillance," *The Independent*, September 14, 2005.

Moscoso, Eunice, "Demand for Data by Feds on Rise. Patriot Act: Businesses Feel Burden of Subpoenas, Court Orders about Patrons," *Atlanta Journal Constitution,* August 17, 2003, E1.

O'Harrow, Jr., Robert, "Financial Database To Screen Accounts: Joint Effort Targets Suspicious Activities," *The Washington Post*, May 30, 2002, at E01.

O'Harrow, Jr., Robert, "U.S. Backs Florida's New Counterterrorism Database: 'Matrix' Offers Law Agencies Faster Access to Americans' Personal Records," *The Washington Post*, August 6, 2003, at A01, available at <http://www.washingtonpost.com/ac2/wp-dyn/A21872-2003Aug5>.

O'Neil, John, and Eric Lichtblau, "Qwest's Refusal of NSA Query's Explained," *The New York Times*, May 12, 2006.

Pagano, Angela, and James Conachy, "Bush's Pay-Off to China over Iraq: Uighur Group Declared 'Terrorist,'" World Socialist Website, September 20, 2002, available at <http://www.wsws.org/articles/2002/sep2002/uigh-s20.shtml>.

Powell, Betsy, "Heavy Security Measures a Way of Life in London," *Toronto Star*, October 10, 2001, at A14.

Privacy International, "What is Wrong with Europe? PI Report Criticises EU Anti-Terror Policies," December 14, 2005, available at <http://www.privacyinternational.org/article.shtml?cmd%5B347%5D=x-347-494877>.

Pusey, Allen, "Experts Wary of Personal Data Use," *The Mercury News*, May 28, 2006, available at <http://www.mercurynews.com/mld/mercurynews/news/politics/14689011.htm>.

Rice-Oxley, Mark, "How Should Britain Tackle Terror?" *The Christian Science Monitor*, November 15, 2005, at 7.

Rise, James, and Eric Lichtblau, "Bush Lets U.S. Spy on Callers Without Courts," *The New York Times*, December 16, 2005, available at <http://www.nytimes.com/2005/12/16/politics/16program.html?ex=1292389200&en=e32072d786623ac1&ei=5090&partner=rssuserland&emc=rss>.

Santoro, Daniel, "El Gobierno enviará en breve una ley antiterrorista al Congreso," *Diario Clarin*, November 3, 2003, available at <http://old.clarin.com/diario/2003/11/03/p-00801.htm>.

Simpson, Glenn R., and Jathon Sapsford, "New Rules for Money-Laundering," *The Wall Street Journal*, April 23, 2002.

Sullivan, Bob, "Are Private Firms Helping Big Brother Too Much?" *MSBNC*, August 20, 2004, available at <http://www.msnbc.msn.com/id/5737239>.

Swarns, Rachel L., "More than 13,000 May Face Deportation," *The New York Times*, June 7, 2003.

Taylor, Jeffrey, "Putin's Policy of Realpolitik," *The Atlantic Monthly*, December 2001, available at <http://www.theatlantic.com/doc/prem/200112/tayler>.

Till, Francis, "Police Win Intercept Rights," *The National Business Review*, July 11, 2003, at 31.

"Washington Subway System Considering Bag Searches: Officials," *Agence France Presse*, July 18, 2005.

Wilson, Giles, "Terrorism Fear Derails Train-Spotters," *BBC NewsOnline*, May 28, 2003, available at <http://212.58.226.30/1/hi/uk/2943304.stm>.

Wong, May, "New Data Protection Law Likely to Reduce Junk Mails, Marketing Ploys," *Channel NewsAsia*, May 21, 2006, available at <http://www.channelnewsasia.com/stories/singaporelocalnews/view/209498/1/.html>.

"World Leaders Express Outrage," *The Guardian* (London), September 11, 2001, available at <http://www.guardian.co.uk /september11 /story/ 0,11209, 600809,00.html>.

Cases

Campbell v. AT&T Communications of California, Cal. Super. Ct., No. CGC-06-45626, complaint filed May 26, 2006.

Driscoll v. Verizon Commc'ns Inc., D.D.C., No. 1:06-cv-00916-RBW, complaint filed May 15, 2006 (95 PRA, May 17, 2006).

European Parliament v. Council of the European Union and European Parliament v. Commission of the European Communities (C-317/04 and C-318/04), available at <http://curia.eu.int/jurisp/cgibin/gettext.pl?where=&lang=en&num=79939469C19040317&doc=T&ouvert=T&seance=ARRET>.

In the Matter of Eli Lilly & Co., No. 012 3214, Agreement Containing Consent Order, available at <http://www.ftc.gov/os/2002/01/lillycmp.pdf>.

In the Matter of Guess? Inc. and Guess.com, Inc., File No. 022 3260, available at <http://www.ftc.gov/opa/2003/06/guess.htm>.

In the Matter of JetBlue Airways and Acxiom Corporation (complaint filed with the Federal Trade Commission).

In the Matter of Northwest Airlines, Docket No. 16939 (complaint filed with the Department of Transportation).

Ludman v. AT&T Inc., D.D.C., No. 1:06-cv-00917-RBW, complaint filed May 15, 2006 (95 PRA, May 17, 2006).

Mayer v. Verizon Commc'ns Inc., S.D.N.Y., No. 1:06-cv-03650-LBS/AJP, complaint filed May 12, 2006 (94 PRA, May 16, 2006).

Phillips v. BellSouth Corp., D.D.C., No. 1:06-cv-00918-RBW, complaint filed May 15, 2006.

Riordon v. Verizon Communications Inc., Cal. Super. Ct., No. CGC-06-45268, complaint filed May 26, 2006.

Legislation and Regulations

1999 Constitution of the Federal Republic of Nigeria, available at <http://www.nigeria-law.org/ConstitutionOfTheFederalRepublicOfNigeria.htm>.

Ant-Terrorism Act, 2002, No. 14/2002 (Uganda), available at <http://www.kituochakatiba.co.ug/anti.htm>.

Anti-Terrorism, Crime and Security Act 2001 (United Kingdom), available at <http://www.hmso.gov.uk/acts/acts2001/20010024.htm>.

Basic Law: Human Dignity and Liberty (5752–1992) (Israel), Passed by the Knesset on the 21st Adar, 5754, March 9, 1994, available at <http://www.mfa.gov.il/mfa/go.asp?MFAH00hi0>.

California Online Privacy Protection Act of 2003—Business and Professions Code Section 22575–22579, available at <http://www.leginfo.ca.gov/cgibin/displaycode?section=bpc&group=22001-23000&file=22575-22579>.

Children's Online Privacy Protection Act of 1998 (United States), 15 U.S.C. 6501 (1999). On October 20, 1999, the FTC issued the final rule implementing COPPA. FTC, Children's Online Privacy Protection Rule; Final Rule 16 CFR Part 312 (1999).

Communications Act of 1934, as amended by the Telecommunications Act of 1996 (United States), 47 U.S.C. 151, available at <http://www.fcc.gov/Reports/1934new.pdf>.

Constitution of the Hashemite Kingdom of Jordan, adopted January 1, 1952, available at <http://www.kinghussein.gov.jo/constitution_jo.html>.

Constitution of India, available at <http://www.oefre.unibe.ch/law/icl /in00000_.html>.

Constitution of Mexico (1917), an English translation of which is available at <http://www.ilstu.edu/class/hist263/docs/1917const.html#TitleIChapterI>.

Constitution of the Republic of Singapore, September 1963, available at <http://statutes.agc.gov.sg/non_version/cgi-bin/cgi_retrieve.pl?&actno=RevedCONST&date=latest&method=part>.

Constitution of the Republic of South Africa, Act 108 of 1996, available at <http://www.info.gov.za/documents/constitution/index.htm>.

Conversione in legge, con modificazioni, del decreto-legge 27 luglio 2005, n. 144, recante misure urgenti per il contrasto del terrorismo internazionale, LEGGE 31 luglio 2005, n.155, Gazzetta Ufficiale N. 177 dell' 1 Agosto 2005, available at <http://www.gazzette.comune.jesi.an.it/2005/177/3.htm>.

Council Directive No. 95/46/EC of 24 October 1995 on the Protection of Individuals with Regard to the Processing of Personal Data and on the Free Movement of Such Data, O.J. L 281/31 (1995).

Council of Europe Convention on Cybercrime, Budapest, 23.X1.2001, available at <http://conventions.coe.int/Treaty/EN/Treaties/Html/185.htm>.

Criminal Code of The Russian Federation, Adopted by the State Duma on May 24, 1996, Adopted by the Federation Council on June 5, 1996, Federal Law No. 64-FZ of June 13, 1996 on the Enforcement of the Criminal Code of the Russian Federation, available at <http://www.russian-criminal-code.com>.

Criminal-Procedural Code of the Russian Federation, No. 174-FZ of December 18, 2001 (with the Amendments and Additions of May 29, July 24, 25, October 31, 2002, June 30, July 4, 7, December 8, 2003, April 22, June 29, December 2, 28, 2004, June 1, 2005), available at <http://legislationline.org/upload/legislations/9a/eb/3a4a5e98a67c25d4fe5eb5170513.htm>.

Electronic Communications Privacy Act, Pub. L. No. 99-508, 100 Stat. 1848 (1986) (codified at 18 U.S.C. 2510–2521, 2701–2710, 3117, 3121–3126 (1986)).

Electronic Communications and Transactions Act (South Africa), Act No. 25 of 2002.

Federal Law No. 114-FZ of July 25, 2002 on the Counteraction of Extremist Activity.

Federal Law on Operational Investigative Activity, No. 144-FZ of August 12, 1995 (Russian Federation).

Law of the Russian Federation "On Mass Media," No. 2124-1 of December 27, 1991 (Russian Federation), as of December 8, 2003 (as amended on January 13, 1995; June 6, 1995; July 19, 1995; December 27, 1995; March 2, 1998; June 20, 2000; August 5, 2000; August 4, 2001; March 21, 2002; July 25, 2002; July 4, 2003; and

December 8, 2003), available at <http:// www.medialaw.ru/e_pages/laws/ russian/massmedia_eng/massmedia_eng.html>.

Omnibus Crime Control and Safe Streets Act of 1968 (United States), 42 U.S.C. §3789d.

Personal Information Protection and Electronic Documents Act, introduced as Bill C-6, assented to April 13, 2000 (Canada), available at <http:// www.privcom.gc.ca/ legislation/02_06_01_e.asp>.

Prevention of Terrorism Act 2005, C. 12, (United Kingdom), available at <http://www.opsi.gov.uk/acts/acts2005/20050002.htm>.

Privacy Act of 1974 (United States), 5 U.S.C. §552a (2000).

Projet de loi relatif à la lutte contre le terrorisme et portant dispositions diverses relatives à la sécurité et aux contrôles frontaliers (France), available at <http://www .senat.fr/dossierleg/pjl05-109.html>.

Protection of Privacy Law 5741–1981, 1011 Laws of the State of Israel 128. Amended by the Protection of Privacy Law (Amendment) 5745–1985.

Regulation of Interception of Communications and Provision of Communication-Related Information Act (South Africa) No. 70 of 2002.

Regulation of Investigatory Powers Act 2000 (c. 23) (United Kingdom), available at <http://www.legislation.hmso.gov.uk/acts/acts2000/20000023.htm>, replacing Interception of Communications Act 1985 (c. 56) (United Kingdom), available at <http://www.archive.official-documents.co.uk/document/cm47/ 4778/4778.htm>.

Suppression of Terrorism Bill, 2003 (Kenya), Kenya gazette Supplement No. 38, publication date April 30, 2003, available at <http://www.ealawsociety.org/ statutes/Kenya%20Suppression%20of%20Terrorism%20Bill%202003.pdf>.

Telecommunications Act (South Africa), Act No. 103 of 1996, as amended.

Terrorism (Suppression of Financing) Act (No. 16 of 2002) (Singapore), available at <http://statutes.agc.gov.sg>.

Terrorism Act 2000 (United Kingdom), chapter 11, available at <http://www.opsi .gov.uk/acts/acts2000/20000011.htm#aofs>.

Terrorism Act 2006 (United Kingdom), C. 11, available at: <http://www.opsi.gov.uk/ acts/acts2006/20060011.htm>.

Terrorism Suppression Act 2002 034 (New Zealand), Commenced: 18 October 2002, available at <http://rangi.knowledge-basket.co.nz/gpacts/public/text/2002/an/ 034.html>.

Policy Documents, Annual Reports, and Other Advisory Documents

Article 29 Data Protection Working Party, Opinion 4/2003 on the Level of Protection ensured in the US for the Transfer of Passengers' Data, 11070/03/EN, adopted on June 13, 2003.

Attorney General of Canada, Annual Report Concerning Investigative Hearings and Recognizance With Conditions for Period of December 24, 2001–December 23 2002, May 2003.

Commission of the European Communities, Brussels, Report From The Commission, Overview of European Union action in response to the events of the 11 September and assessment of their likely economic impact, October 17, 2001, COM(2001) 611 final.

Commission Staff Working Document—The implementation of Commission Decision 520/2000/EC on the adequate protection of personal data provided by the Safe Harbour privacy Principles and related Frequently Asked Questions issued by the US Department of Commerce, available at <http://europa.eu.int/comm/internal_market/privacy/docs/adequacy/sec-2004-1323_en.pdf>.

Council of Europe Parliamentary Assembly, Recommendation 1534 (2001), Democracies Facing Terrorism, September 26, 2001 (28th Sitting), available at <http://assembly.coe.int/main.asp?Link=/documents/workingdocs/doc01/edoc9282.htm>.

Department of the Solicitor General of Canada, Annual Report on the Use of Arrest Without Warrant Pursuant to the Antiterrorism Act 2002, May 2003.

Discussion Paper 109 (Project 124), Privacy and Data Protection (South Africa), available at <http://www.doj.gov.za/salrc/dpapers.htm>.

Financial Action Task Force on Money Laundering, "Nine Special Recommendations on Terrorist Financing," available at <http://www.fatf-gafi.org/document/9/0,2340,en_32250379_32236920_34032073_1_1_1_1,00.html>.

Government Accounting Office Report, "Data Mining: Federal Efforts Cover a Wide Range of Uses," May 2004, available at <http://www.epic.org/privacy/profiling/gao_dm_rpt.pdf>.

International Bar Association, Task Force On International Terrorism, International Terrorism: Legal Challenges And Responses (2004).

Uganda Human Rights Commission, Annual Report January 2001–September 2002 (2003).

UN Counter-Terrorism Committee, Reports of Member States, available at <http://www.un.org/Docs/sc/committees/1373/submitted_reports.html>.

United Nations Human Rights Committee, Comments on Russian Federation, U.N. Doc. CCPR/C/79/Add.54 (1995), available at <http:/ /sim.law.uu.nl/SIM/CaseLaw/uncom.nsf/0/9172bc5146972b6dc125663c00343b49?OpenDocument>.

U.S. Department of State, "Singapore: Country Reports on Human Rights Practices – 2002," March 31, 2003, available at <http://www.state.gov/g/drl/rls/hrrpt/2002/18263.htm>.

U.S. Department of State, "United Arab Emirates: Country Reports on Human Rights Practices—2005," released by the Bureau of Democracy, Human Rights, and Labor, March 8, 2006, available at <http://www.state.gov/g/drl/rls/hrrpt/2005/61701.htm>.

Index

Colleges and universities, sharing student information with government, 44

Colombia: guerilla groups, clamp down on, 8–9; terrorism incidents, 131

Communications Act, customer information disclosures under, 40

Communications Decency Act of 1996, 168

Communication streams, Electronic Communications Privacy Act (ECPA), 21

Communication surveillance, U.K., 110–11

Computer Assisted Passenger Profiling System (CAPPS). *See* CAPPS

Computer Processed Personal Data Protection Law of 1995, Taiwan, 140

Consumer Credit Reporting Reform Act of 1996, 166

Consumers: concerns of, 9–10; FACTA protections for, 27–28

Control orders, 108–10

Convention for the Protection of Human Rights and Fundamental Freedoms, 162

Convention on Cybercrime, Council of Europe, 70, 99–102, 115

Convention on the Prevention of Terrorism, Council of Europe, 115

Convention on the Rights of the Child, 162

COPPA. *See* Children's Online Privacy Protection Act (COPPA)

Corporations, participation in counterterrorism efforts. *See* Data sharing between private companies and government

Council of Europe: Convention on the Prevention of Terrorism, 115; response to September 11th attacks, 6–7

Council of Europe Cybercrime Convention, 70, 99–102, 115

Counteraction of Terrorism, Russia, 116

Counteraction to Extremist Activities, Russia, 115

Counter-Terrorism Act, New Zealand, 150–51

Counterterrorism measures: Africa (*See* Africa); Australia, 147–49; border control, 56–57; Canada, 123–26; Europe (*See* Europe); Middle East (*See* Middle East); New Zealand, 150–52; privacy considerations, 57–58; private companies participation in (*See* Data sharing between private companies and government); propaganda, 58–59; Russia, 112–17; secrecy surrounding, 59; South America (*See* South America); troubling issues, 58–59; USA PATRIOT Act (*See* USA PATRIOT Act)

Covered Entities, HIPAA, 15–16

Credit information, FACTA provisions, 27

Cybercrime Convention, Council of Europe, 70, 99–102, 115

Cyber Security Research and Development Act, 171

Daschle, Tom, 34

Data Accountability and Trust Act, 174

Data mining/sharing systems, 44–53; abuse potential, 55; accuracy issues, 54–55; CAPPS, 47; CAPPS II, 47–49; Carnivore (DCS1000), 45–46; criticisms of, 54–56; effectiveness of, 56; errors, 54–55; invasions of privacy, 55–56; MATRIX, 51–53; mistakes, 54–55; NSEERS, 49, 50; presumption of guilt, 56; Secure Flight, 49; security concerns, 55; TALON, 49–51; Terrorism Information Awareness (TIA), 46–47

Data Protection Act, Tunisia, 64, 67

Data Protection Convention, 101–2

Data Protection Directive, European. *See* European Data Protection Directive

Data Retention Directive, EU, 96–99

Data Security Notification Law (S.B. 1386), California, 28–29

Data sharing between private companies and government, 9–10, 37–44, 157;

Hancock, Nathan, 147
Health Insurance Portability and
    Accountability Act (HIPAA),
    14–16, 165
HIPAA. *See* Health Insurance Portability
    and Accountability Act (HIPAA)
Hong Kong, privacy rights, 138
Hosein, Gus, 117
Human rights: Convention for the
    Protection of Human Rights and
    Fundamental Freedoms, 162;
    Uganda, 68–69, 75; United Nations
    Human Rights Commission, 114;
    Universal Declaration of Human
    Rights, 161
Human Rights Watch: ATCS Act concerns,
    108; French counterterrorism
    measures concerns, 104

Identity theft, FACTA provisions, 27–28
India: counterterrorism measures, 144;
    pre-9/11 privacy rights, 139;
    Prevention of Terrorism Act
    (POTA), 144; Public Financial
    Institutions Act, 139; Terrorists and
    Disruptive Activities (Prevention)
    Act (TADA), 144
Indonesia: Bali nightclub attacks, 141,
    146; counterterrorism measures, 146
Informatics Law of 1984, Brazil, 130
Information sharing, intragovernmental, 35
Intelligence Authorization Act for Fiscal
    Year 1999, 167
Intelligence Reform and Terrorism
    Prevention Act of 2004, 56
Interception Bill, Australia, 148, 149
International banking transaction data,
    information sharing with
    governments, 43–44
International Convention for the
    Suppression of Terrorism Bombings,
    ratification of: Brazil, 134; Canada,
    124; Kenya, 70; Mexico, 128
International Convention for the
    Suppression of the Financing of
    Terrorism of December 9, 1999, 5;

Brazilian ratification of, 134; Canadian
    ratification of, 124; Kenyan ratification
    of, 70; Mexican ratification of, 128
International Covenant on Civil and
    Political Rights, 161
International response to September 11th
    attacks, 8–10
Internet: Australian surveillance of, 149;
    Canadian surveillance of, 125–26;
    Children's Online Privacy Protection
    Act (COPPA), 18–20, 167; effect of,
    1; French data retention law, 103–4;
    Italian surveillance of, 105; Middle
    East usage, 62–65; New Zealand
    surveillance of, 152
Iraq, privacy rights, 63
Israel: Basic Law on Human Dignity
    and Freedom, 63; pre-9/11 privacy
    rights, 63–64; Protection of Privacy
    Law, 64
Italy, counterterrorism measures, 102,
    104–5

Japan: Personal Information Protection Act
    (PIPA), 145; post-9/11 privacy rights,
    145; pre-9/11 privacy rights, 139
JetBlue Airways, sharing of customer
    information with TSA, 42
Jordan: counterterrorism efforts, 66;
    Electronic Transaction Act (ETA), 66;
    post-9/11 privacy rights, 66; pre-9/11
    privacy rights, 64
Junk Fax Prevention Act of 2005, 173
Justice and Home Affairs, EU, 91

Kenya, counterterrorism measures, 69–70
Khusui, 62
Krouthammer, Charles, 158
Kurdistan Workers' Party (PKK), Turkish
    clamp down on, 8

Law on Communications, Russia, 116
Law on Information, Informatisation and
    Protection of Information (LIIPI),
    Russia, 113
Law on Mass Media, Russia, 115, 116

Organization of American States (OAS) Inter-American Convention Against Terrorism, 134, 135

PADI. *See* Professional Association of Diving Instructors (PADI)
Personal Data Protection Act, Argentina, 130
Personal Data Protection Law, Colima Mexico, 126, 127–28
Personal information, Canadian Act definition of, 120
Personal Information and Privacy Protection Act, California, 22
Personal Information Protection Act (PIPA), Japan, 145
Personal Information Protection and Electronic Documents Act (Canadian Act), 120–23
Peru, 131
Petco, FTC enforcement action against, 30–31
Philippines, counterterrorism measures, 146
Physical surveillance, U.K., 111
PIPA. *See* Personal Information Protection Act (PIPA), Japan
PKK. *See* Kurdistan Workers' Party (PKK)
PLCP. *See* Federal Law for Consumer Protection (PLCP), Mexico
POTA. *See* Prevention of Terrorism Act (POTA), India
Prevention of Terrorism Act 2005, U.K., 108–10
Prevention of Terrorism Act (POTA), India, 144
Privacy: concept in Middle East, 62; concerns regarding, 10–11; data sharing between private companies and government (*See* Data sharing between private companies and government); debate surrounding, 156–57; effect of technology on, 1; etymology of, 156; government's concerns regarding, 57–58; right to, 1; September 11th terrorist attacks, effect of (*See* September 11th terrorist

attacks); surveys, 10–11; views of, jurisdictional, 1
Privacy Act of 1974, 58, 164
Privacy Act of 1993, New Zealand, 150
Privacy Amendment (Private Sector) Act of 2000, Australia, 147
Privacy Commissioner: Canada, 123; Hong Kong, 138; New Zealand, 150
Privacy in international instruments, 159–62
Privacy International report, 2005, 117
Privacy officers, designation of, 58
Private companies, participation in counterterrorism efforts. *See* Data sharing between private companies and government
Professional Association of Diving Instructors (PADI), sharing of customer data with government, 44
Propaganda, 58–59
Protection of Computer Processed Personal Data Act of 1990, Japan, 139
Protection of Computer Processed Personal Data Held by Administrative Organs Act of 1988, Japan, 139
Public Financial Institutions Act, India, 139
Putin, Vladimir, 115, 116

Quest data, refusal to allow NSA collection of, 39

Ratner, Michael, 156
REAL ID Act of 2005, 173
Regulation of Investigatory Powers act 2000 (RIPA), U.K., 90, 110–11
RIPA. *See* Regulation of Investigatory Powers act 2000 (RIPA), U.K.
Russia: Chechan rebels, clamp down on, 8, 114–15; Counteraction of Terrorism, 116; Counteraction to Extremist Activities, 115; counterterrorism efforts, 112–17; Criminal-Procedural Code, proposed changes to, 116; data protection laws, 112–13; international cooperation, 115; Law on Communications, 116; Law on

Information, Informatisation and Protection of Information (LIIPI), 113; Law on Mass Media, 115, 116; Law on Operational Investigation Activity, 114; legislative developments, 115–16; Moscow theatre hostage incident, 115; post-9/11 privacy rights, 114–16; pre-9/11 privacy rights, 112–14; proposed legislation, 116; September 11th attacks, actions after, 8

Sadat, Anwar, 63
Safe Harbors program, U.S., 84–86, 175–76
SA Interception Act, 70–71
Sarbanes-Oxley Act of 2002, 171
Sarkozy, Nicolas, 103
Schwartz, Ari, 52
Search warrants, 35
Secure Flight, 49
Seisint, 51–53
September 11th terrorist attacks: African response to (*See* Africa); Asian response to (*See* Asia); Australian response to (*See* Australia); Canadian response to, 123–26; effect of, 2–3, 155; EU response to (*See* European Union (EU)); initial response to, 2–10, 92–93; international response to, 8–10; legislation in response to, 3–8, 33–36; Mexican response to, 126–28; Middle East response to (*See* Middle East); New Zealand response to (*See* New Zealand); privacy in U.S. prior to (*See* United States); Russian response to (*See* Russia); South American response to (*See* South America); U. S. response to, 2–10
SIM cards, 72
Singapore: counterterrorism measures, 145–46; post-9/11 privacy rights, 145; pre-9/11 privacy rights, 139; surveillance activities, 146; Terrorism (Suppression of Financing) Act, 146

Society for Worldwide Interbank Financial Transactions (SWIFT). *See* SWIFT (Society for Worldwide Interbank Financial Transactions)
South Africa: Electronic Communications and Transactions Act (ECTA), 71; post-9/11 counterterrorism measures, 70–73; post-9/11 privacy rights, 72–73; pre-9/11 privacy rights, 68; SA Interception Act, 70–71; subscriber identity module (SIM) card, 72; surveillance activities, 70–71
South America: (*See also* specific nation/state); counterterrorism measures, 131–35; pre-9/11 privacy rights, 129–31; terrorism incidents, 131
South Korea, privacy rights, 139–40
Spain: counterterrorism efforts, 105; ETA terrorist group, 89, 105; Madrid train bombings, 102, 103, 105, 125; pre-9/11 counterterrorism measures, 89
Standards for Safeguarding Customer Information, FTC, 18
State privacy laws: post-9/11, 28–30; pre-9/11, 22
Stored Communications Act, 171
Stored information, Electronic Communications Privacy Act (ECPA), 21
Subscriber identity module (SIM) cards, 72
Suppression of Terrorism Bill, Kenya, 69–70
Surveillance, 3; Australia, 148–49; Canada, 125–26; China, 143; closed-circuit television (CCTV), 36, 99, 111, 125, 143; Electronic Communications Privacy Act (ECPA), 20–22; Europe, 99, 117; France, 103; increase in, 36–37; Italy, 104–5; Mexico, 128; New Zealand, 152; Russia, 116; Singapore, 146; South Africa, 70–71; United Kingdom, 36, 99, 110–11; USA PATRIOT Act, under, 21–22; video surveillance software market, 36; wiretapping (*See* Wiretapping)

About the Author

Jacqueline Klosek, a Certified Information Privacy Professional, is an attorney with Goodwin Procter LLP in New York City, where she practices in the Intellectual Property Transactions and Strategies Practice Area. Her practice focuses on advising clients on cutting-edge issues related to the intersection of law and technology, with a particular focus on data privacy and security. She is the author of three books.